CREATED BY **JOSS WHEDON**

JORDIE **BELLAIRE** JEREMY **LAMBERT** RAMON **BACHS** ANDRÉS **GENOLET**

Buffy the vampire slayer™

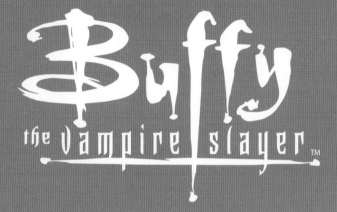

VOLUME FIVE **THE BIGGEST BAD**

Published by
BOOM! STUDIOS

Series Designer
Michelle Ankley

Collection Designer
Scott Newman

Assistant Editor
Gavin Gronenthal

Associate Editor
Jonathan Manning

Editor
Jeanine Schaefer

Special Thanks to **Sierra Hahn**, **Becca J. Sadowsky**, and **Nicole Spiegel** & **Carol Roeder**.

Ross Richie CEO & Founder
Joy Huffman CFO
Matt Gagnon Editor-in-Chief
Filip Sablik President, Publishing & Marketing
Stephen Christy President, Development
Lance Kreiter Vice President, Licensing & Merchandising
Arune Singh Vice President, Marketing
Bryce Carlson Vice President, Editorial & Creative Strategy
Kate Henning Director, Operations
Spencer Simpson Director, Sales
Scott Newman Manager, Production Design
Elyse Strandberg Manager, Finance
Sierra Hahn Executive Editor
Jeanine Schaefer Executive Editor
Dafna Pleban Senior Editor
Shannon Watters Senior Editor
Eric Harburn Senior Editor
Sophie Philips-Roberts Associate Editor
Amanda LaFranco Associate Editor
Jonathan Manning Associate Editor
Gavin Gronenthal Assistant Editor
Gwen Waller Assistant Editor

Allyson Gronowitz Assistant Editor
Ramiro Portnoy Assistant Editor
Kenzie Rzonca Assistant Editor
Shelby Netschke Editorial Assistant
Michelle Ankley Design Coordinator
Marie Krupina Production Designer
Grace Park Production Designer
Chelsea Roberts Production Designer
Samantha Knapp Production Design Assistant
José Meza Live Events Lead
Stephanie Hocutt Digital Marketing Lead
Esther Kim Marketing Coordinator
Breanna Sarpy Live Events Coordinator
Amanda Lawson Marketing Assistant
Holly Aitchison Digital Sales Coordinator
Morgan Perry Retail Sales Coordinator
Megan Christopher Operations Coordinator
Rodrigo Hernandez Operations Coordinator
Zipporah Smith Operations Assistant
Jason Lee Senior Accountant
Sabrina Lesin Accounting Assistant

BUFFY THE VAMPIRE SLAYER Volume Five, April 2021. Published by BOOM! Studios, a division of Boom Entertainment, Inc. © 2021 20th Television. Originally published in single magazine form as BUFFY THE VAMPIRE SLAYER No. 17-20. © 2020 20th Television. BOOM! Studios™ and the BOOM! Studios logo are trademarks of Boom Entertainment, Inc., registered in various countries and categories. All characters, events, and institutions depicted herein are fictional. Any similarity between any of the names, characters, persons, events, and/or institutions in this publication to actual names, characters, and persons, whether living or dead, events, and/or institutions is unintended and purely coincidental. BOOM! Studios does not read or accept unsolicited submissions of ideas, stories, or artwork.

BOOM! Studios, 5670 Wilshire Boulevard, Suite 400, Los Angeles, CA 90036-5679. Printed in China. First Printing.

ISBN: 978-1-68415-654-2, eISBN: 978-1-64668-139-6

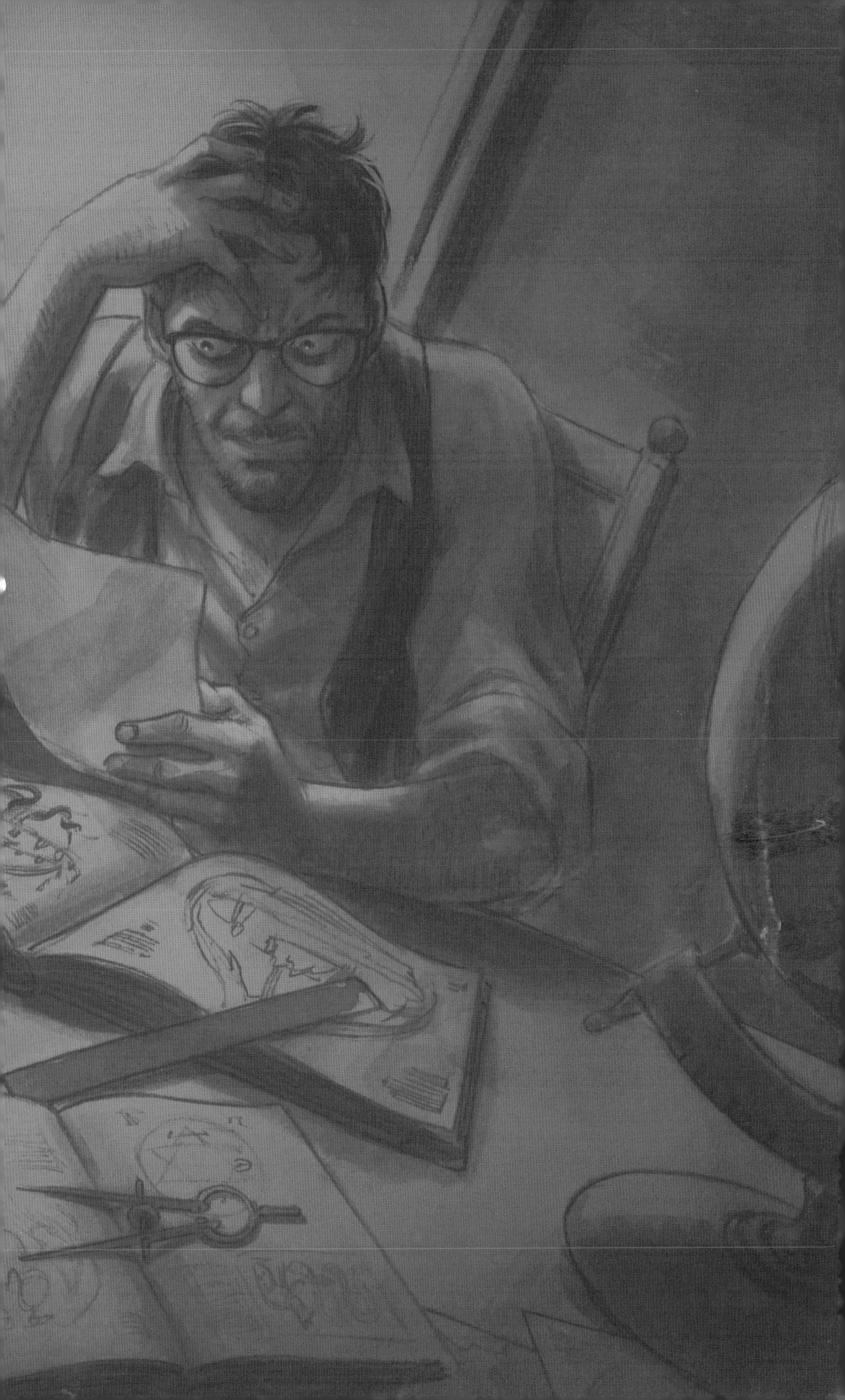

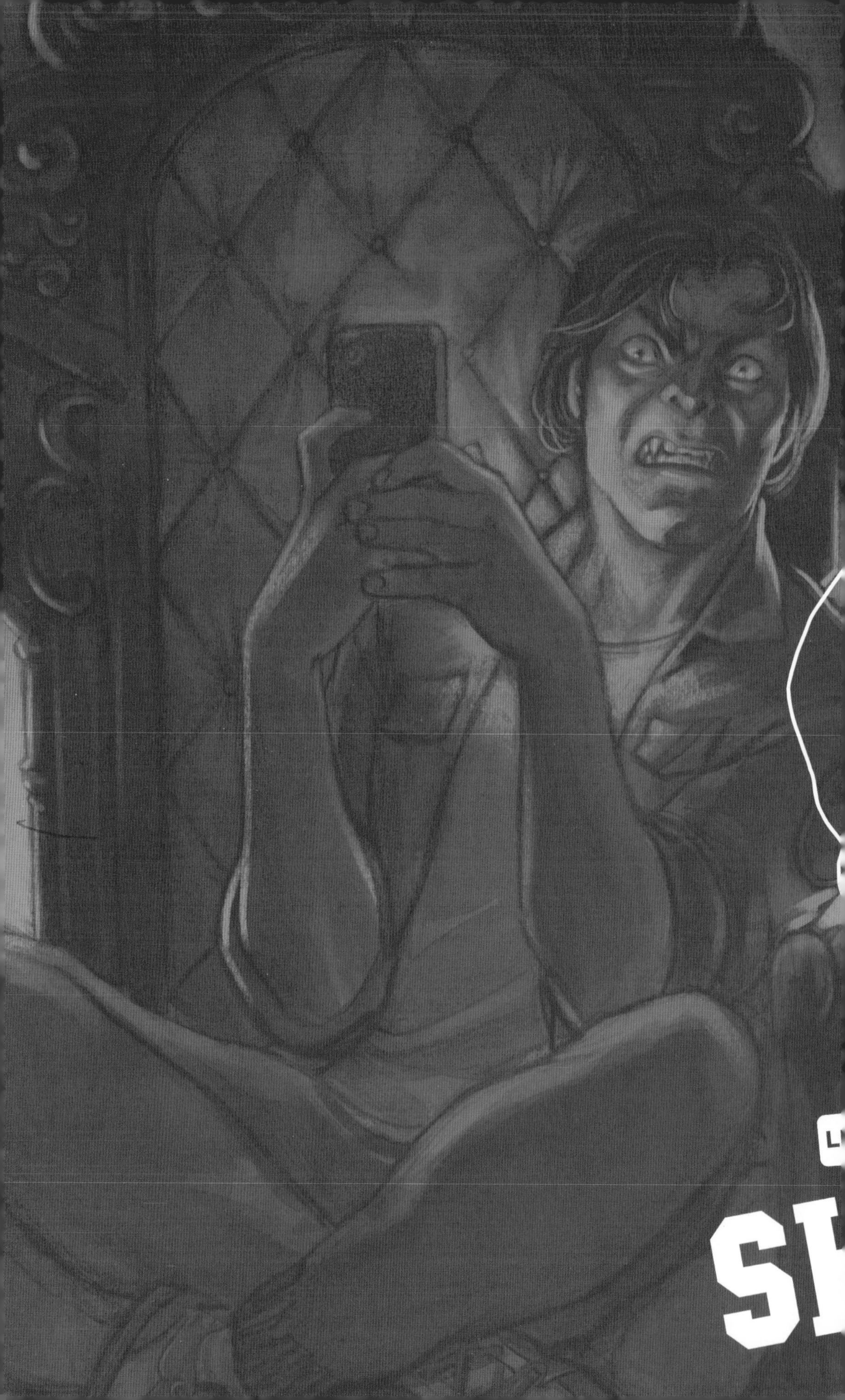

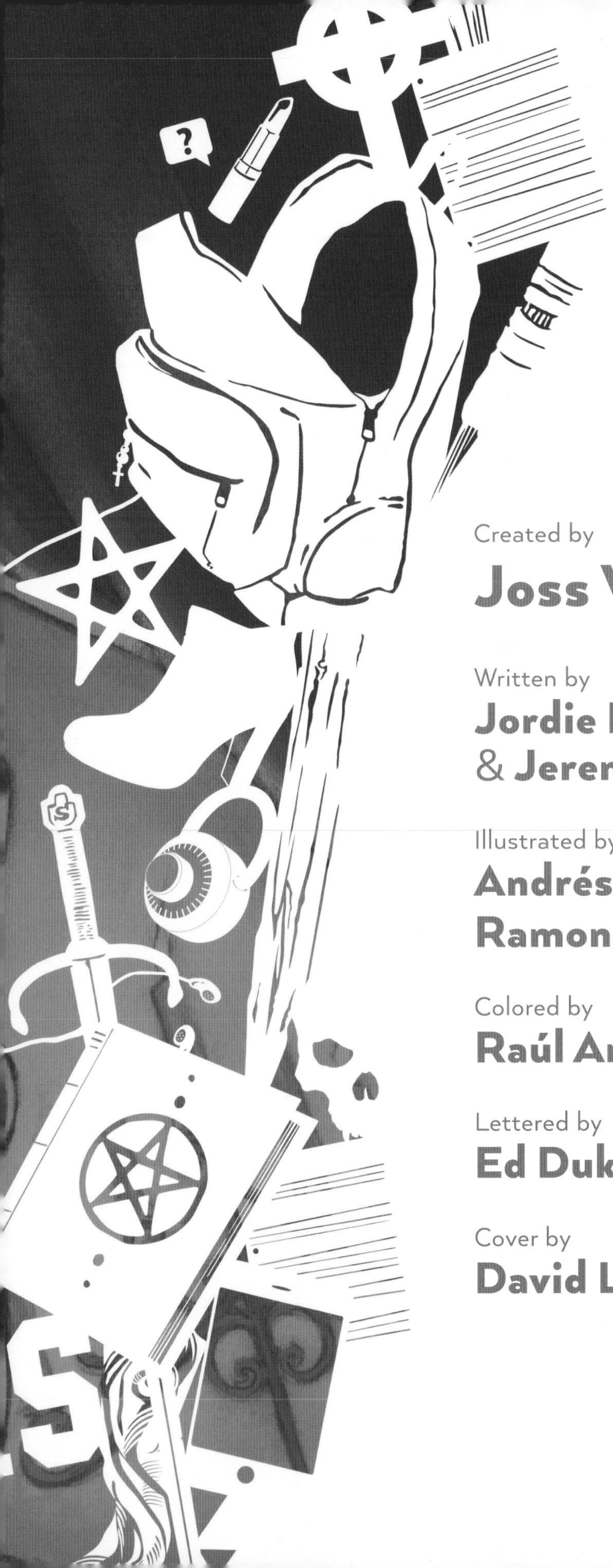

Created by
Joss Whedon

Written by
Jordie Bellaire
& **Jeremy Lambert**

Illustrated by
Andrés Genolet (Chapter 17)
Ramon Bachs (Chapters 18-20)

Colored by
Raúl Angulo

Lettered by
Ed Dukeshire

Cover by
David López

CHAPTER
SEVENTEEN

Issue Seventeen Cover by **David López**

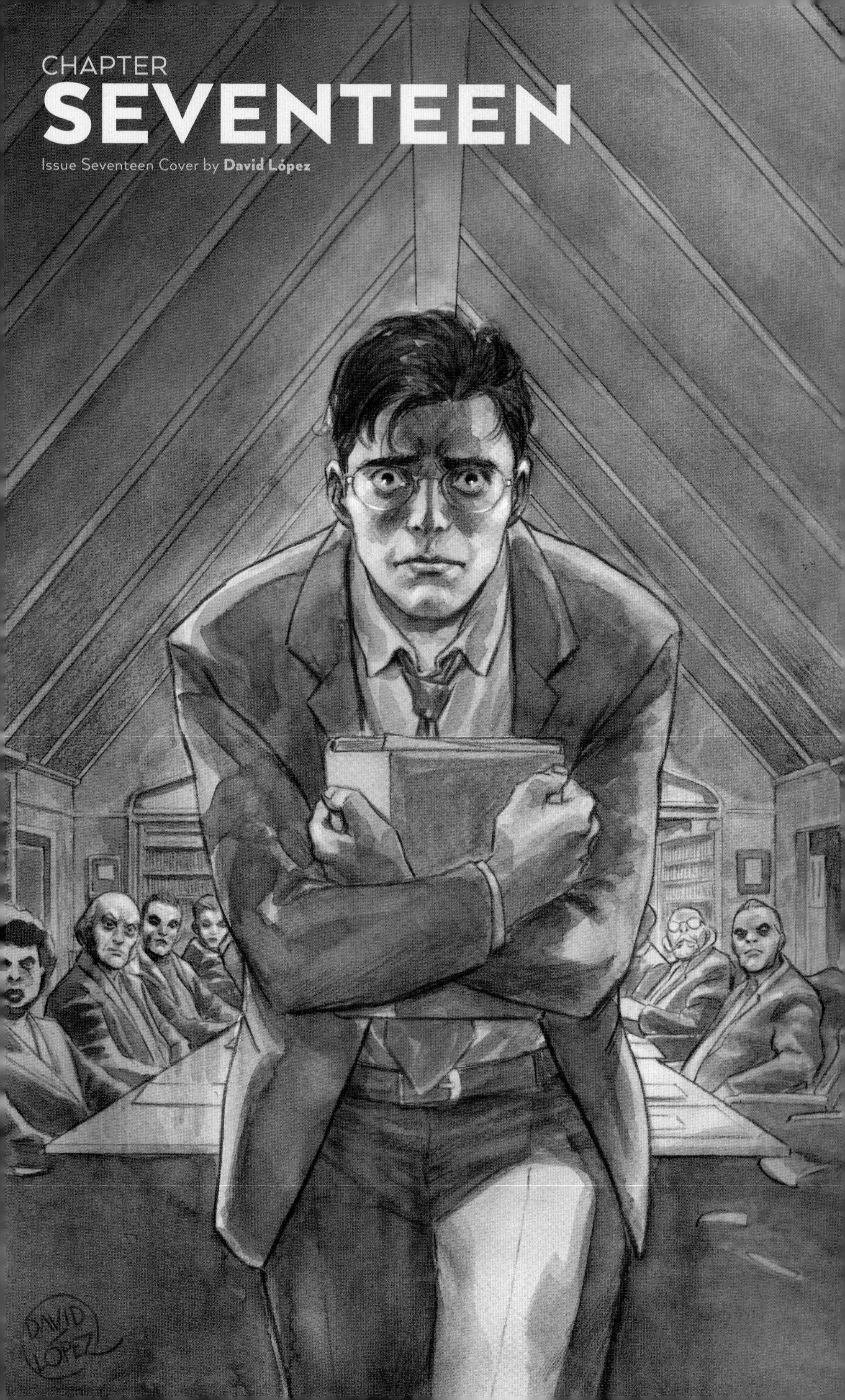

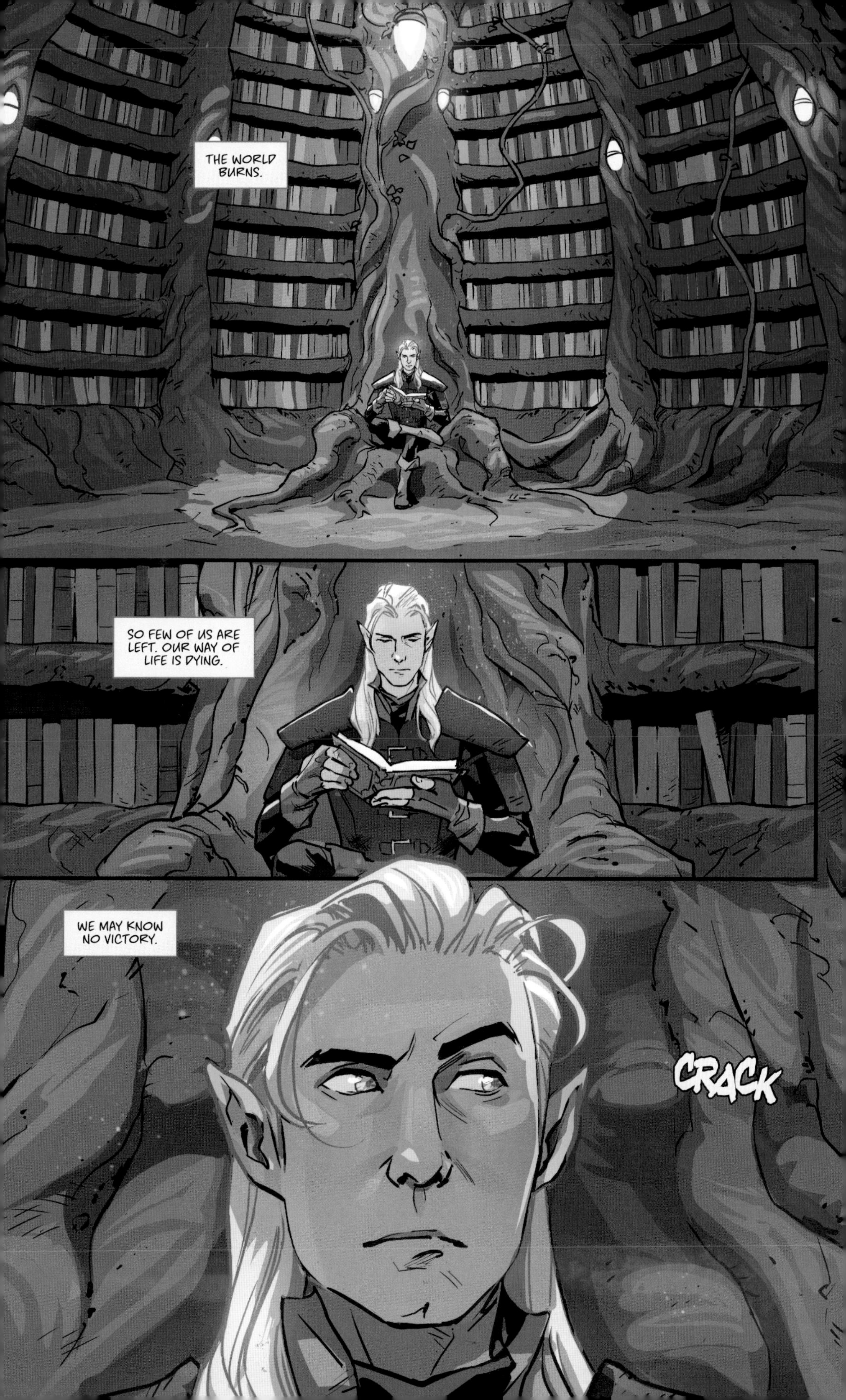
THE WORLD BURNS.
SO FEW OF US ARE LEFT. OUR WAY OF LIFE IS DYING.
WE MAY KNOW NO VICTORY.
CRACK

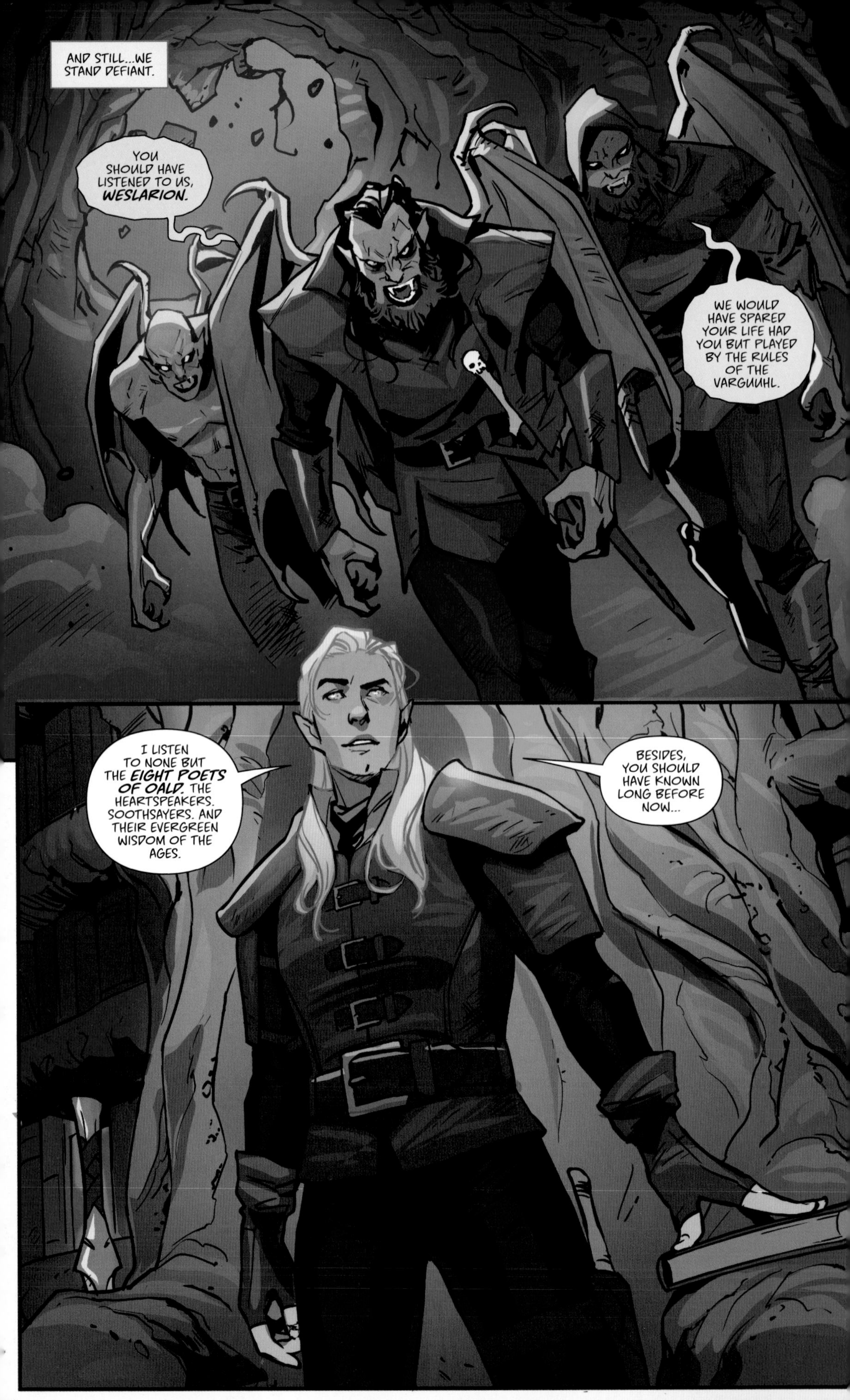
AND STILL...WE STAND DEFIANT.
YOU SHOULD HAVE LISTENED TO US, **WESLARION.**
WE WOULD HAVE SPARED YOUR LIFE HAD YOU BUT PLAYED BY THE RULES OF THE VARGUUHL.
I LISTEN TO NONE BUT THE **EIGHT POETS OF OALD**. THE HEARTSPEAKERS. SOOTHSAYERS. AND THEIR EVERGREEN WISDOM OF THE AGES.
BESIDES, YOU SHOULD HAVE KNOWN LONG BEFORE NOW...

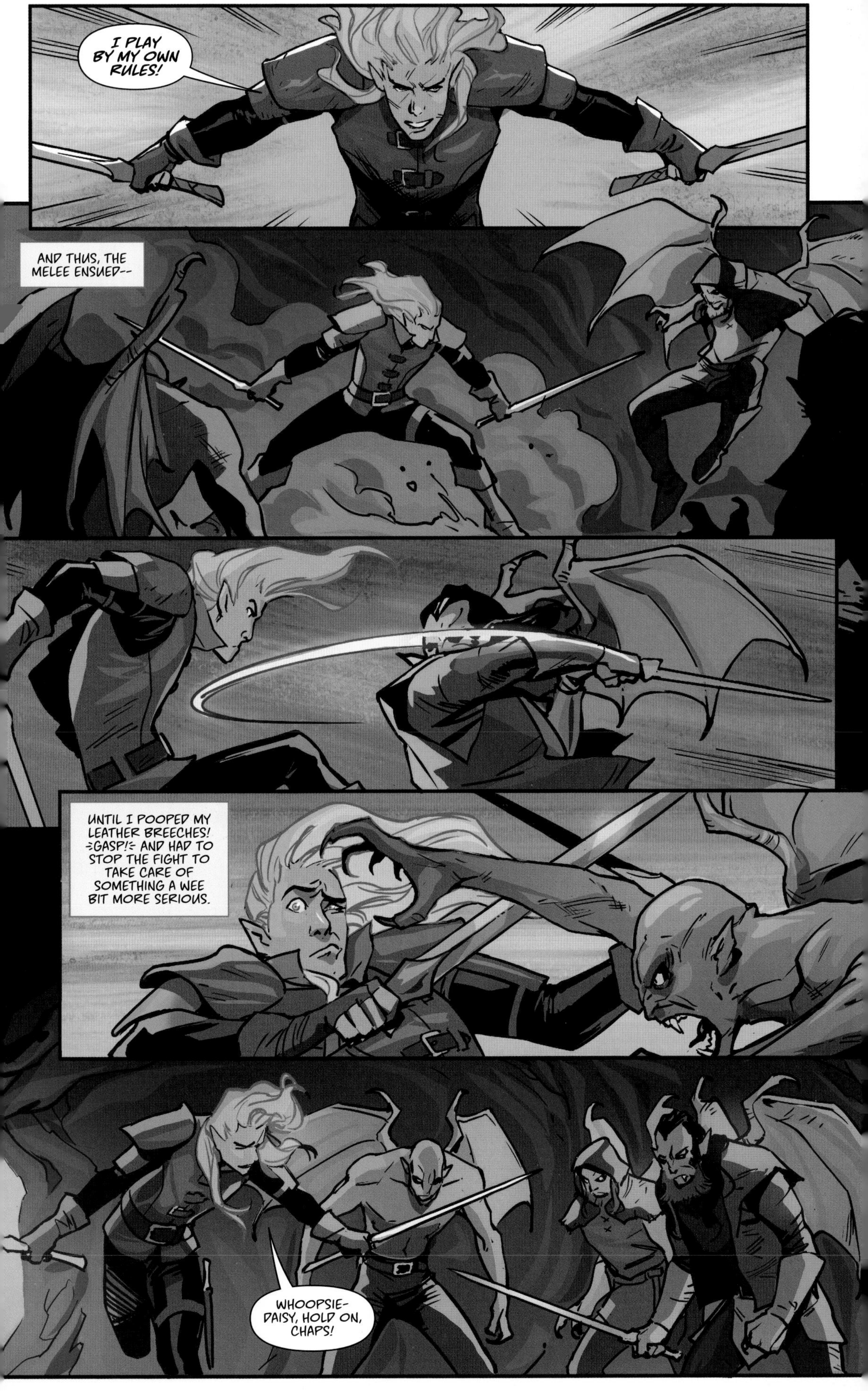
I PLAY BY MY OWN RULES!
AND THUS, THE MELEE ENSUED--
UNTIL I POOPED MY LEATHER BREECHES! =GASP!= AND HAD TO STOP THE FIGHT TO TAKE CARE OF SOMETHING A WEE BIT MORE SERIOUS.
WHOOPSIE-DAISY, HOLD ON, CHAPS!

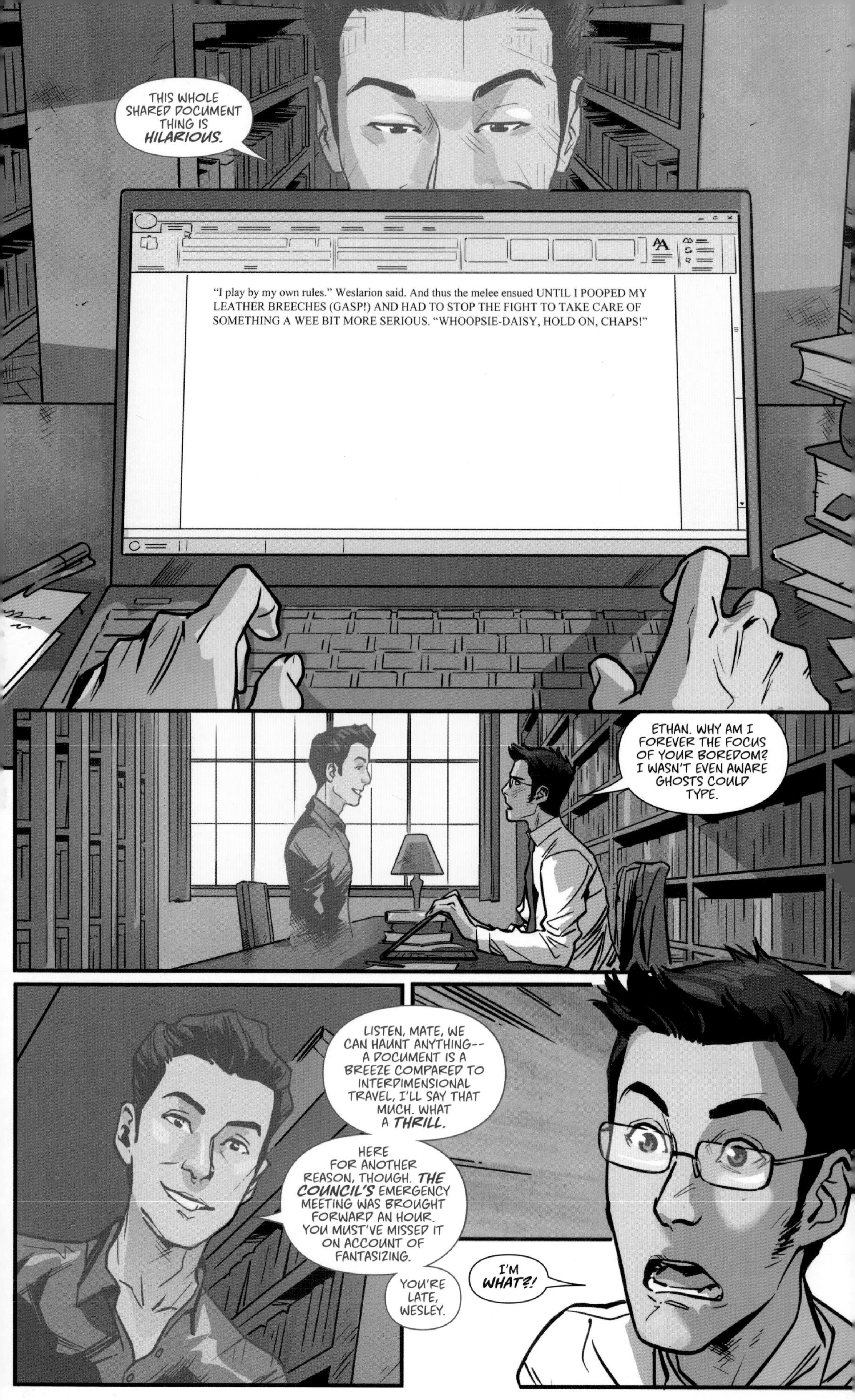
THIS WHOLE SHARED DOCUMENT THING IS HILARIOUS.
"I play by my own rules." Weslarion said. And thus the melee ensued UNTIL I POOPED MY LEATHER BREECHES (GASP!) AND HAD TO STOP THE FIGHT TO TAKE CARE OF SOMETHING A WEE BIT MORE SERIOUS. "WHOOPSIE-DAISY, HOLD ON, CHAPS!"
ETHAN. WHY AM I FOREVER THE FOCUS OF YOUR BOREDOM? I WASN'T EVEN AWARE GHOSTS COULD TYPE.
LISTEN, MATE, WE CAN HAUNT ANYTHING-- A DOCUMENT IS A BREEZE COMPARED TO INTERDIMENSIONAL TRAVEL, I'LL SAY THAT MUCH. WHAT A THRILL.
HERE FOR ANOTHER REASON, THOUGH. THE COUNCIL'S EMERGENCY MEETING WAS BROUGHT FORWARD AN HOUR. YOU MUST'VE MISSED IT ON ACCOUNT OF FANTASIZING.
YOU'RE LATE, WESLEY.
I'M WHAT?!

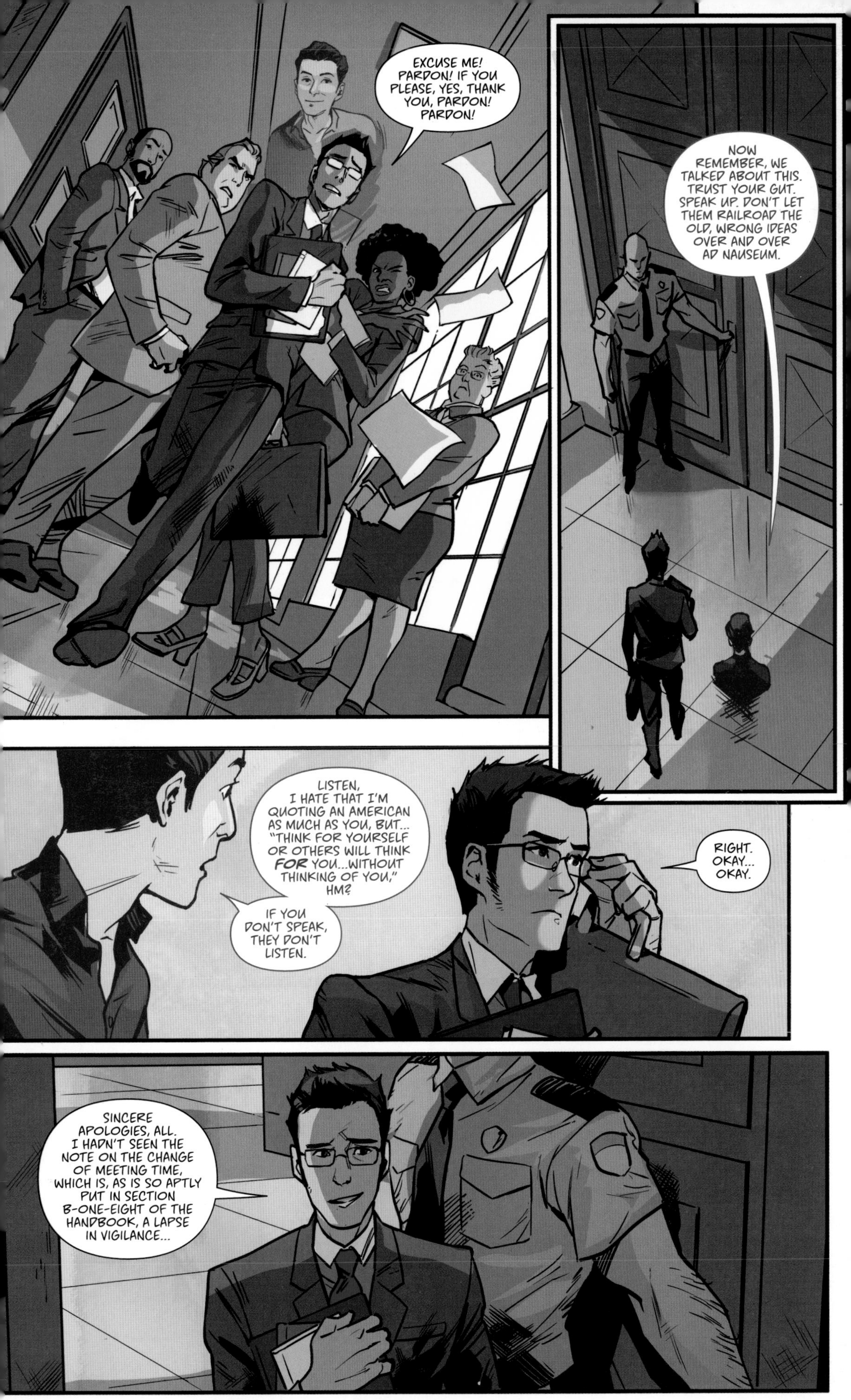
EXCUSE ME! PARDON! IF YOU PLEASE, YES, THANK YOU, PARDON! PARDON!
NOW REMEMBER, WE TALKED ABOUT THIS. TRUST YOUR GUT. SPEAK UP. DON'T LET THEM RAILROAD THE OLD, WRONG IDEAS OVER AND OVER AD NAUSEUM.
LISTEN, I HATE THAT I'M QUOTING AN AMERICAN AS MUCH AS YOU, BUT... "THINK FOR YOURSELF OR OTHERS WILL THINK **FOR** YOU...WITHOUT THINKING OF YOU," HM?
IF YOU DON'T SPEAK, THEY DON'T LISTEN.
RIGHT. OKAY... OKAY.
SINCERE APOLOGIES, ALL. I HADN'T SEEN THE NOTE ON THE CHANGE OF MEETING TIME, WHICH IS, AS IS SO APTLY PUT IN SECTION B-ONE-EIGHT OF THE HANDBOOK, A LAPSE IN VIGILANCE...

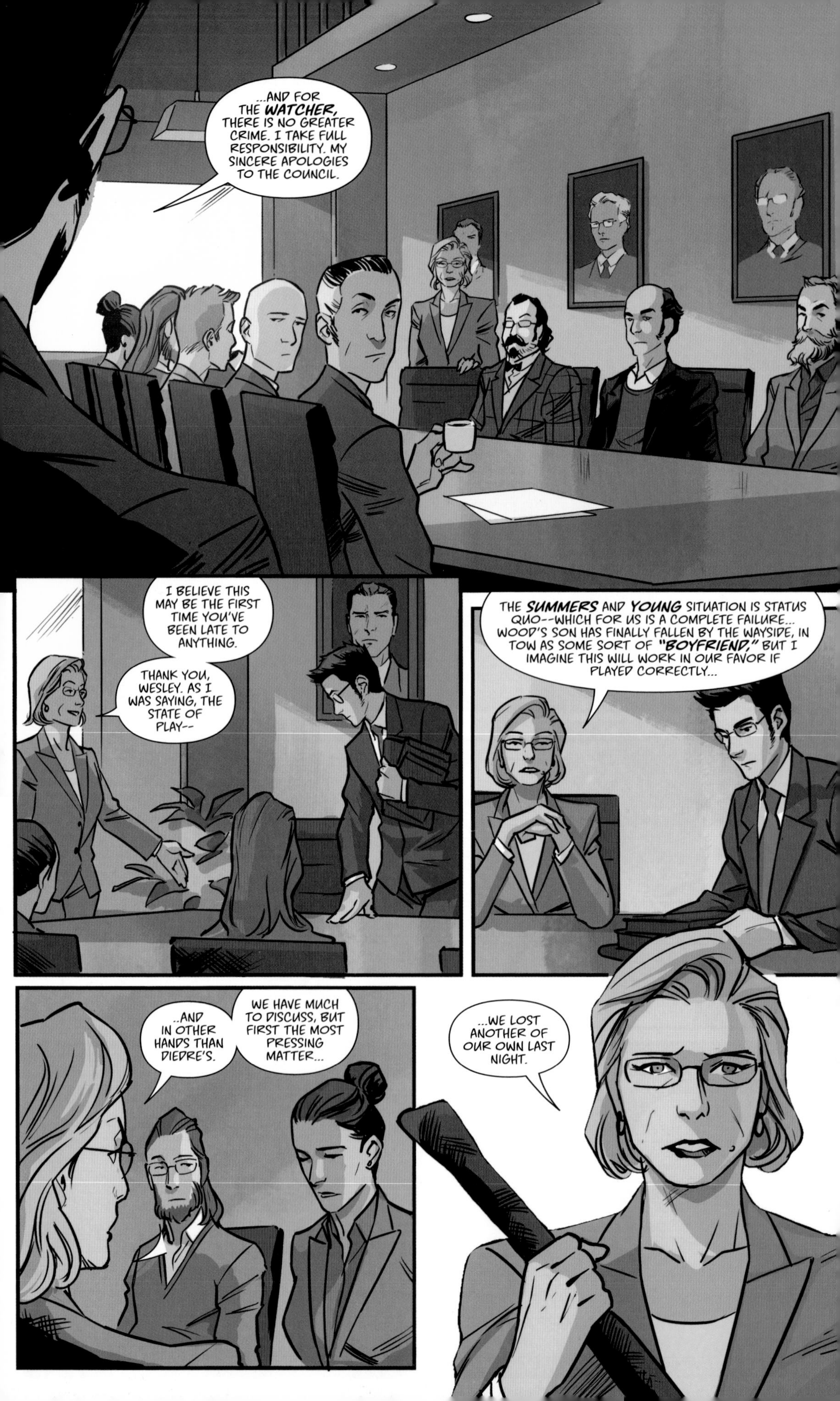
...AND FOR THE WATCHER, THERE IS NO GREATER CRIME. I TAKE FULL RESPONSIBILITY. MY SINCERE APOLOGIES TO THE COUNCIL.
I BELIEVE THIS MAY BE THE FIRST TIME YOU'VE BEEN LATE TO ANYTHING.
THANK YOU, WESLEY. AS I WAS SAYING, THE STATE OF PLAY--
THE SUMMERS AND YOUNG SITUATION IS STATUS QUO--WHICH FOR US IS A COMPLETE FAILURE... WOOD'S SON HAS FINALLY FALLEN BY THE WAYSIDE, IN TOW AS SOME SORT OF "BOYFRIEND," BUT I IMAGINE THIS WILL WORK IN OUR FAVOR IF PLAYED CORRECTLY...
..AND IN OTHER HANDS THAN DIEDRE'S.
WE HAVE MUCH TO DISCUSS, BUT FIRST THE MOST PRESSING MATTER...
...WE LOST ANOTHER OF OUR OWN LAST NIGHT.

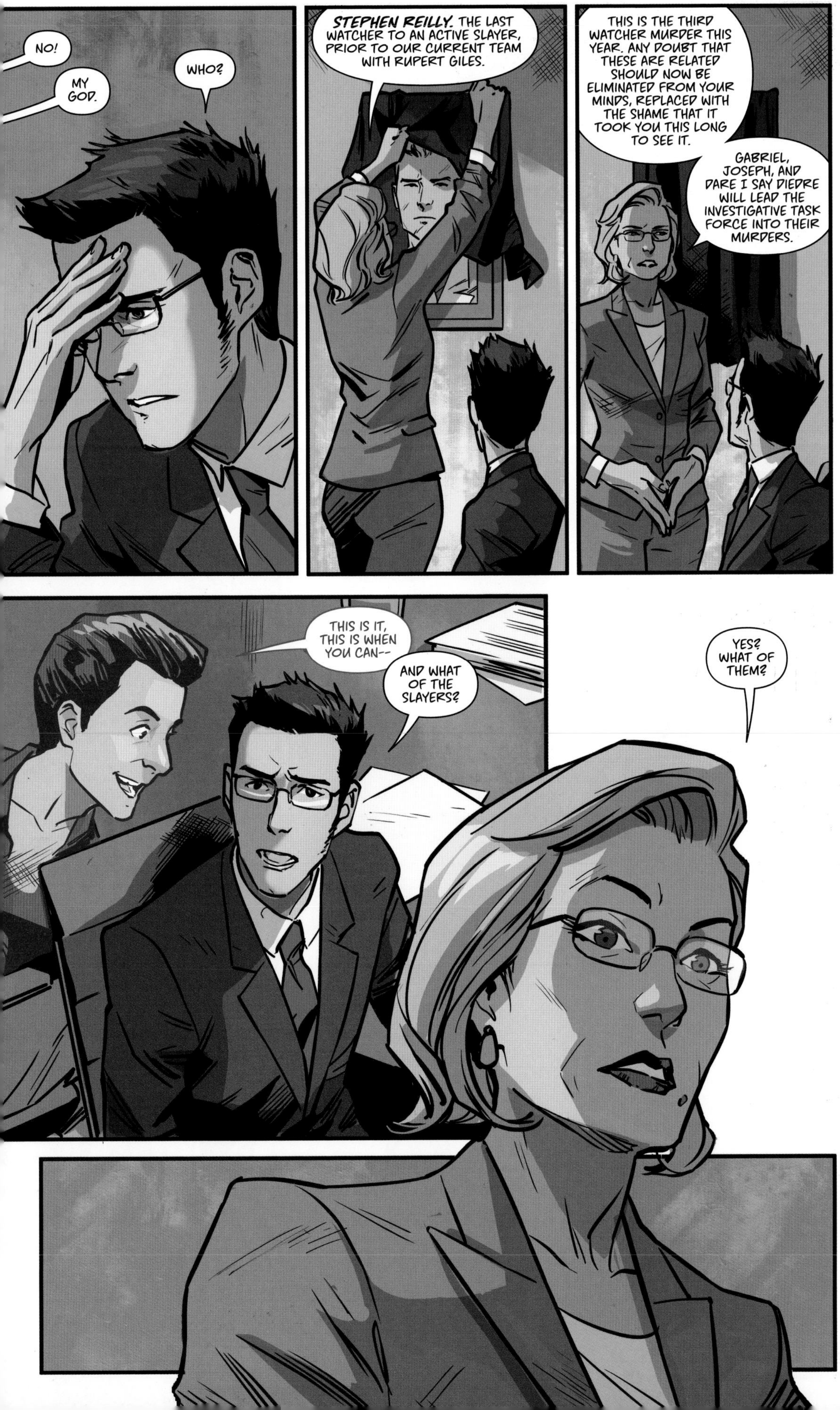
NO!
MY GOD.
WHO?
STEPHEN REILLY. THE LAST WATCHER TO AN ACTIVE SLAYER, PRIOR TO OUR CURRENT TEAM WITH RUPERT GILES.
THIS IS THE THIRD WATCHER MURDER THIS YEAR. ANY DOUBT THAT THESE ARE RELATED SHOULD NOW BE ELIMINATED FROM YOUR MINDS, REPLACED WITH THE SHAME THAT IT TOOK YOU THIS LONG TO SEE IT.
GABRIEL, JOSEPH, AND DARE I SAY DIEDRE WILL LEAD THE INVESTIGATIVE TASK FORCE INTO THEIR MURDERS.
THIS IS IT, THIS IS WHEN YOU CAN--
AND WHAT OF THE SLAYERS?
YES? WHAT OF THEM?

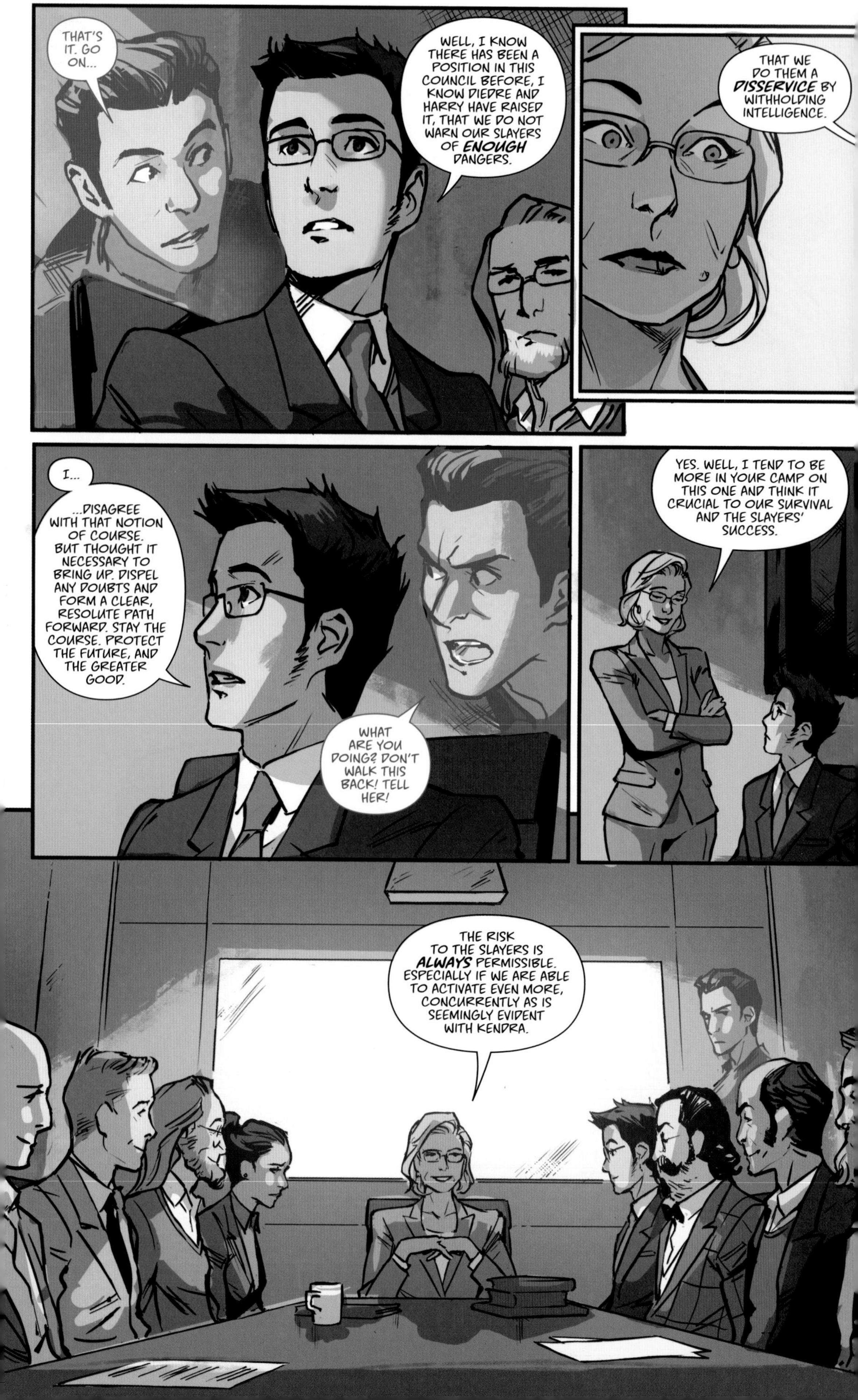
THAT'S IT. GO ON...
WELL, I KNOW THERE HAS BEEN A POSITION IN THIS COUNCIL BEFORE, I KNOW DIEDRE AND HARRY HAVE RAISED IT, THAT WE DO NOT WARN OUR SLAYERS OF ENOUGH DANGERS.
THAT WE DO THEM A DISSERVICE BY WITHHOLDING INTELLIGENCE.
I...
...DISAGREE WITH THAT NOTION OF COURSE. BUT THOUGHT IT NECESSARY TO BRING UP. DISPEL ANY DOUBTS AND FORM A CLEAR, RESOLUTE PATH FORWARD. STAY THE COURSE. PROTECT THE FUTURE, AND THE GREATER GOOD.
WHAT ARE YOU DOING? DON'T WALK THIS BACK! TELL HER!
YES. WELL, I TEND TO BE MORE IN YOUR CAMP ON THIS ONE AND THINK IT CRUCIAL TO OUR SURVIVAL AND THE SLAYERS' SUCCESS.
THE RISK TO THE SLAYERS IS ALWAYS PERMISSIBLE. ESPECIALLY IF WE ARE ABLE TO ACTIVATE EVEN MORE, CONCURRENTLY AS IS SEEMINGLY EVIDENT WITH KENDRA.

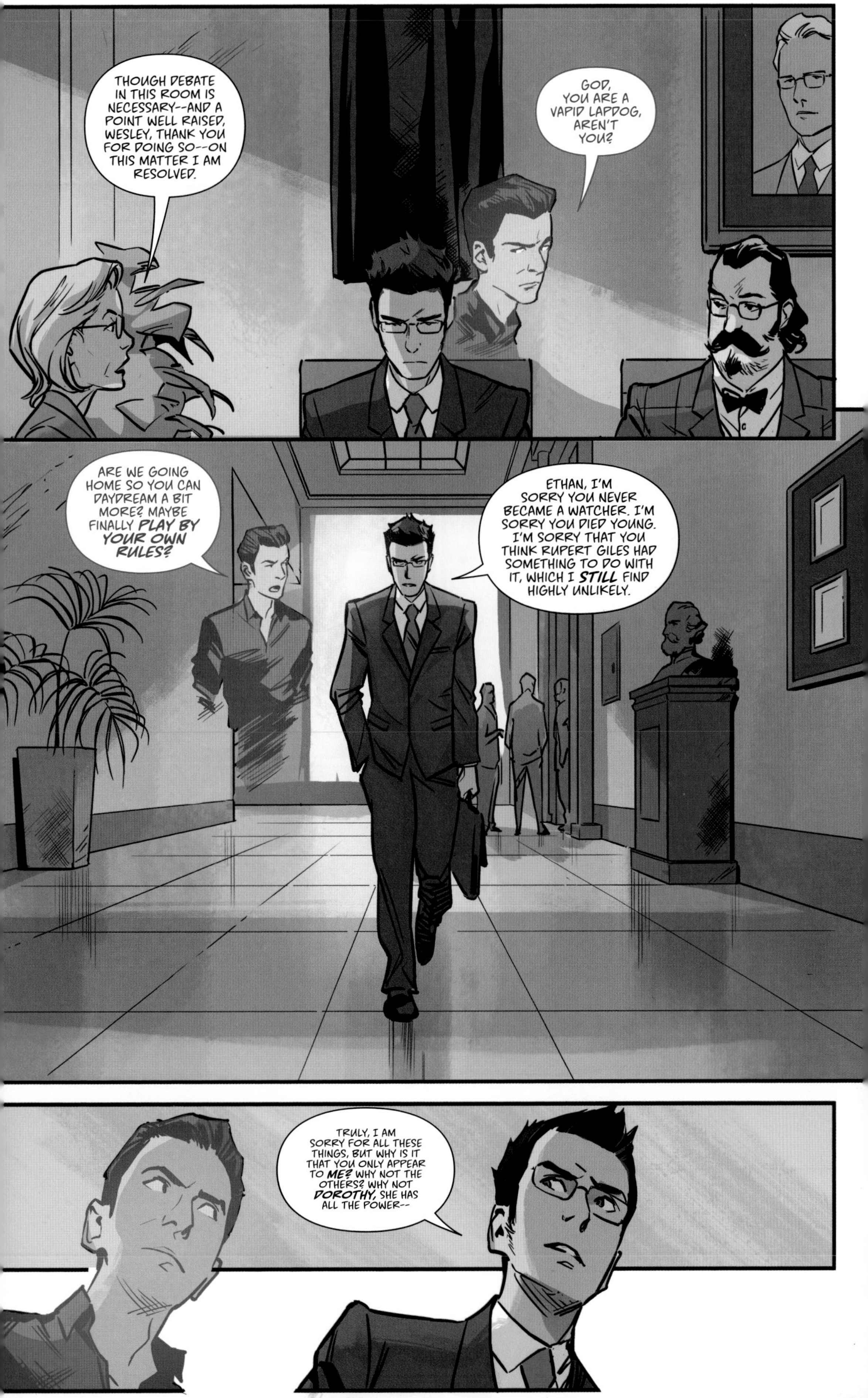
THOUGH DEBATE IN THIS ROOM IS NECESSARY--AND A POINT WELL RAISED, WESLEY, THANK YOU FOR DOING SO--ON THIS MATTER I AM RESOLVED.
GOD, YOU ARE A VAPID LAPDOG, AREN'T YOU?
ARE WE GOING HOME SO YOU CAN DAYDREAM A BIT MORE? MAYBE FINALLY PLAY BY YOUR OWN RULES?
ETHAN, I'M SORRY YOU NEVER BECAME A WATCHER. I'M SORRY YOU DIED YOUNG. I'M SORRY THAT YOU THINK RUPERT GILES HAD SOMETHING TO DO WITH IT, WHICH I STILL FIND HIGHLY UNLIKELY.
TRULY, I AM SORRY FOR ALL THESE THINGS, BUT WHY IS IT THAT YOU ONLY APPEAR TO ME? WHY NOT THE OTHERS? WHY NOT DOROTHY, SHE HAS ALL THE POWER--

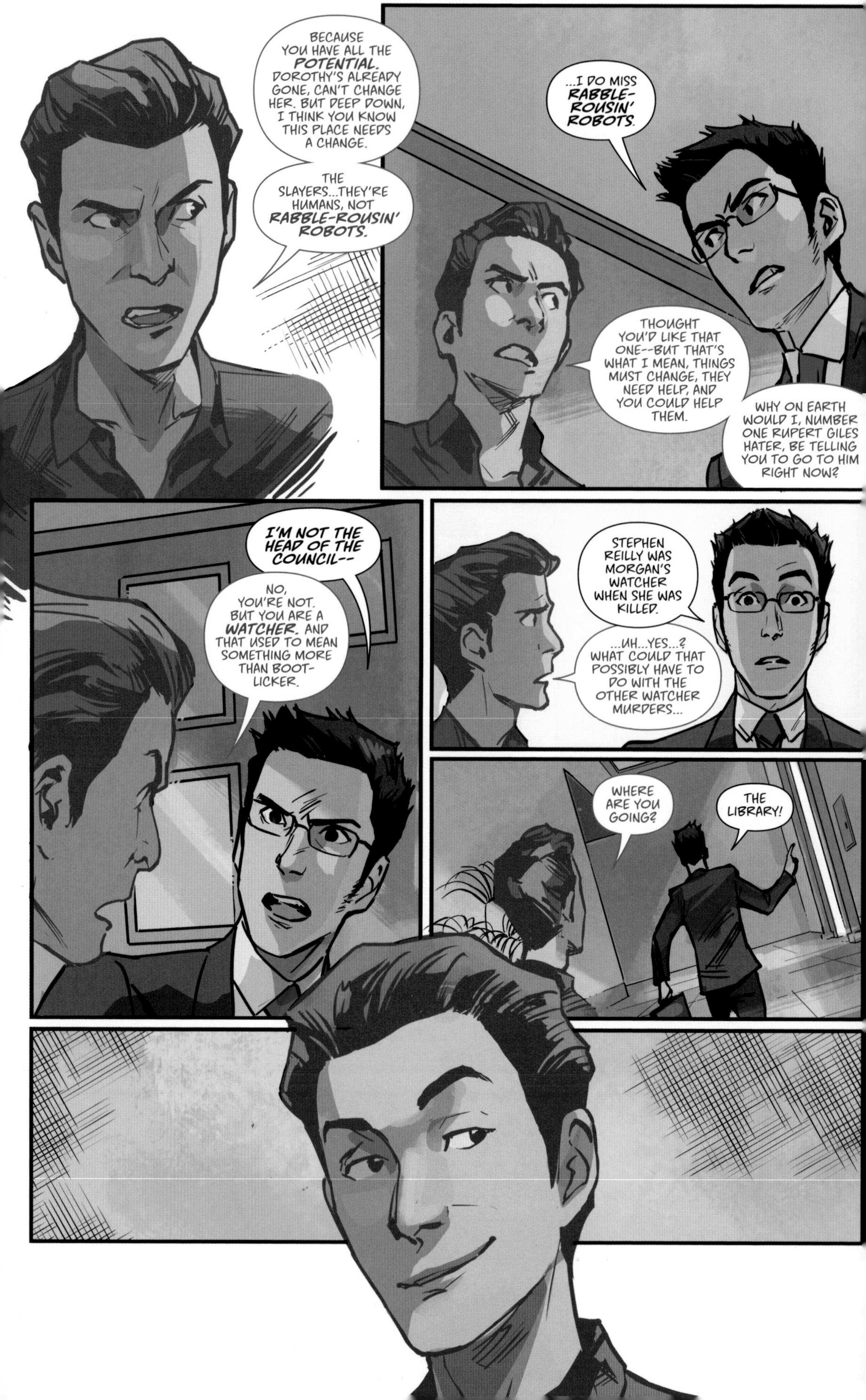
BECAUSE YOU HAVE ALL THE POTENTIAL. DOROTHY'S ALREADY GONE, CAN'T CHANGE HER. BUT DEEP DOWN, I THINK YOU KNOW THIS PLACE NEEDS A CHANGE.
THE SLAYERS...THEY'RE HUMANS, NOT RABBLE-ROUSIN' ROBOTS.
...I DO MISS RABBLE-ROUSIN' ROBOTS.
THOUGHT YOU'D LIKE THAT ONE--BUT THAT'S WHAT I MEAN, THINGS MUST CHANGE, THEY NEED HELP, AND YOU COULD HELP THEM.
WHY ON EARTH WOULD I, NUMBER ONE RUPERT GILES HATER, BE TELLING YOU TO GO TO HIM RIGHT NOW?
I'M NOT THE HEAD OF THE COUNCIL--
NO, YOU'RE NOT. BUT YOU ARE A WATCHER. AND THAT USED TO MEAN SOMETHING MORE THAN BOOT-LICKER.
STEPHEN REILLY WAS MORGAN'S WATCHER WHEN SHE WAS KILLED.
...UH...YES...? WHAT COULD THAT POSSIBLY HAVE TO DO WITH THE OTHER WATCHER MURDERS...
WHERE ARE YOU GOING?
THE LIBRARY!

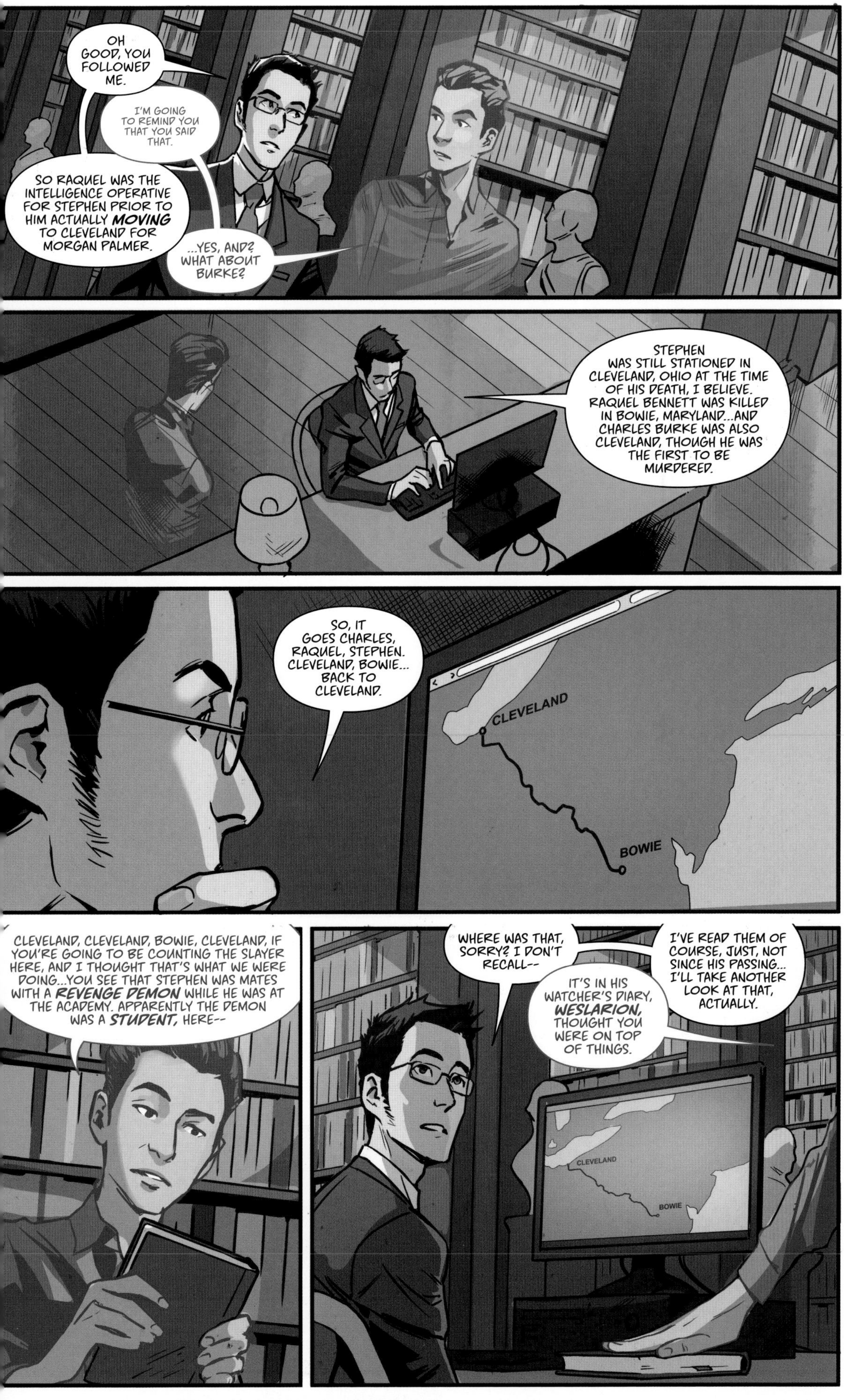
OH GOOD, YOU FOLLOWED ME.
I'M GOING TO REMIND YOU THAT YOU SAID THAT.
SO RAQUEL WAS THE INTELLIGENCE OPERATIVE FOR STEPHEN PRIOR TO HIM ACTUALLY MOVING TO CLEVELAND FOR MORGAN PALMER.
...YES, AND? WHAT ABOUT BURKE?
STEPHEN WAS STILL STATIONED IN CLEVELAND, OHIO AT THE TIME OF HIS DEATH, I BELIEVE. RAQUEL BENNETT WAS KILLED IN BOWIE, MARYLAND...AND CHARLES BURKE WAS ALSO CLEVELAND, THOUGH HE WAS THE FIRST TO BE MURDERED.
SO, IT GOES CHARLES, RAQUEL, STEPHEN. CLEVELAND, BOWIE... BACK TO CLEVELAND.
CLEVELAND
BOWIE
CLEVELAND, CLEVELAND, BOWIE, CLEVELAND, IF YOU'RE GOING TO BE COUNTING THE SLAYER HERE, AND I THOUGHT THAT'S WHAT WE WERE DOING...YOU SEE THAT STEPHEN WAS MATES WITH A REVENGE DEMON WHILE HE WAS AT THE ACADEMY. APPARENTLY THE DEMON WAS A STUDENT, HERE--
WHERE WAS THAT, SORRY? I DON'T RECALL--
IT'S IN HIS WATCHER'S DIARY, WESLARION, THOUGHT YOU WERE ON TOP OF THINGS.
I'VE READ THEM OF COURSE, JUST, NOT SINCE HIS PASSING... I'LL TAKE ANOTHER LOOK AT THAT, ACTUALLY.
CLEVELAND
BOWIE

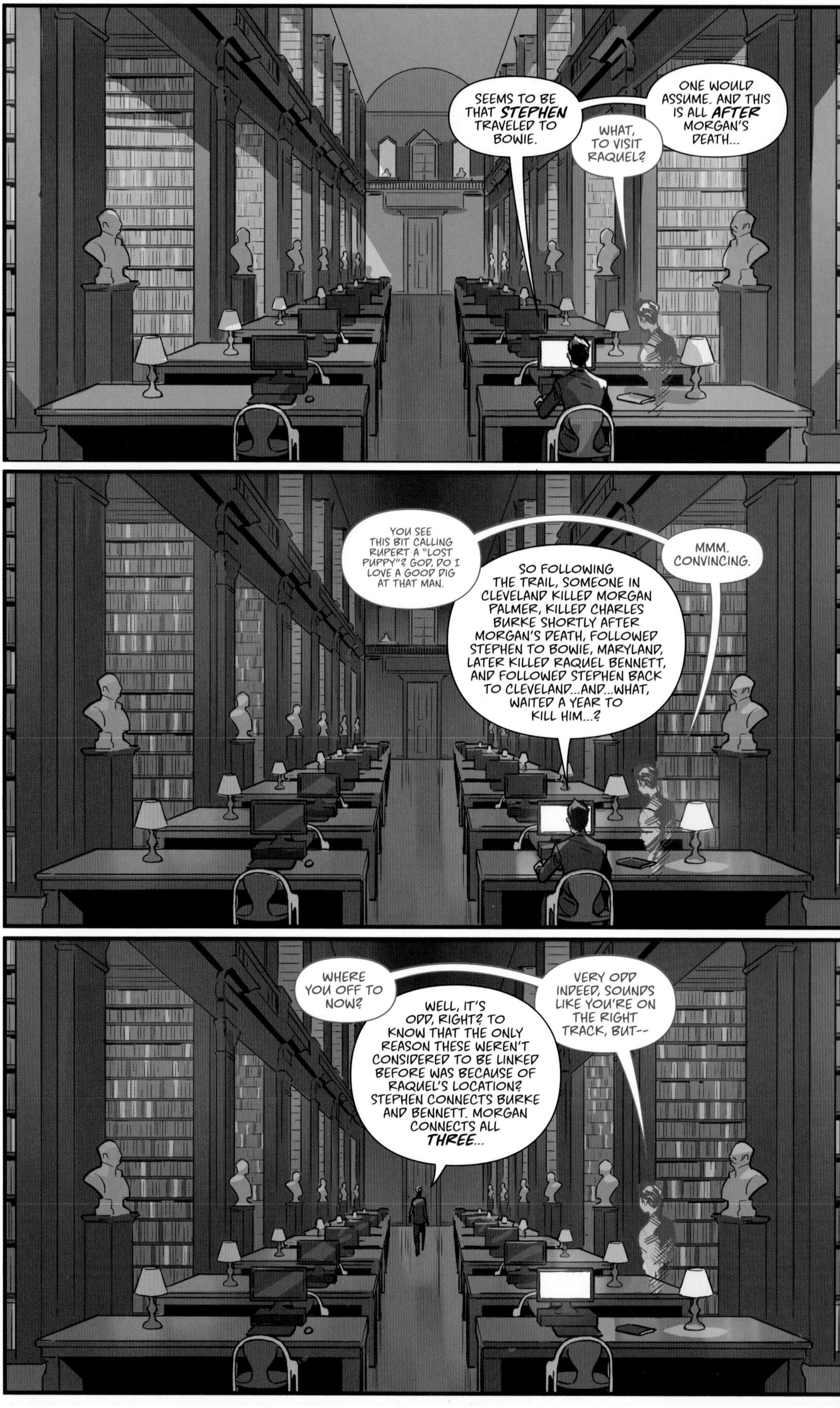
SEEMS TO BE THAT STEPHEN TRAVELED TO BOWIE.
WHAT, TO VISIT RAQUEL?
ONE WOULD ASSUME. AND THIS IS ALL AFTER MORGAN'S DEATH...
YOU SEE THIS BIT CALLING RUPERT A "LOST PUPPY"? GOD, DO I LOVE A GOOD DIG AT THAT MAN.
SO FOLLOWING THE TRAIL, SOMEONE IN CLEVELAND KILLED MORGAN PALMER, KILLED CHARLES BURKE SHORTLY AFTER MORGAN'S DEATH, FOLLOWED STEPHEN TO BOWIE, MARYLAND, LATER KILLED RAQUEL BENNETT, AND FOLLOWED STEPHEN BACK TO CLEVELAND...AND...WHAT, WAITED A YEAR TO KILL HIM...?
MMM. CONVINCING.
WHERE YOU OFF TO NOW?
WELL, IT'S ODD, RIGHT? TO KNOW THAT THE ONLY REASON THESE WEREN'T CONSIDERED TO BE LINKED BEFORE WAS BECAUSE OF RAQUEL'S LOCATION? STEPHEN CONNECTS BURKE AND BENNETT. MORGAN CONNECTS ALL THREE...
VERY ODD INDEED, SOUNDS LIKE YOU'RE ON THE RIGHT TRACK, BUT--

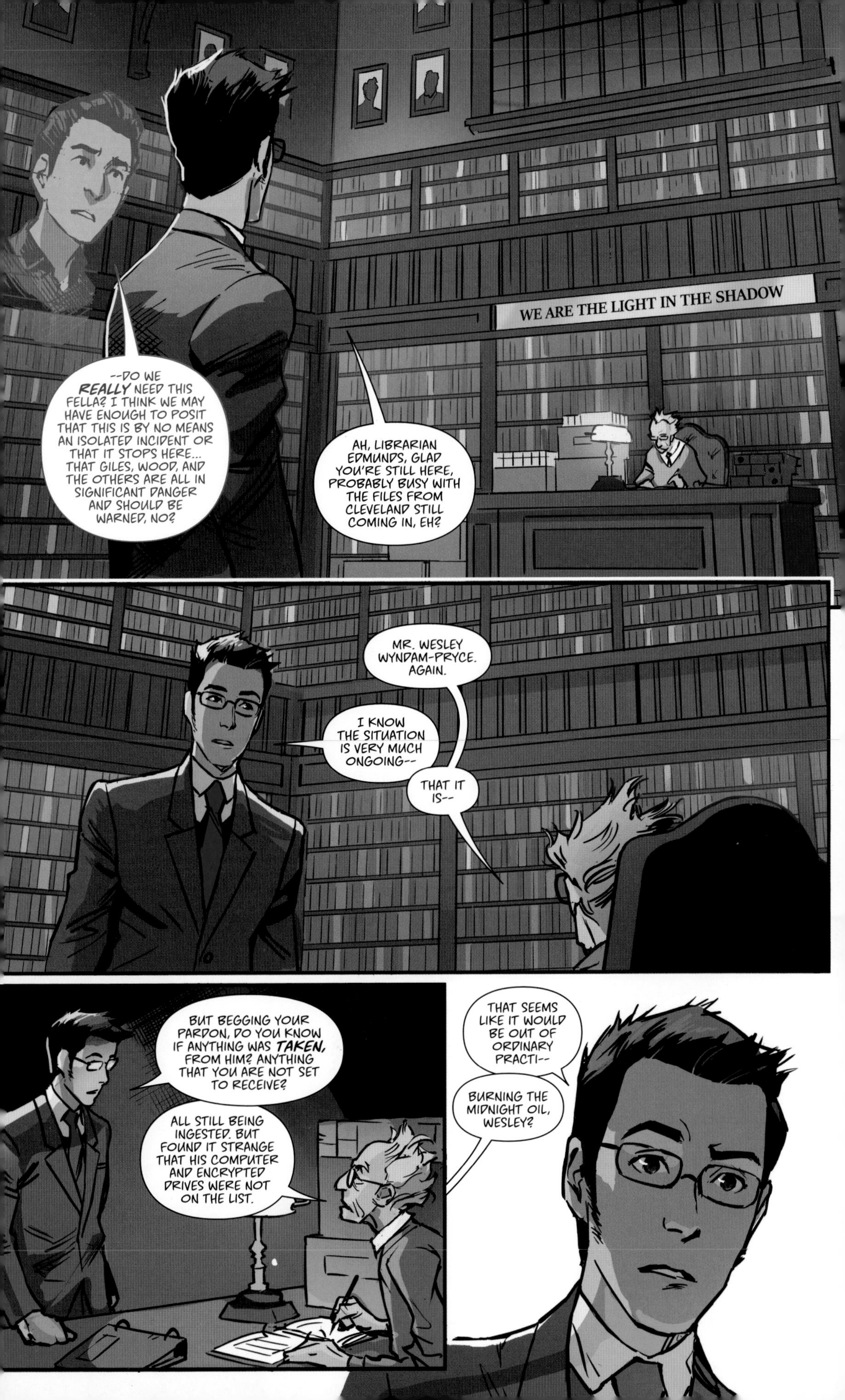

WE ARE THE LIGHT IN THE SHADOW
--DO WE REALLY NEED THIS FELLA? I THINK WE MAY HAVE ENOUGH TO POSIT THAT THIS IS BY NO MEANS AN ISOLATED INCIDENT OR THAT IT STOPS HERE... THAT GILES, WOOD, AND THE OTHERS ARE ALL IN SIGNIFICANT DANGER AND SHOULD BE WARNED, NO?
AH, LIBRARIAN EDMUNDS, GLAD YOU'RE STILL HERE, PROBABLY BUSY WITH THE FILES FROM CLEVELAND STILL COMING IN, EH?
MR. WESLEY WYNDAM-PRYCE. AGAIN.
I KNOW THE SITUATION IS VERY MUCH ONGOING--
THAT IT IS--
BUT BEGGING YOUR PARDON, DO YOU KNOW IF ANYTHING WAS TAKEN, FROM HIM? ANYTHING THAT YOU ARE NOT SET TO RECEIVE?
ALL STILL BEING INGESTED. BUT FOUND IT STRANGE THAT HIS COMPUTER AND ENCRYPTED DRIVES WERE NOT ON THE LIST.
THAT SEEMS LIKE IT WOULD BE OUT OF ORDINARY PRACTI--
BURNING THE MIDNIGHT OIL, WESLEY?

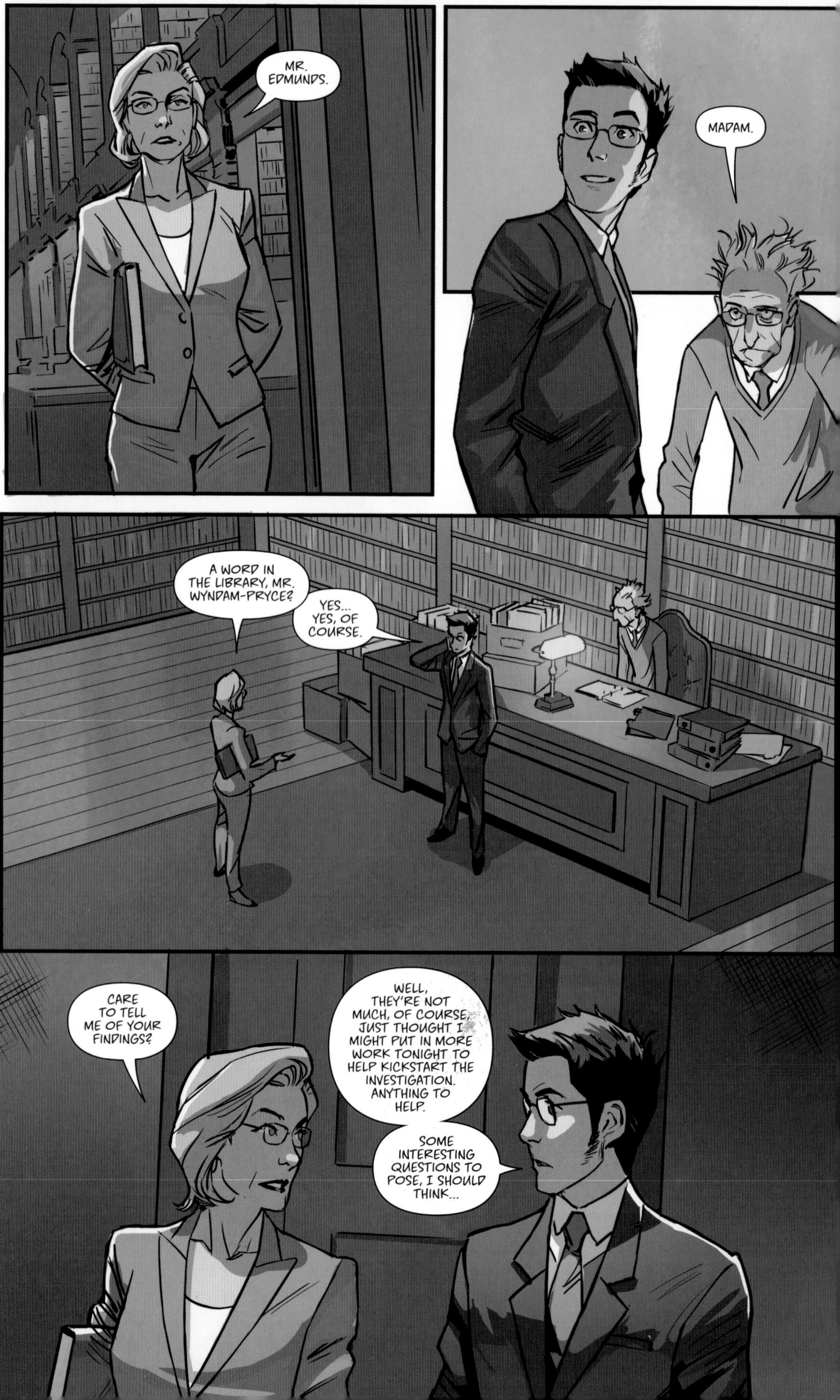
MR. EDMUNDS.
MADAM.
A WORD IN THE LIBRARY, MR. WYNDAM-PRYCE?
YES... YES, OF COURSE.
CARE TO TELL ME OF YOUR FINDINGS?
WELL, THEY'RE NOT MUCH, OF COURSE, JUST THOUGHT I MIGHT PUT IN MORE WORK TONIGHT TO HELP KICKSTART THE INVESTIGATION. ANYTHING TO HELP.
SOME INTERESTING QUESTIONS TO POSE, I SHOULD THINK...

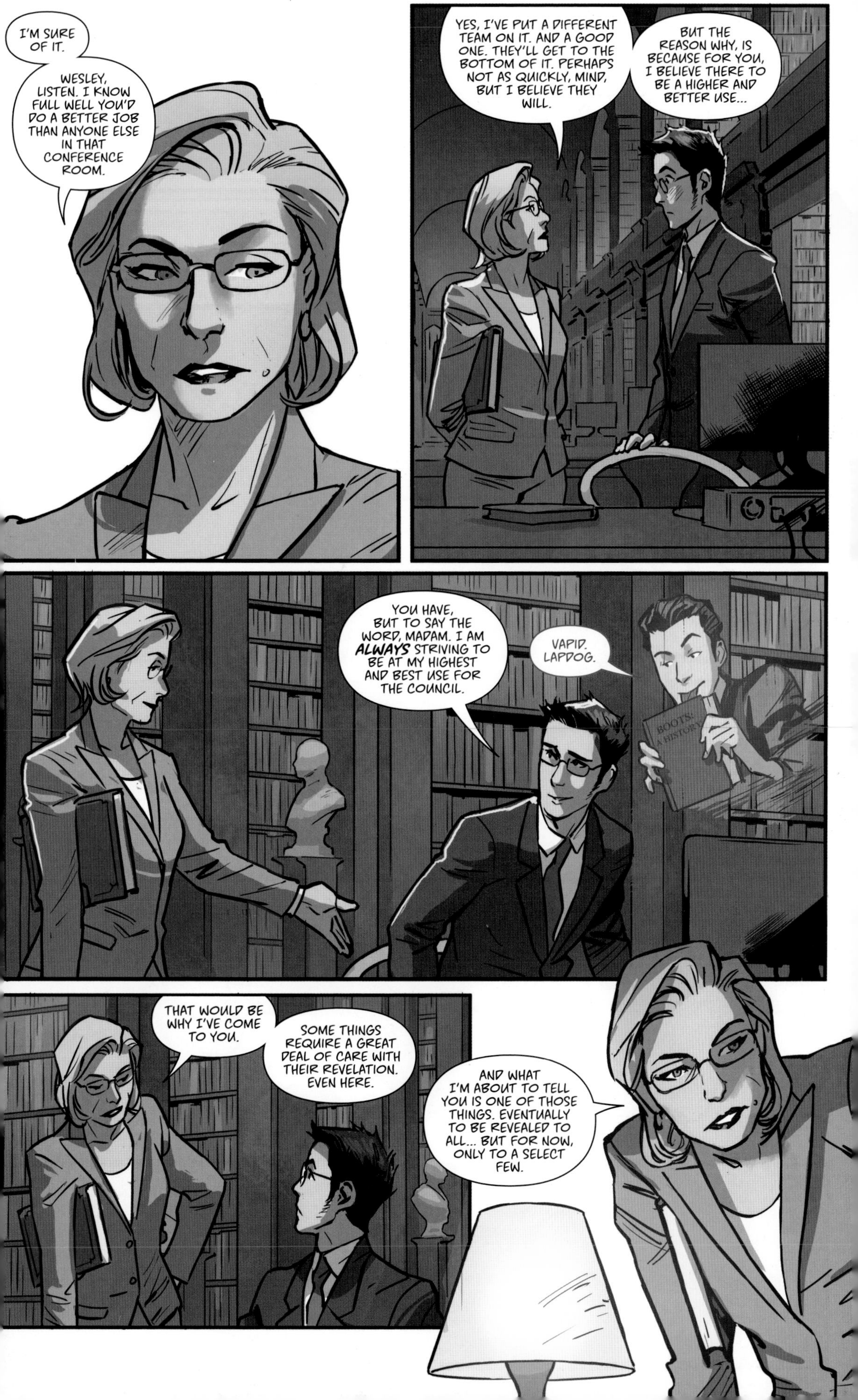
I'M SURE OF IT.
WESLEY, LISTEN. I KNOW FULL WELL YOU'D DO A BETTER JOB THAN ANYONE ELSE IN THAT CONFERENCE ROOM.
YES, I'VE PUT A DIFFERENT TEAM ON IT. AND A GOOD ONE. THEY'LL GET TO THE BOTTOM OF IT. PERHAPS NOT AS QUICKLY, MIND, BUT I BELIEVE THEY WILL.
BUT THE REASON WHY, IS BECAUSE FOR YOU, I BELIEVE THERE TO BE A HIGHER AND BETTER USE...
YOU HAVE, BUT TO SAY THE WORD, MADAM. I AM ALWAYS STRIVING TO BE AT MY HIGHEST AND BEST USE FOR THE COUNCIL.
VAPID. LAPDOG.
BOOTS: A HISTORY
THAT WOULD BE WHY I'VE COME TO YOU.
SOME THINGS REQUIRE A GREAT DEAL OF CARE WITH THEIR REVELATION. EVEN HERE.
AND WHAT I'M ABOUT TO TELL YOU IS ONE OF THOSE THINGS. EVENTUALLY TO BE REVEALED TO ALL... BUT FOR NOW, ONLY TO A SELECT FEW.

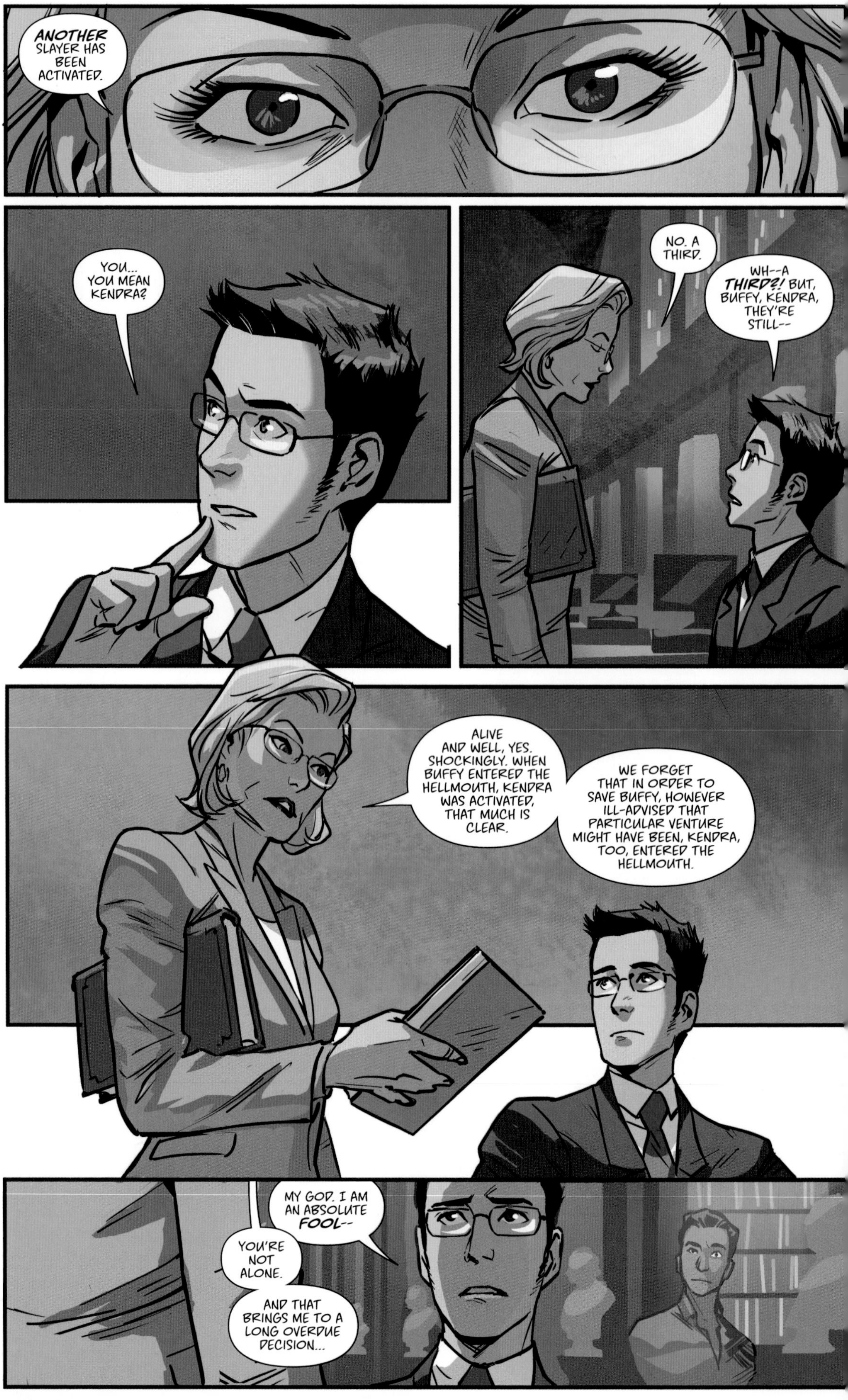
ANOTHER SLAYER HAS BEEN ACTIVATED.
YOU... YOU MEAN KENDRA?
NO. A THIRD.
WH--A THIRD?! BUT, BUFFY, KENDRA, THEY'RE STILL--
ALIVE AND WELL, YES. SHOCKINGLY. WHEN BUFFY ENTERED THE HELLMOUTH, KENDRA WAS ACTIVATED, THAT MUCH IS CLEAR.
WE FORGET THAT IN ORDER TO SAVE BUFFY, HOWEVER ILL-ADVISED THAT PARTICULAR VENTURE MIGHT HAVE BEEN, KENDRA, TOO, ENTERED THE HELLMOUTH.
MY GOD. I AM AN ABSOLUTE FOOL--
YOU'RE NOT ALONE.
AND THAT BRINGS ME TO A LONG OVERDUE DECISION...

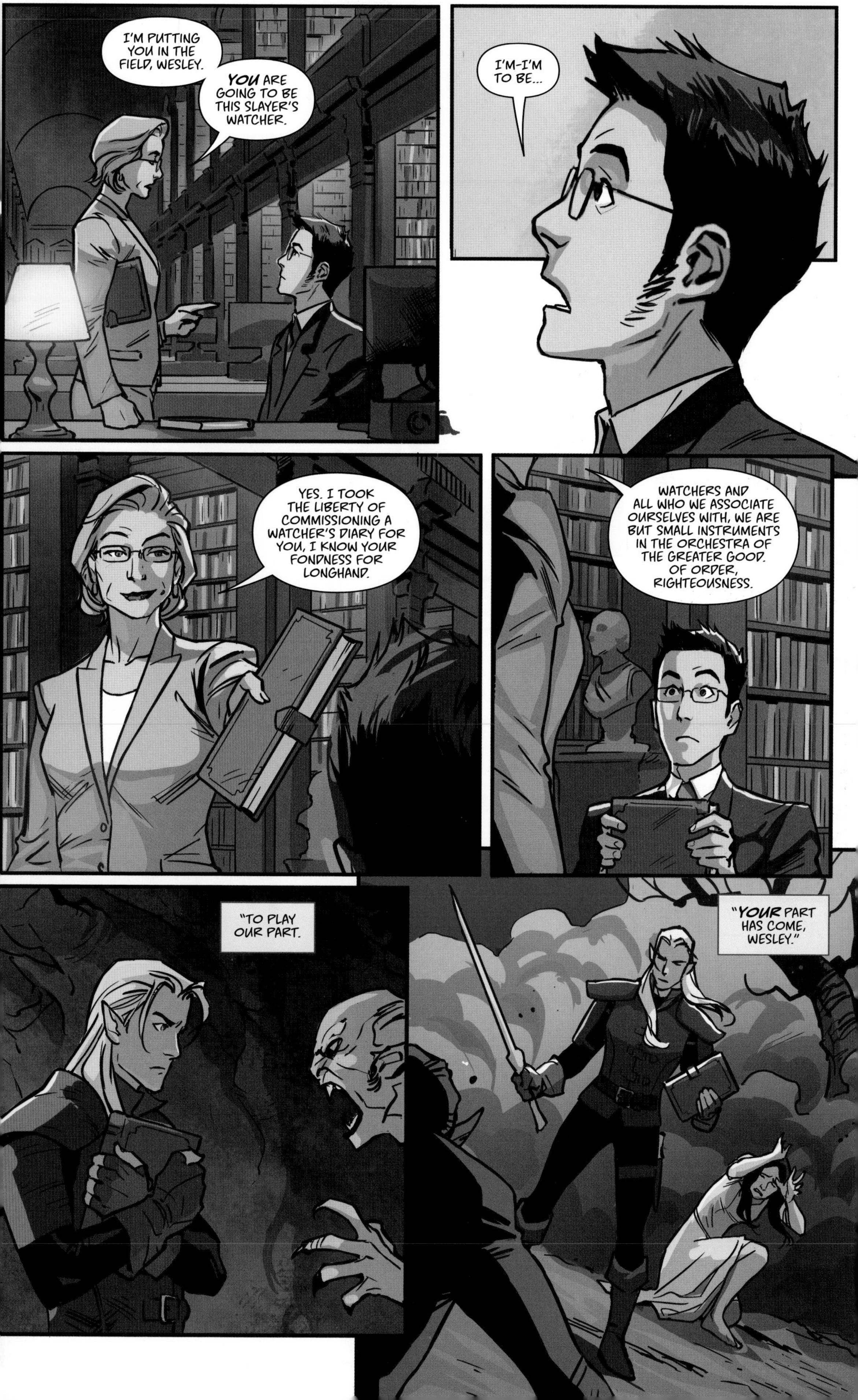
I'M PUTTING YOU IN THE FIELD, WESLEY.
YOU ARE GOING TO BE THIS SLAYER'S WATCHER.
I'M-I'M TO BE...
YES. I TOOK THE LIBERTY OF COMMISSIONING A WATCHER'S DIARY FOR YOU, I KNOW YOUR FONDNESS FOR LONGHAND.
WATCHERS AND ALL WHO WE ASSOCIATE OURSELVES WITH, WE ARE BUT SMALL INSTRUMENTS IN THE ORCHESTRA OF THE GREATER GOOD. OF ORDER, RIGHTEOUSNESS.
"TO PLAY OUR PART.
"YOUR PART HAS COME, WESLEY."

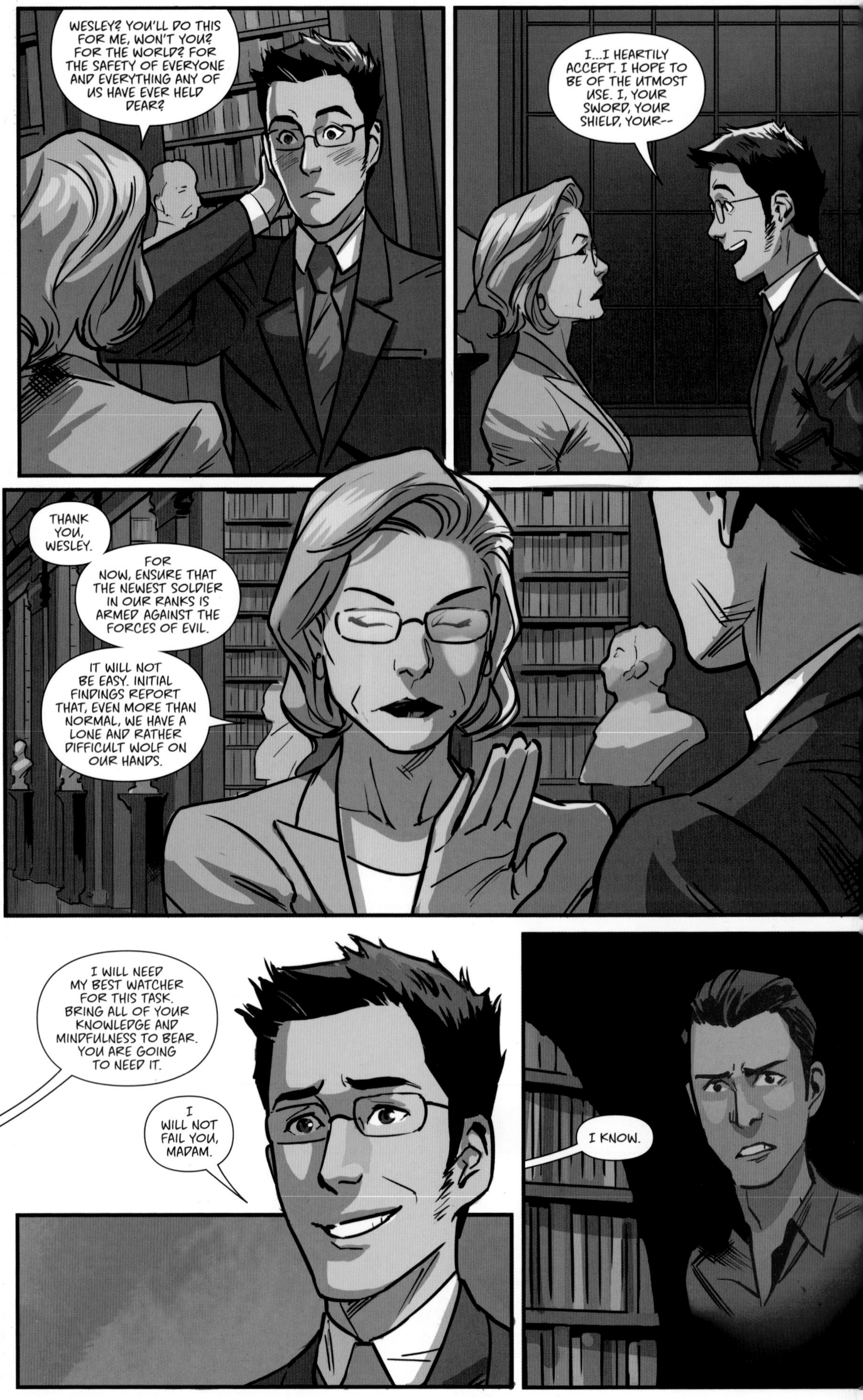
WESLEY? YOU'LL DO THIS FOR ME, WON'T YOU? FOR THE WORLD? FOR THE SAFETY OF EVERYONE AND EVERYTHING ANY OF US HAVE EVER HELD DEAR?
I...I HEARTILY ACCEPT. I HOPE TO BE OF THE UTMOST USE. I, YOUR SWORD, YOUR SHIELD, YOUR--
THANK YOU, WESLEY.
FOR NOW, ENSURE THAT THE NEWEST SOLDIER IN OUR RANKS IS ARMED AGAINST THE FORCES OF EVIL.
IT WILL NOT BE EASY. INITIAL FINDINGS REPORT THAT, EVEN MORE THAN NORMAL, WE HAVE A LONE AND RATHER DIFFICULT WOLF ON OUR HANDS.
I WILL NEED MY BEST WATCHER FOR THIS TASK. BRING ALL OF YOUR KNOWLEDGE AND MINDFULNESS TO BEAR. YOU ARE GOING TO NEED IT.
I WILL NOT FAIL YOU, MADAM.
I KNOW.

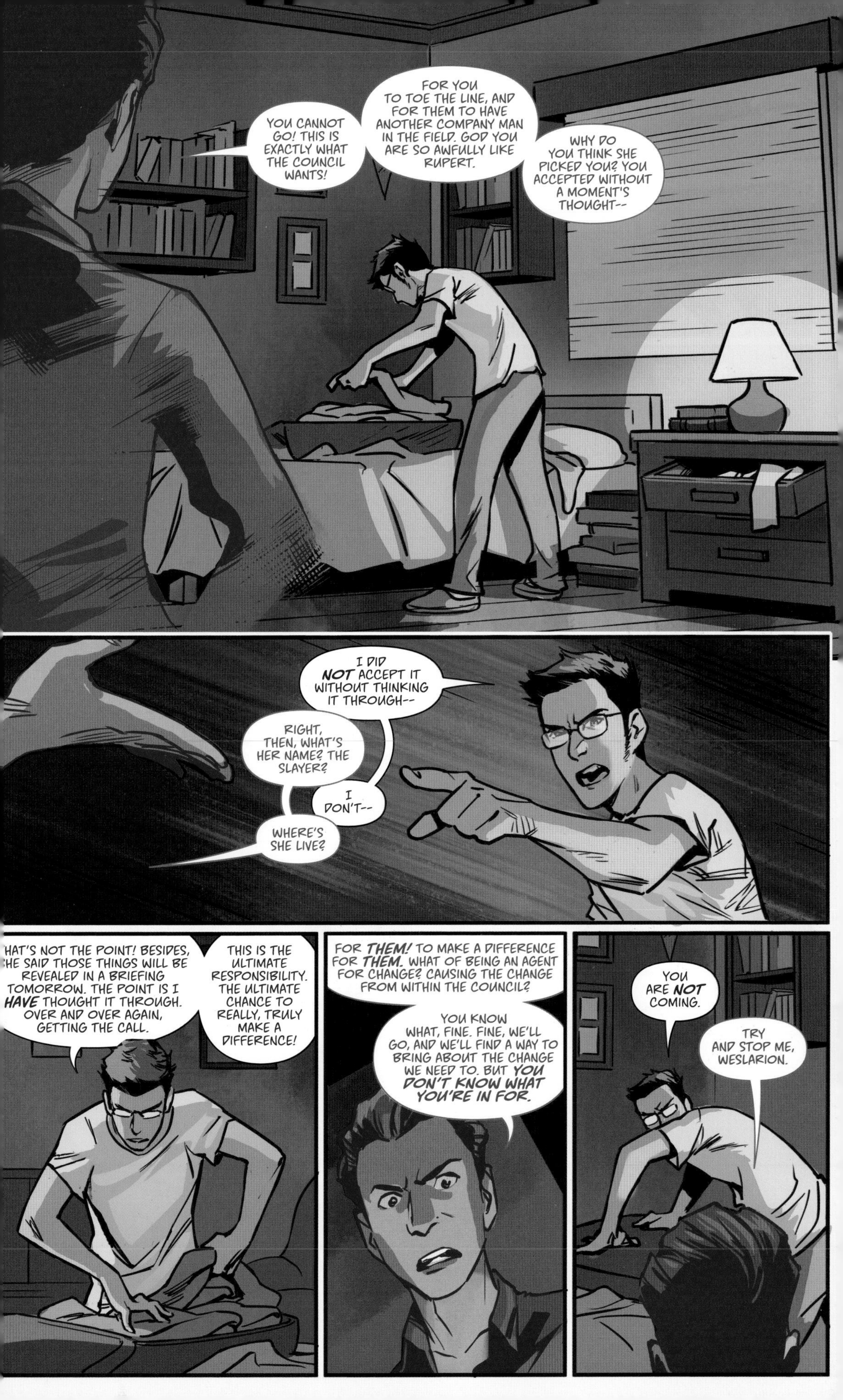
YOU CANNOT GO! THIS IS EXACTLY WHAT THE COUNCIL WANTS!
FOR YOU TO TOE THE LINE, AND FOR THEM TO HAVE ANOTHER COMPANY MAN IN THE FIELD. GOD YOU ARE SO AWFULLY LIKE RUPERT.
WHY DO YOU THINK SHE PICKED YOU? YOU ACCEPTED WITHOUT A MOMENT'S THOUGHT--
I DID NOT ACCEPT IT WITHOUT THINKING IT THROUGH--
RIGHT, THEN, WHAT'S HER NAME? THE SLAYER?
I DON'T--
WHERE'S SHE LIVE?
HAT'S NOT THE POINT! BESIDES, HE SAID THOSE THINGS WILL BE REVEALED IN A BRIEFING TOMORROW. THE POINT IS I HAVE THOUGHT IT THROUGH. OVER AND OVER AGAIN, GETTING THE CALL.
THIS IS THE ULTIMATE RESPONSIBILITY. THE ULTIMATE CHANCE TO REALLY, TRULY MAKE A DIFFERENCE!
FOR THEM! TO MAKE A DIFFERENCE FOR THEM. WHAT OF BEING AN AGENT FOR CHANGE? CAUSING THE CHANGE FROM WITHIN THE COUNCIL?
YOU KNOW WHAT, FINE. FINE, WE'LL GO, AND WE'LL FIND A WAY TO BRING ABOUT THE CHANGE WE NEED TO. BUT YOU DON'T KNOW WHAT YOU'RE IN FOR.
YOU ARE NOT COMING.
TRY AND STOP ME, WESLARION.

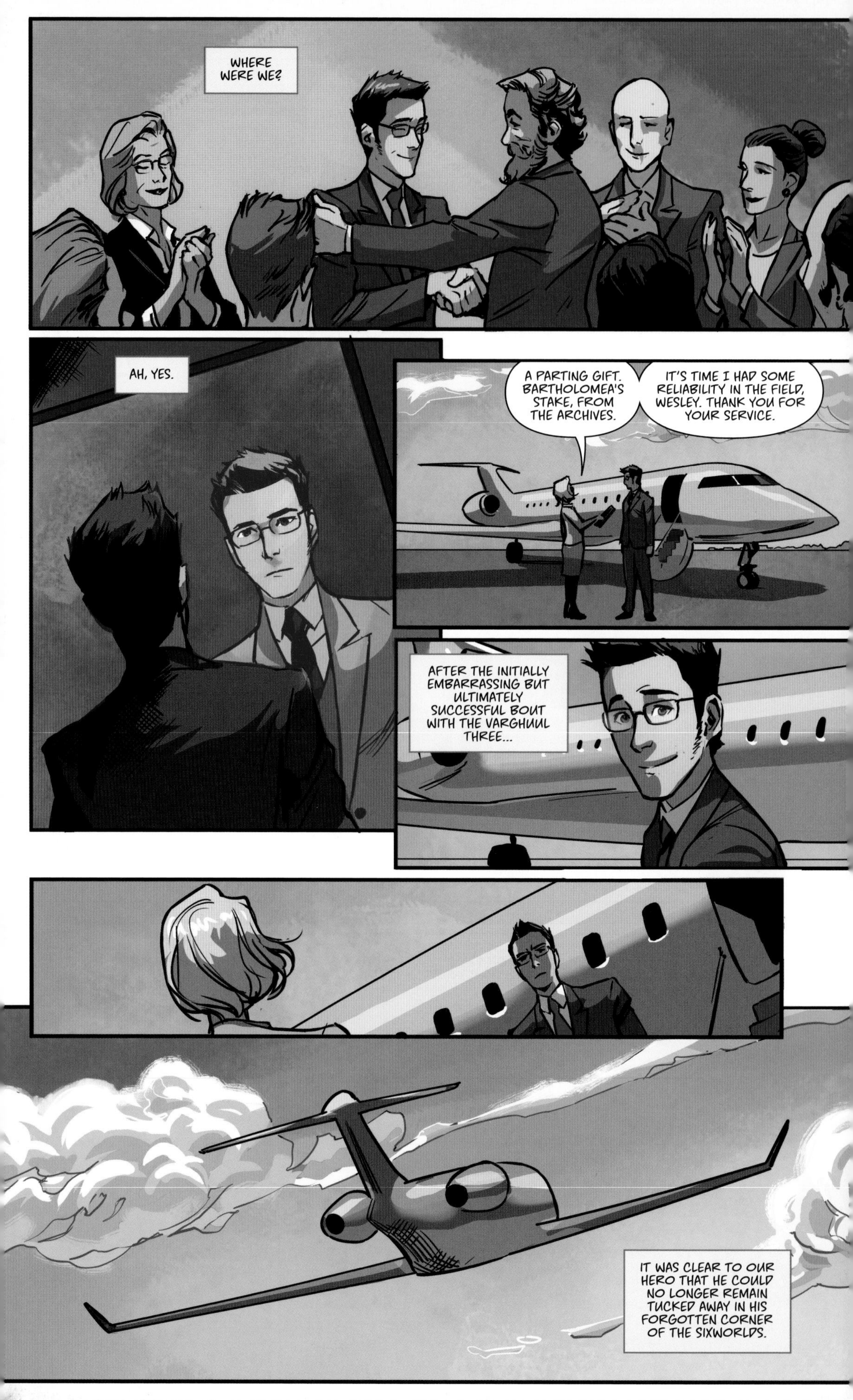
WHERE WERE WE?
AH, YES.
A PARTING GIFT. BARTHOLOMEA'S STAKE, FROM THE ARCHIVES.
IT'S TIME I HAD SOME RELIABILITY IN THE FIELD, WESLEY. THANK YOU FOR YOUR SERVICE.
AFTER THE INITIALLY EMBARRASSING BUT ULTIMATELY SUCCESSFUL BOUT WITH THE VARGHUUL THREE...
IT WAS CLEAR TO OUR HERO THAT HE COULD NO LONGER REMAIN TUCKED AWAY IN HIS FORGOTTEN CORNER OF THE SIXWORLDS.

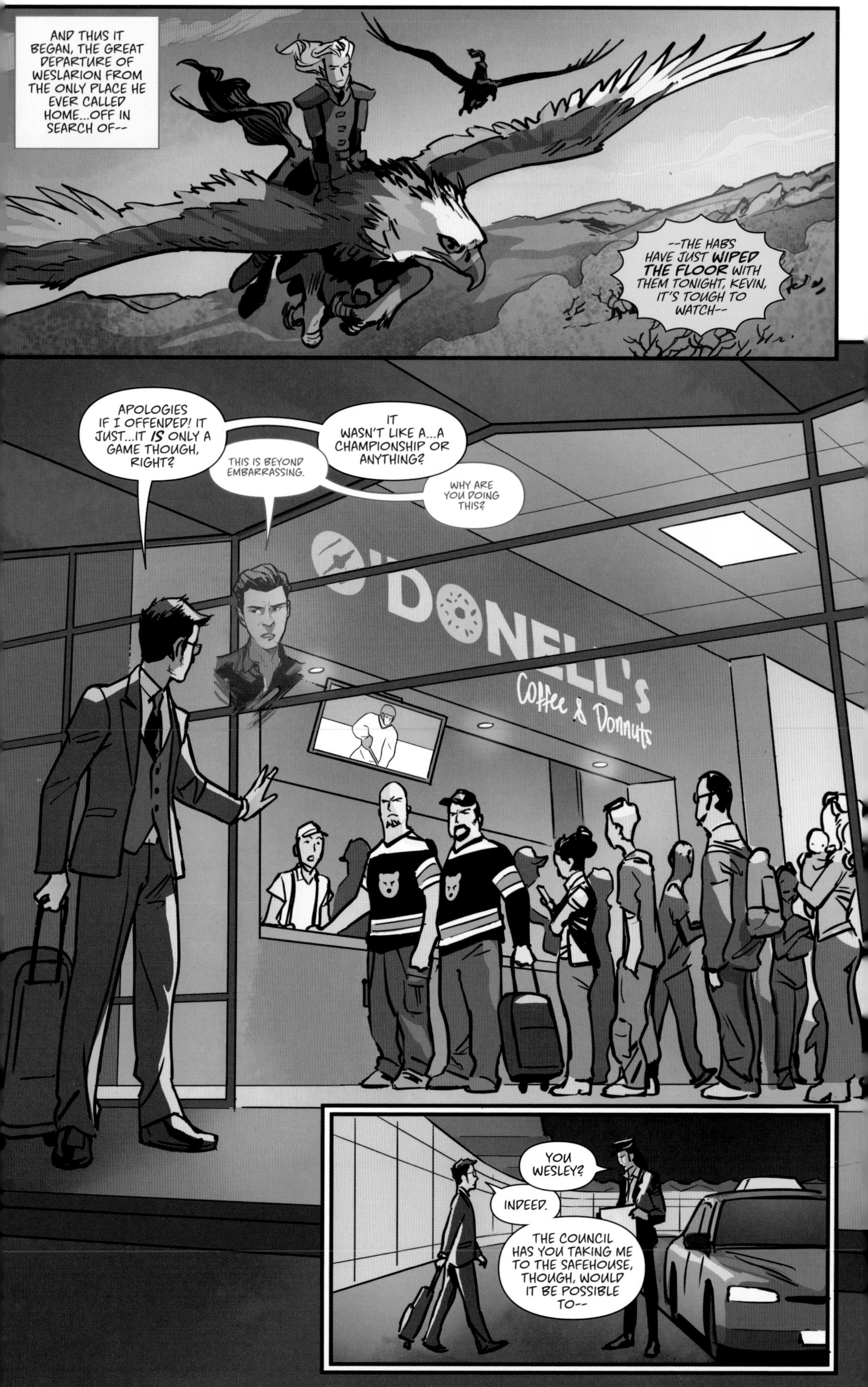
AND THUS IT BEGAN, THE GREAT DEPARTURE OF WESLARION FROM THE ONLY PLACE HE EVER CALLED HOME...OFF IN SEARCH OF--
--THE HABS HAVE JUST **WIPED THE FLOOR** WITH THEM TONIGHT, KEVIN, IT'S TOUGH TO WATCH--
APOLOGIES IF I OFFENDED! IT JUST...IT ***IS*** ONLY A GAME THOUGH, RIGHT?
IT WASN'T LIKE A...A CHAMPIONSHIP OR ANYTHING?
THIS IS BEYOND EMBARRASSING.
WHY ARE YOU DOING THIS?
YOU WESLEY?
INDEED.
THE COUNCIL HAS YOU TAKING ME TO THE SAFEHOUSE, THOUGH, WOULD IT BE POSSIBLE TO--

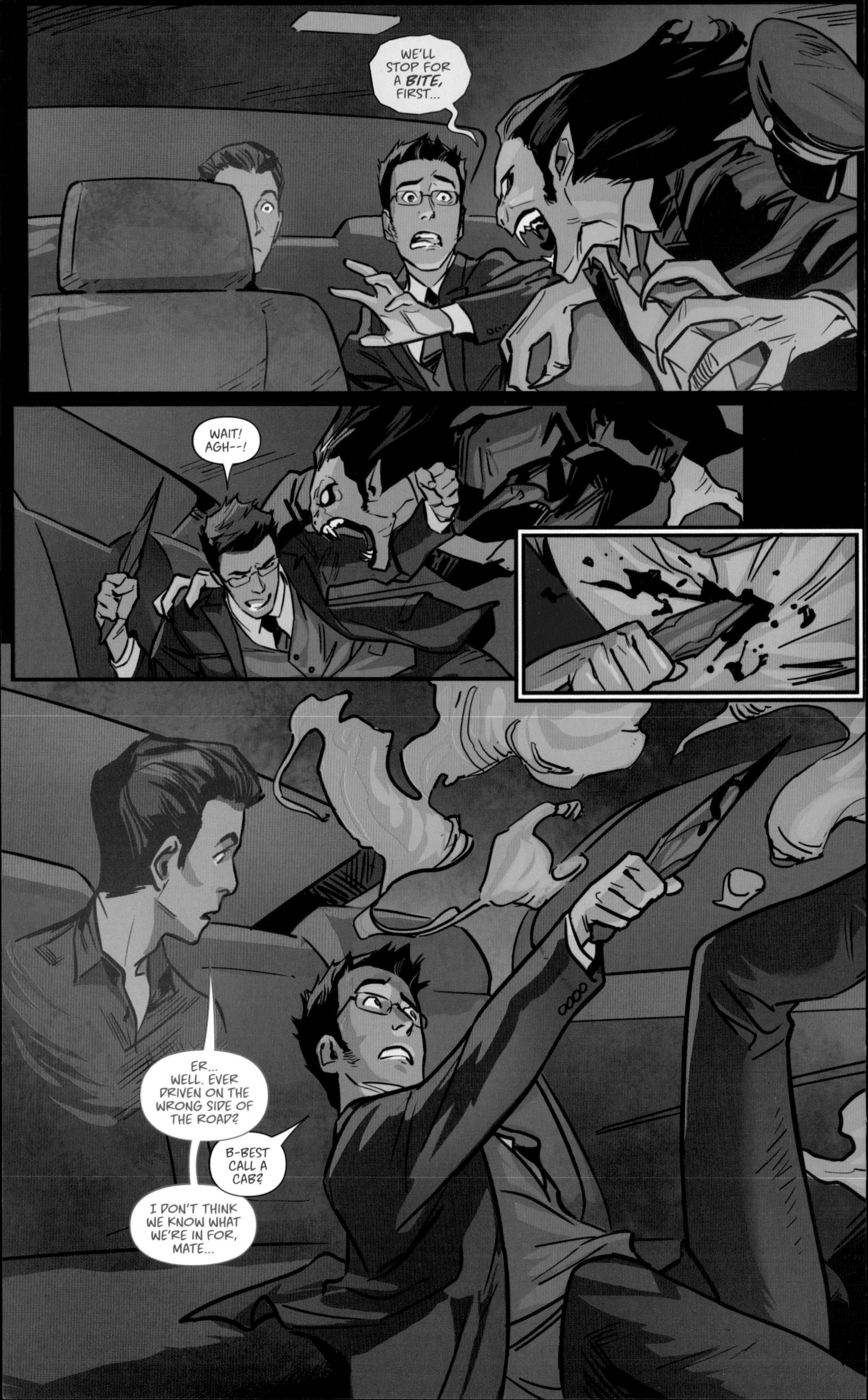
WE'LL STOP FOR A BITE, FIRST...
WAIT! AGH--!
ER... WELL. EVER DRIVEN ON THE WRONG SIDE OF THE ROAD?
B-BEST CALL A CAB?
I DON'T THINK WE KNOW WHAT WE'RE IN FOR, MATE...

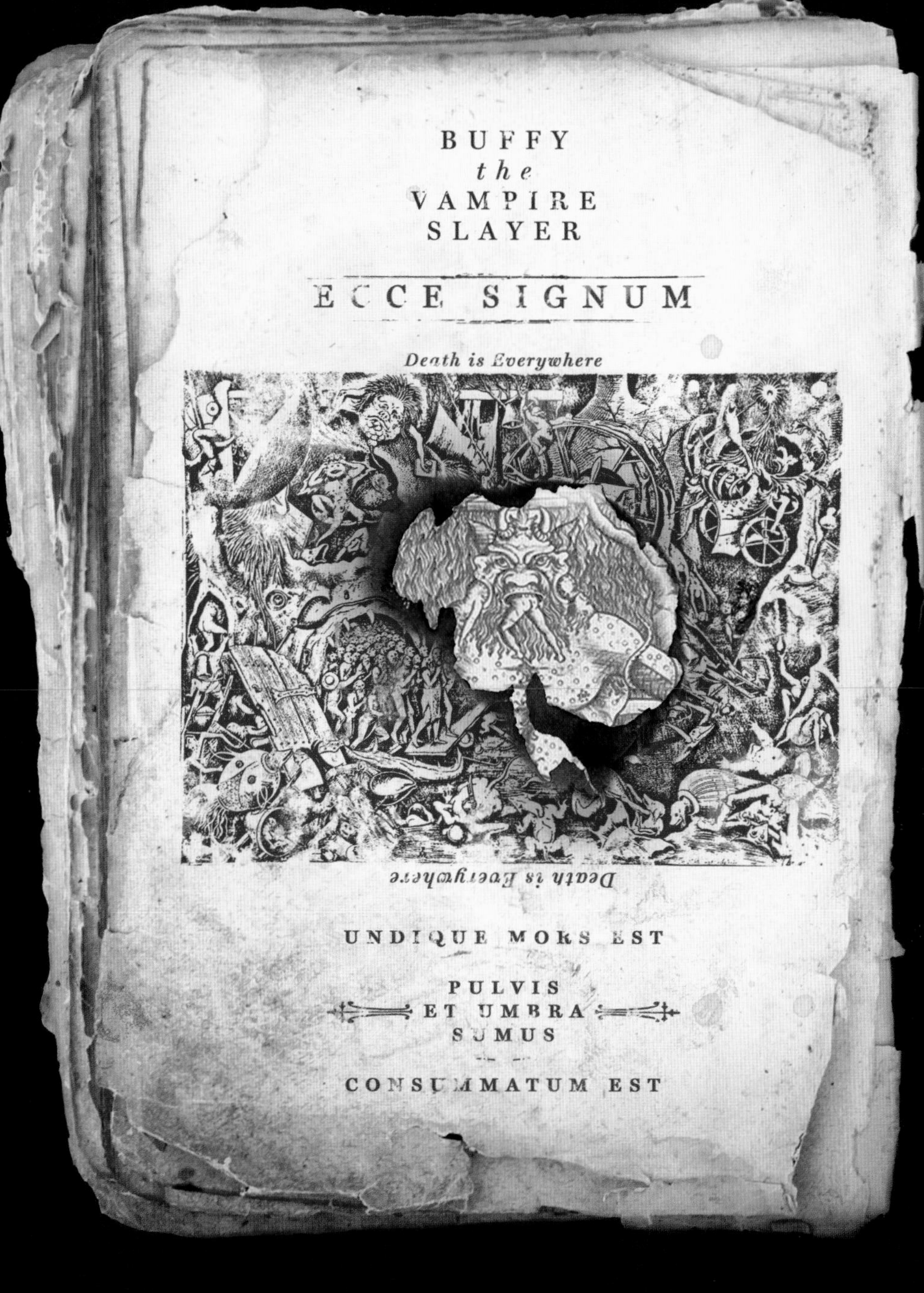
BUFFY
the
VAMPIRE
SLAYER
ECCE SIGNUM
Death is Everywhere
Death is Everywhere
UNDIQUE MORS EST
PULVIS
ET UMBRA
SUMUS
CONSUMMATUM EST

Issue Seventeen Ring of Fire Cover by **Becca Carey**

CHAPTER
EIGHTEEN

Issue Eighteen Cover by **David López**

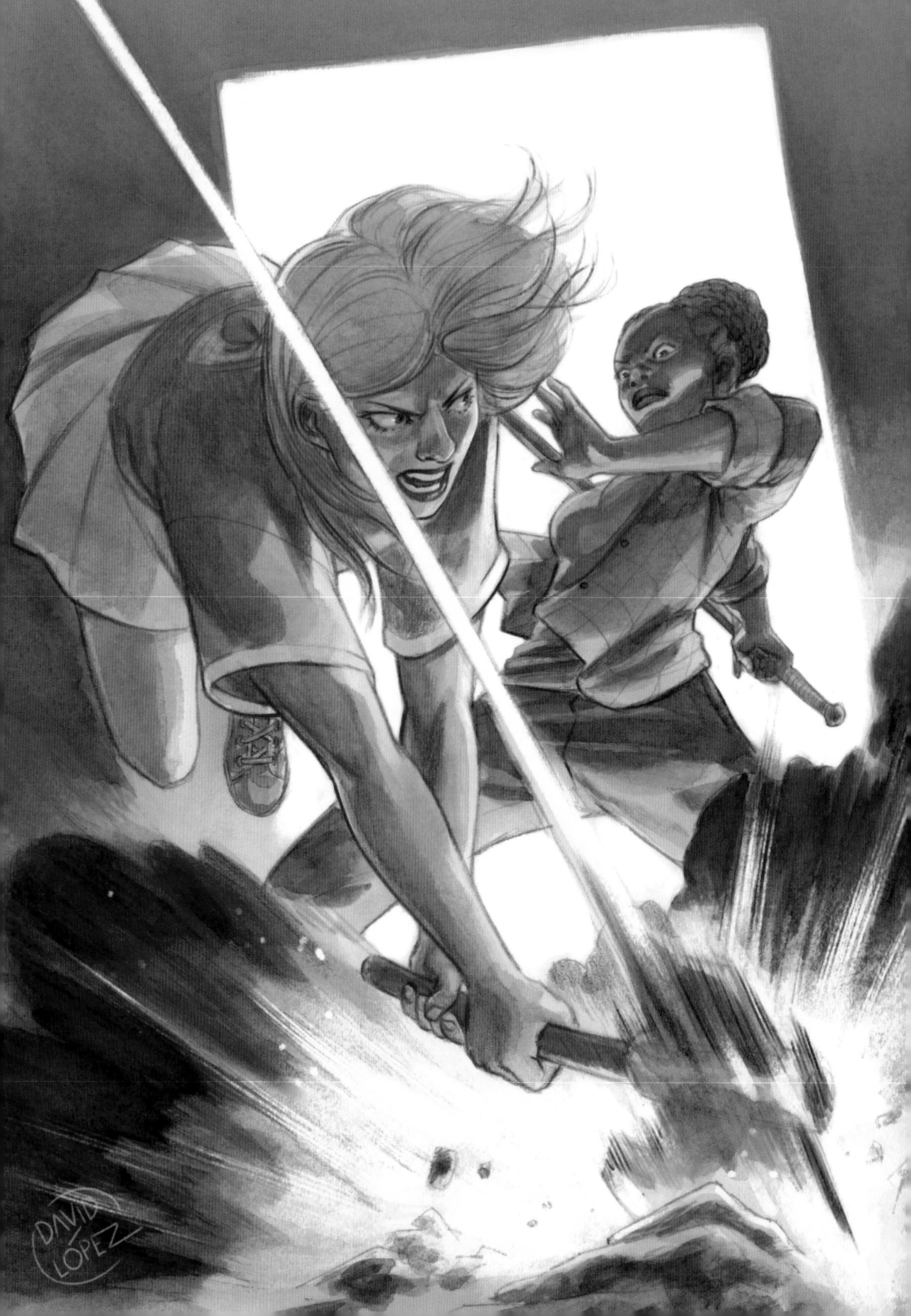
DAVID LÓPEZ

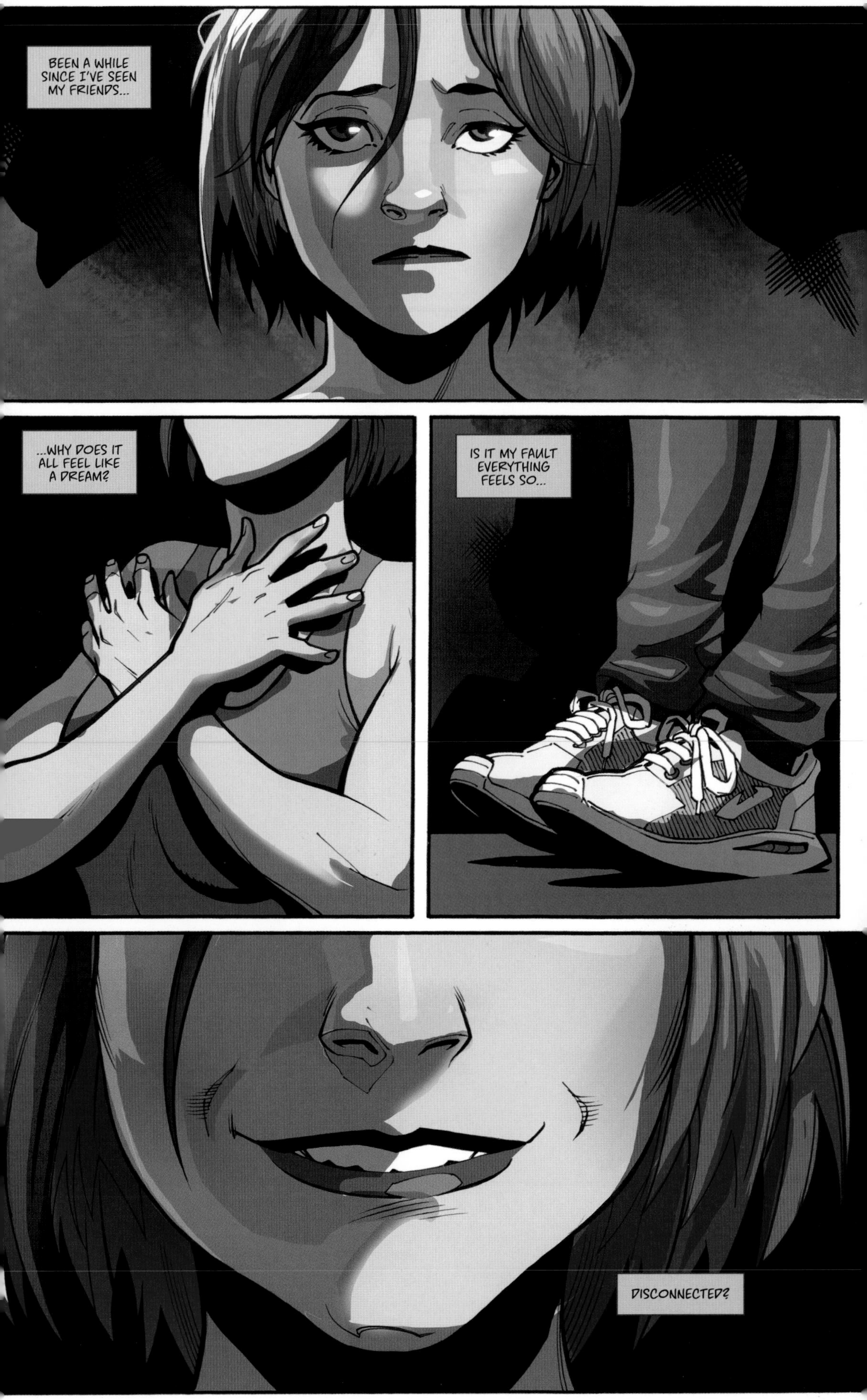
BEEN A WHILE SINCE I'VE SEEN MY FRIENDS...
...WHY DOES IT ALL FEEL LIKE A DREAM?
IS IT MY FAULT EVERYTHING FEELS SO...
DISCONNECTED?

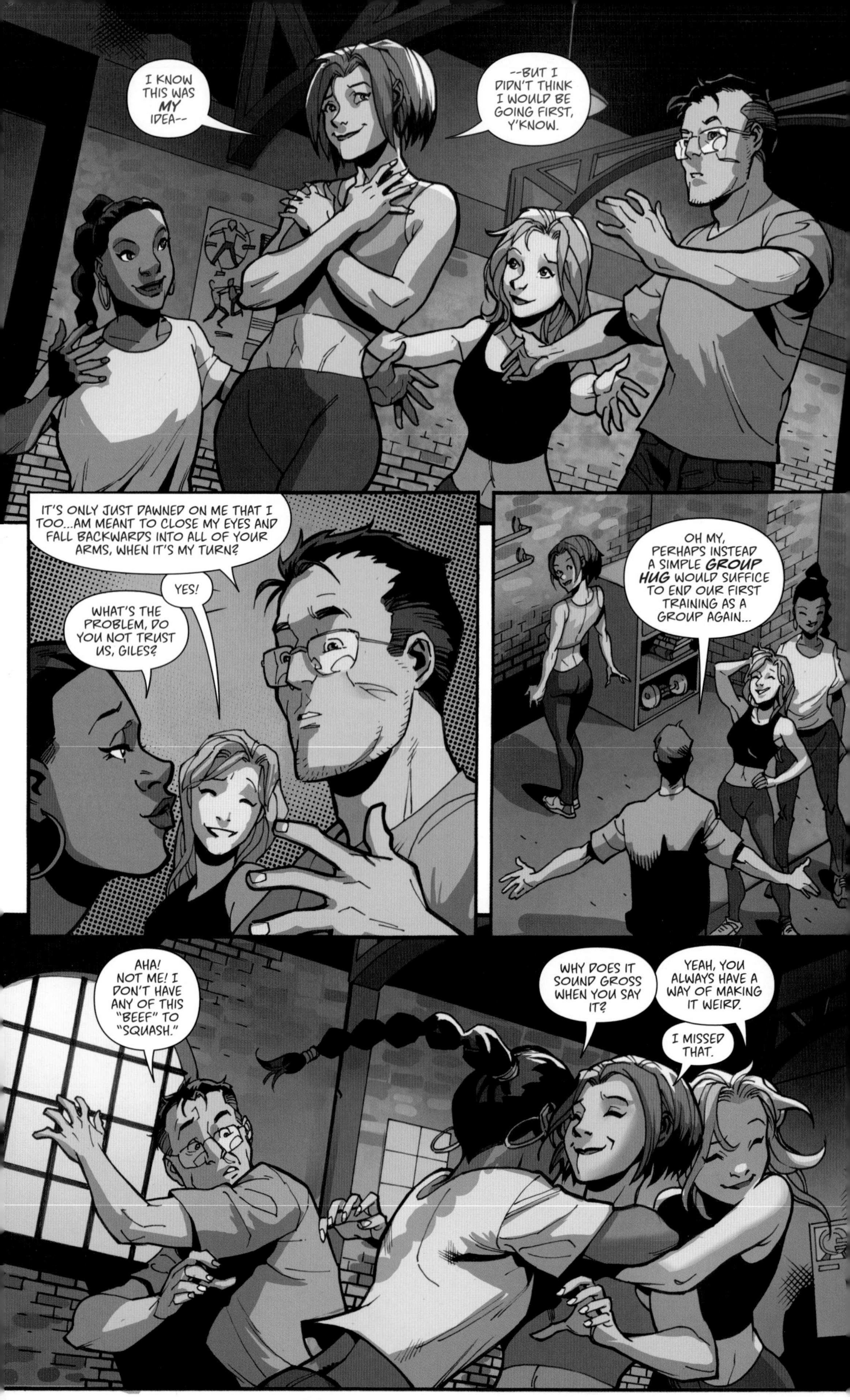
I KNOW THIS WAS MY IDEA--
--BUT I DIDN'T THINK I WOULD BE GOING FIRST, Y'KNOW.
IT'S ONLY JUST DAWNED ON ME THAT I TOO...AM MEANT TO CLOSE MY EYES AND FALL BACKWARDS INTO ALL OF YOUR ARMS, WHEN IT'S MY TURN?
YES!
WHAT'S THE PROBLEM, DO YOU NOT TRUST US, GILES?
OH MY, PERHAPS INSTEAD A SIMPLE GROUP HUG WOULD SUFFICE TO END OUR FIRST TRAINING AS A GROUP AGAIN...
AHA! NOT ME! I DON'T HAVE ANY OF THIS "BEEF" TO "SQUASH."
WHY DOES IT SOUND GROSS WHEN YOU SAY IT?
YEAH, YOU ALWAYS HAVE A WAY OF MAKING IT WEIRD.
I MISSED THAT.

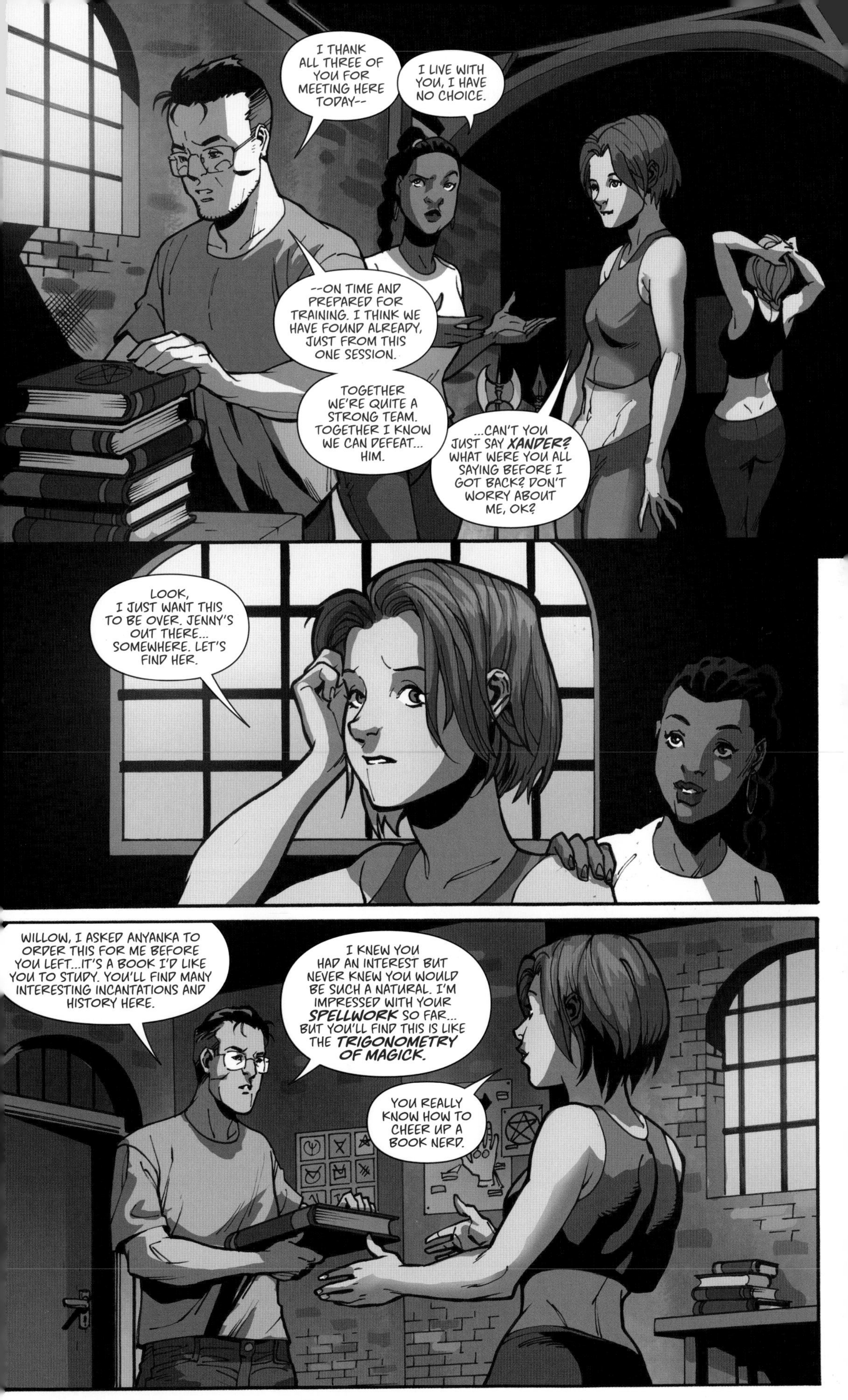
I THANK ALL THREE OF YOU FOR MEETING HERE TODAY--
I LIVE WITH YOU, I HAVE NO CHOICE.
--ON TIME AND PREPARED FOR TRAINING. I THINK WE HAVE FOUND ALREADY, JUST FROM THIS ONE SESSION.
TOGETHER WE'RE QUITE A STRONG TEAM. TOGETHER I KNOW WE CAN DEFEAT... HIM.
...CAN'T YOU JUST SAY XANDER? WHAT WERE YOU ALL SAYING BEFORE I GOT BACK? DON'T WORRY ABOUT ME, OK?
LOOK, I JUST WANT THIS TO BE OVER. JENNY'S OUT THERE... SOMEWHERE. LET'S FIND HER.
WILLOW, I ASKED ANYANKA TO ORDER THIS FOR ME BEFORE YOU LEFT...IT'S A BOOK I'D LIKE YOU TO STUDY. YOU'LL FIND MANY INTERESTING INCANTATIONS AND HISTORY HERE.
I KNEW YOU HAD AN INTEREST BUT NEVER KNEW YOU WOULD BE SUCH A NATURAL. I'M IMPRESSED WITH YOUR SPELLWORK SO FAR... BUT YOU'LL FIND THIS IS LIKE THE TRIGONOMETRY OF MAGICK.
YOU REALLY KNOW HOW TO CHEER UP A BOOK NERD.

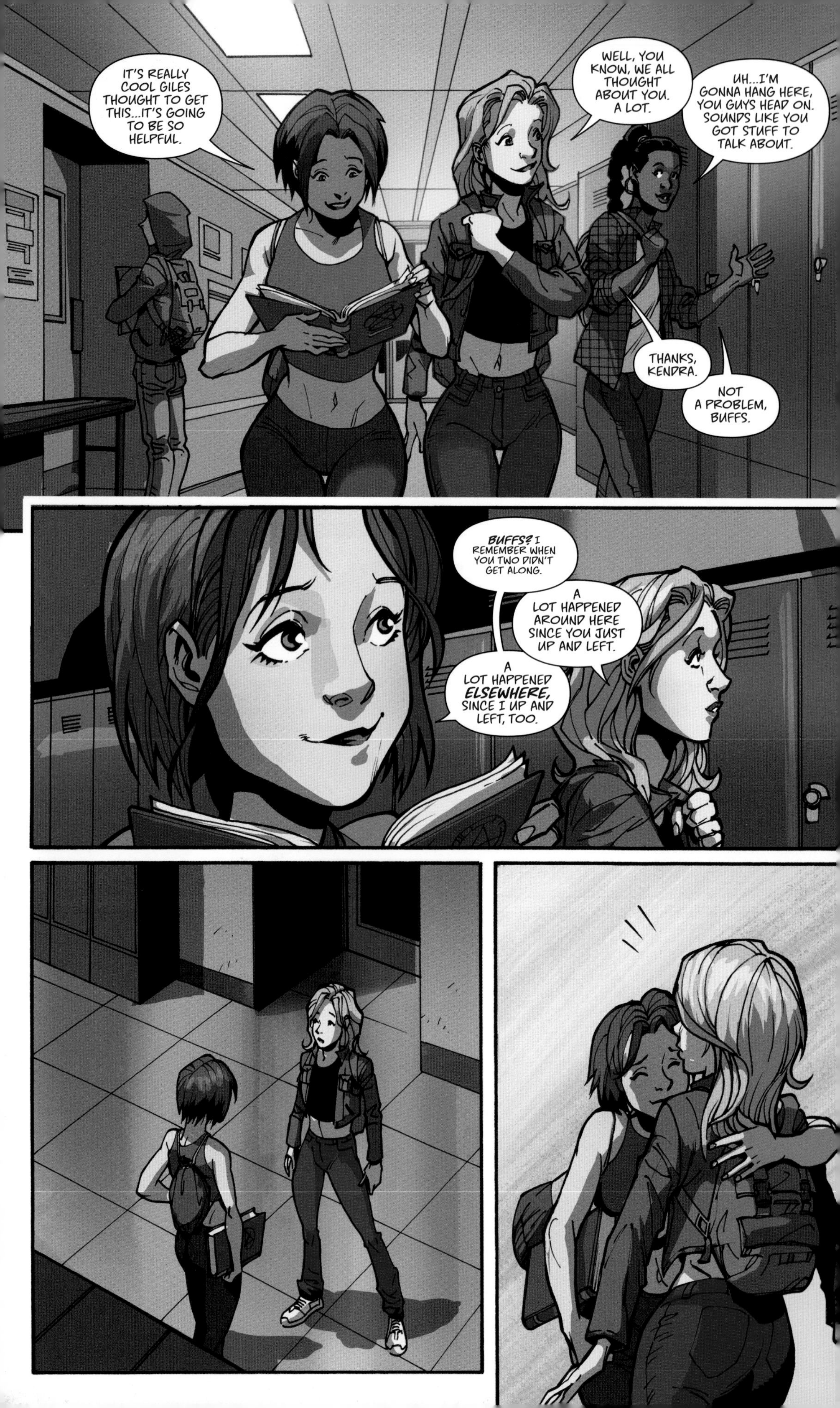
IT'S REALLY COOL GILES THOUGHT TO GET THIS...IT'S GOING TO BE SO HELPFUL.
WELL, YOU KNOW, WE ALL THOUGHT ABOUT YOU. A LOT.
UH...I'M GONNA HANG HERE, YOU GUYS HEAD ON. SOUNDS LIKE YOU GOT STUFF TO TALK ABOUT.
THANKS, KENDRA.
NOT A PROBLEM, BUFFS.
BUFFS? I REMEMBER WHEN YOU TWO DIDN'T GET ALONG.
A LOT HAPPENED AROUND HERE SINCE YOU JUST UP AND LEFT.
A LOT HAPPENED ELSEWHERE, SINCE I UP AND LEFT, TOO.

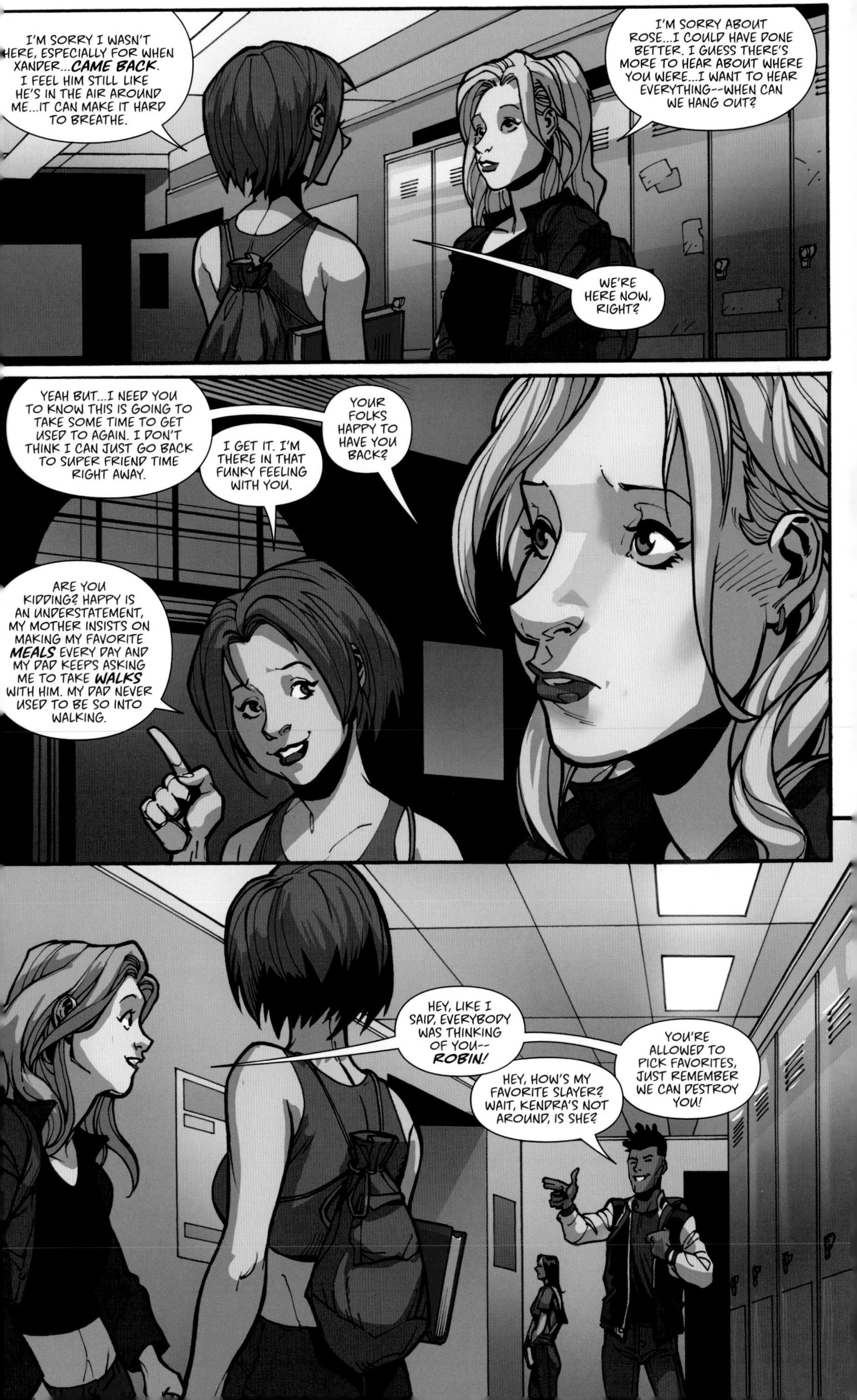
I'M SORRY I WASN'T HERE, ESPECIALLY FOR WHEN XANDER...CAME BACK. I FEEL HIM STILL LIKE HE'S IN THE AIR AROUND ME...IT CAN MAKE IT HARD TO BREATHE.
I'M SORRY ABOUT ROSE...I COULD HAVE DONE BETTER. I GUESS THERE'S MORE TO HEAR ABOUT WHERE YOU WERE...I WANT TO HEAR EVERYTHING--WHEN CAN WE HANG OUT?
WE'RE HERE NOW, RIGHT?
YEAH BUT...I NEED YOU TO KNOW THIS IS GOING TO TAKE SOME TIME TO GET USED TO AGAIN. I DON'T THINK I CAN JUST GO BACK TO SUPER FRIEND TIME RIGHT AWAY.
I GET IT. I'M THERE IN THAT FUNKY FEELING WITH YOU.
YOUR FOLKS HAPPY TO HAVE YOU BACK?
ARE YOU KIDDING? HAPPY IS AN UNDERSTATEMENT, MY MOTHER INSISTS ON MAKING MY FAVORITE MEALS EVERY DAY AND MY DAD KEEPS ASKING ME TO TAKE WALKS WITH HIM. MY DAD NEVER USED TO BE SO INTO WALKING.
HEY, LIKE I SAID, EVERYBODY WAS THINKING OF YOU--ROBIN!
HEY, HOW'S MY FAVORITE SLAYER? WAIT, KENDRA'S NOT AROUND, IS SHE?
YOU'RE ALLOWED TO PICK FAVORITES, JUST REMEMBER WE CAN DESTROY YOU!

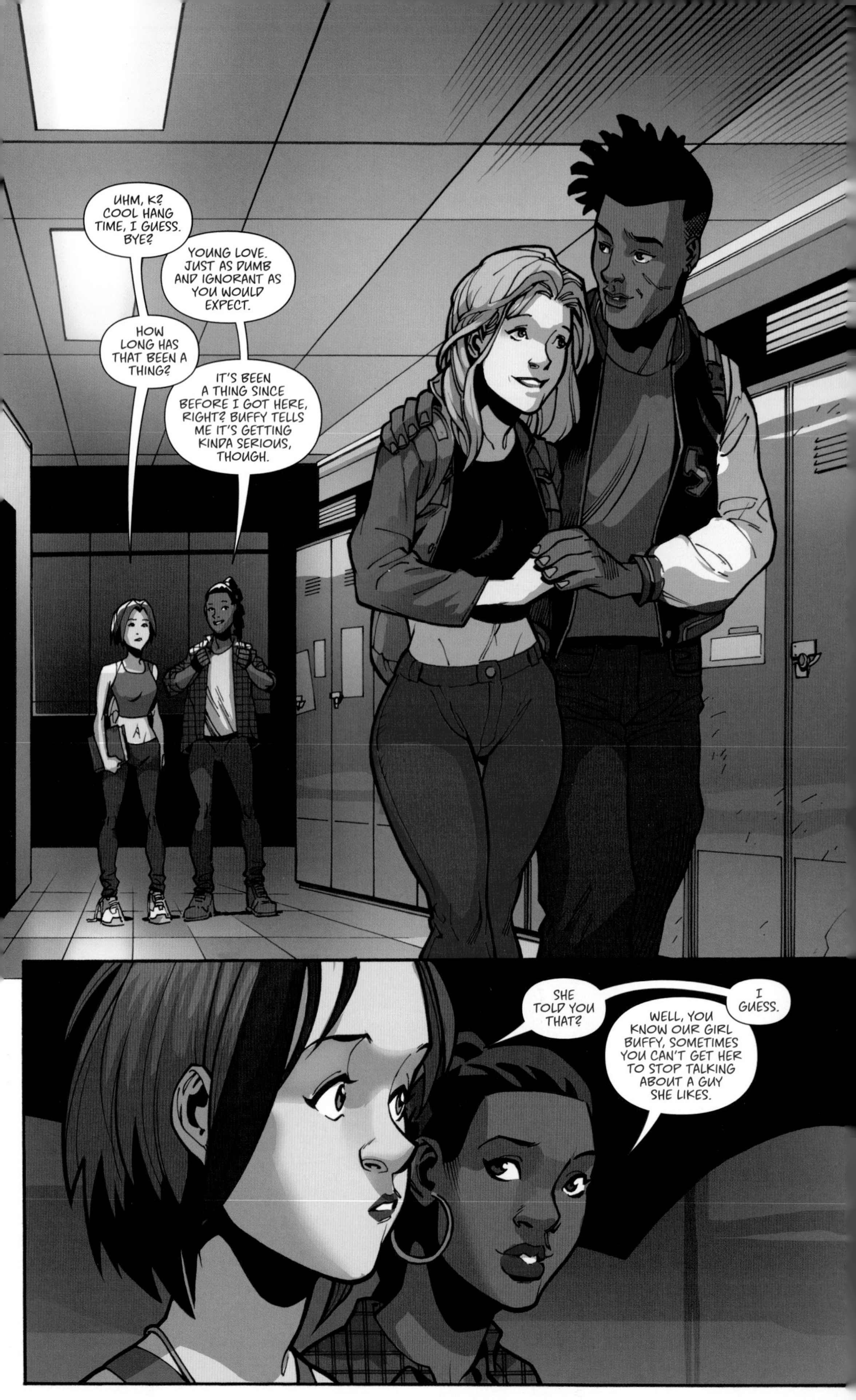
UHM, K? COOL HANG TIME, I GUESS. BYE?
YOUNG LOVE. JUST AS DUMB AND IGNORANT AS YOU WOULD EXPECT.
HOW LONG HAS THAT BEEN A THING?
IT'S BEEN A THING SINCE BEFORE I GOT HERE, RIGHT? BUFFY TELLS ME IT'S GETTING KINDA SERIOUS, THOUGH.
SHE TOLD YOU THAT?
I GUESS.
WELL, YOU KNOW OUR GIRL BUFFY, SOMETIMES YOU CAN'T GET HER TO STOP TALKING ABOUT A GUY SHE LIKES.

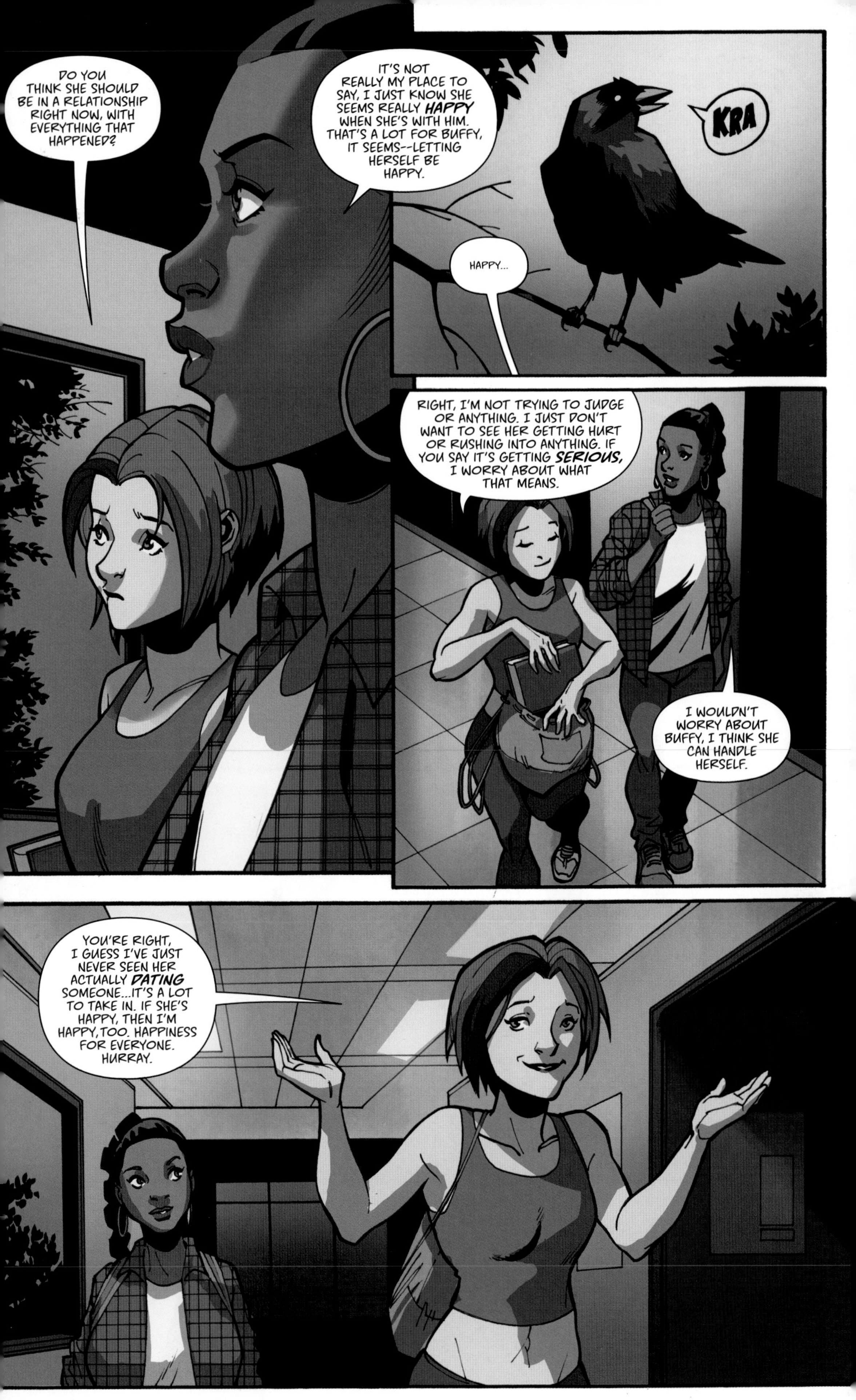
DO YOU THINK SHE SHOULD BE IN A RELATIONSHIP RIGHT NOW, WITH EVERYTHING THAT HAPPENED?
IT'S NOT REALLY MY PLACE TO SAY, I JUST KNOW SHE SEEMS REALLY HAPPY WHEN SHE'S WITH HIM. THAT'S A LOT FOR BUFFY, IT SEEMS--LETTING HERSELF BE HAPPY.
KRA
HAPPY...
RIGHT, I'M NOT TRYING TO JUDGE OR ANYTHING. I JUST DON'T WANT TO SEE HER GETTING HURT OR RUSHING INTO ANYTHING. IF YOU SAY IT'S GETTING SERIOUS, I WORRY ABOUT WHAT THAT MEANS.
I WOULDN'T WORRY ABOUT BUFFY, I THINK SHE CAN HANDLE HERSELF.
YOU'RE RIGHT, I GUESS I'VE JUST NEVER SEEN HER ACTUALLY DATING SOMEONE...IT'S A LOT TO TAKE IN. IF SHE'S HAPPY, THEN I'M HAPPY,TOO. HAPPINESS FOR EVERYONE. HURRAY.

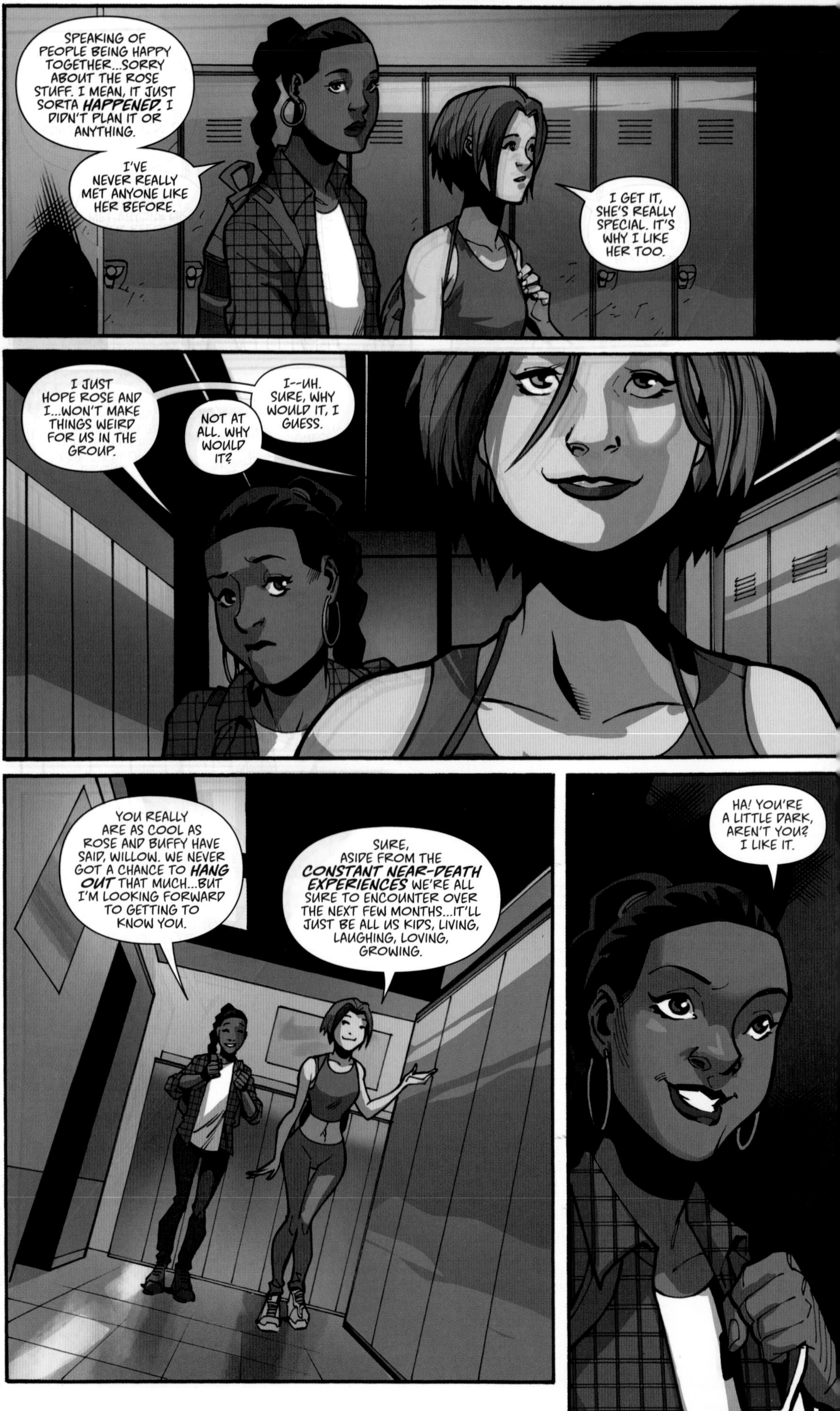

SPEAKING OF PEOPLE BEING HAPPY TOGETHER...SORRY ABOUT THE ROSE STUFF. I MEAN, IT JUST SORTA HAPPENED. I DIDN'T PLAN IT OR ANYTHING.
I'VE NEVER REALLY MET ANYONE LIKE HER BEFORE.
I GET IT, SHE'S REALLY SPECIAL. IT'S WHY I LIKE HER TOO.
I JUST HOPE ROSE AND I...WON'T MAKE THINGS WEIRD FOR US IN THE GROUP.
I--UH. SURE, WHY WOULD IT, I GUESS.
NOT AT ALL. WHY WOULD IT?
YOU REALLY ARE AS COOL AS ROSE AND BUFFY HAVE SAID, WILLOW. WE NEVER GOT A CHANCE TO HANG OUT THAT MUCH...BUT I'M LOOKING FORWARD TO GETTING TO KNOW YOU.
SURE, ASIDE FROM THE CONSTANT NEAR-DEATH EXPERIENCES WE'RE ALL SURE TO ENCOUNTER OVER THE NEXT FEW MONTHS...IT'LL JUST BE ALL US KIDS, LIVING, LAUGHING, LOVING, GROWING.
HA! YOU'RE A LITTLE DARK, AREN'T YOU? I LIKE IT.

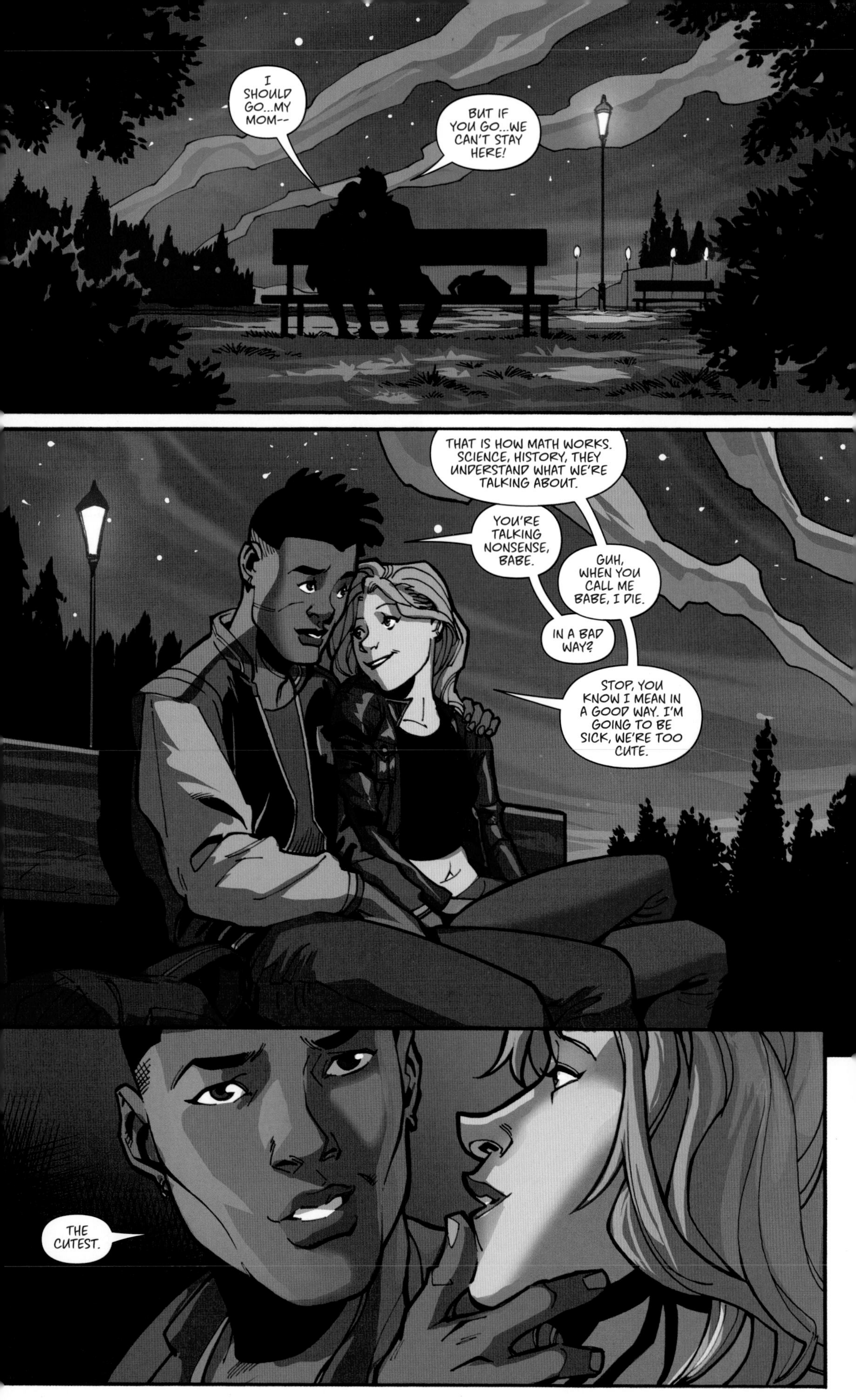
I SHOULD GO...MY MOM--
BUT IF YOU GO...WE CAN'T STAY HERE!
THAT IS HOW MATH WORKS. SCIENCE, HISTORY, THEY UNDERSTAND WHAT WE'RE TALKING ABOUT.
YOU'RE TALKING NONSENSE, BABE.
GUH, WHEN YOU CALL ME BABE, I DIE.
IN A BAD WAY?
STOP, YOU KNOW I MEAN IN A GOOD WAY. I'M GOING TO BE SICK, WE'RE TOO CUTE.
THE CUTEST.

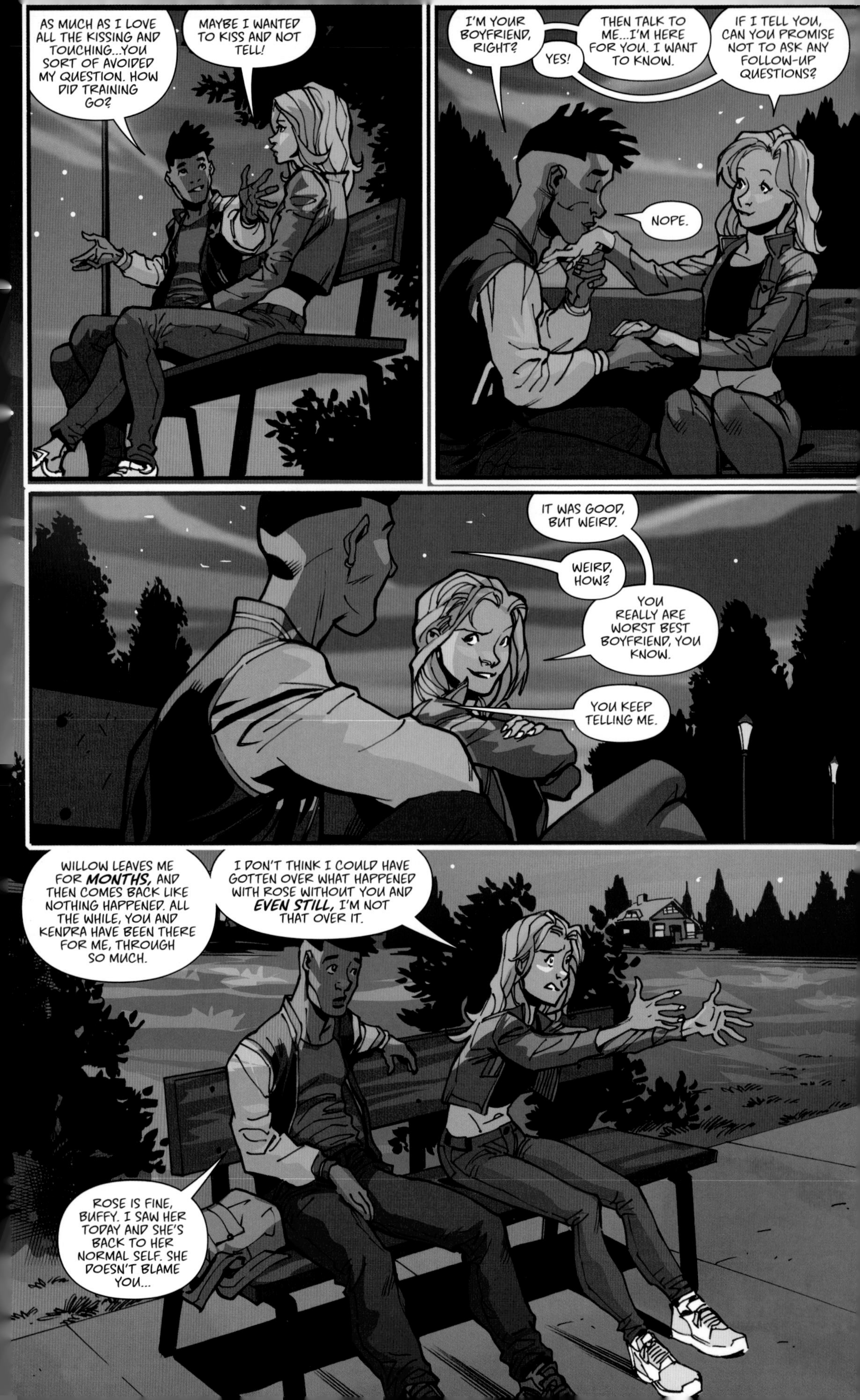
AS MUCH AS I LOVE ALL THE KISSING AND TOUCHING...YOU SORT OF AVOIDED MY QUESTION. HOW DID TRAINING GO?
MAYBE I WANTED TO KISS AND NOT TELL!
I'M YOUR BOYFRIEND, RIGHT?
YES!
THEN TALK TO ME...I'M HERE FOR YOU. I WANT TO KNOW.
IF I TELL YOU, CAN YOU PROMISE NOT TO ASK ANY FOLLOW-UP QUESTIONS?
NOPE.
IT WAS GOOD, BUT WEIRD.
WEIRD, HOW?
YOU REALLY ARE WORST BEST BOYFRIEND, YOU KNOW.
YOU KEEP TELLING ME.
WILLOW LEAVES ME FOR **MONTHS,** AND THEN COMES BACK LIKE NOTHING HAPPENED. ALL THE WHILE, YOU AND KENDRA HAVE BEEN THERE FOR ME, THROUGH SO MUCH.
I DON'T THINK I COULD HAVE GOTTEN OVER WHAT HAPPENED WITH ROSE WITHOUT YOU AND **EVEN STILL,** I'M NOT THAT OVER IT.
ROSE IS FINE, BUFFY. I SAW HER TODAY AND SHE'S BACK TO HER NORMAL SELF. SHE DOESN'T BLAME YOU...

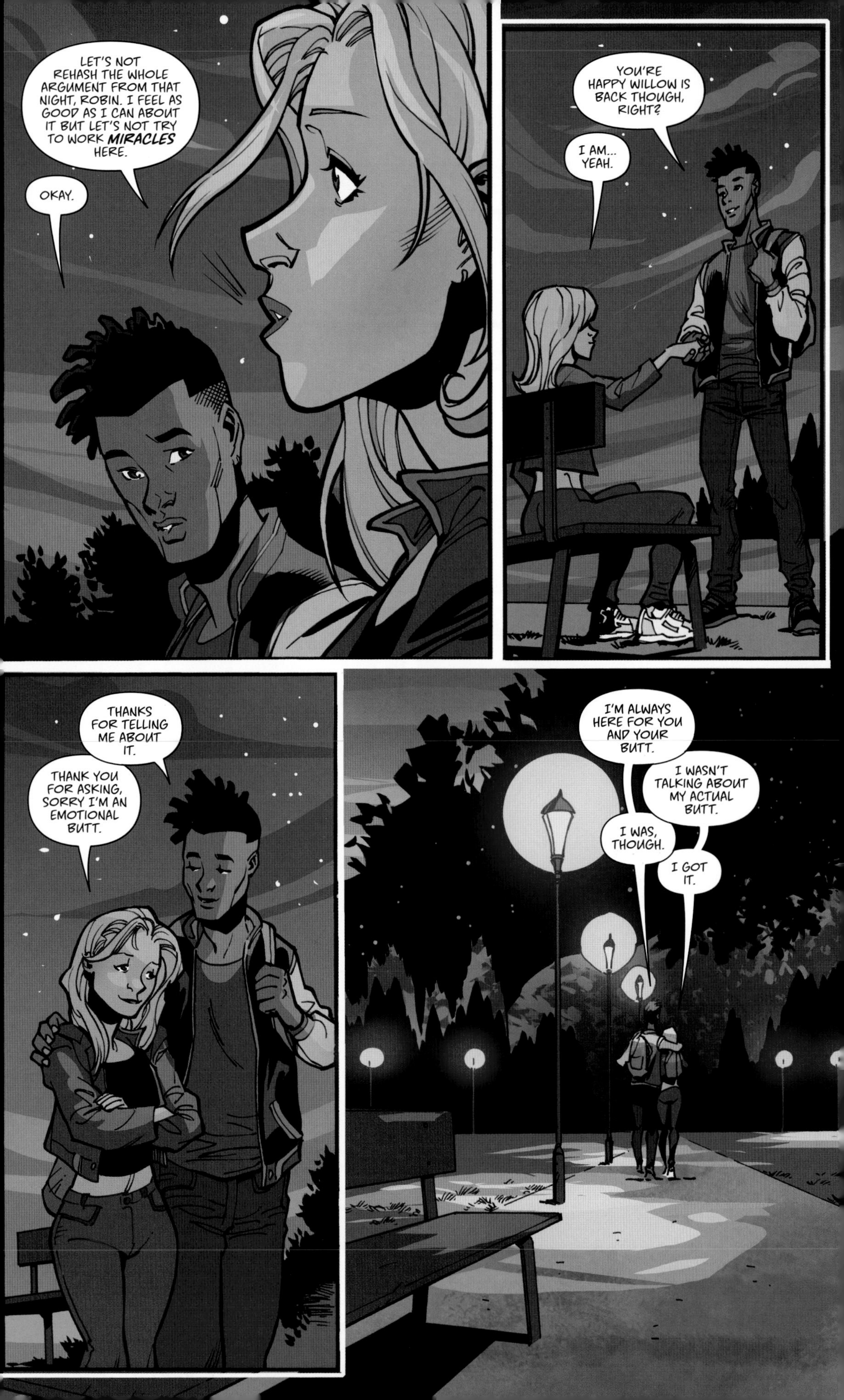
LET'S NOT REHASH THE WHOLE ARGUMENT FROM THAT NIGHT, ROBIN. I FEEL AS GOOD AS I CAN ABOUT IT BUT LET'S NOT TRY TO WORK *MIRACLES* HERE.
OKAY.
YOU'RE HAPPY WILLOW IS BACK THOUGH, RIGHT?
I AM... YEAH.
THANKS FOR TELLING ME ABOUT IT.
THANK YOU FOR ASKING, SORRY I'M AN EMOTIONAL BUTT.
I'M ALWAYS HERE FOR YOU AND YOUR BUTT.
I WASN'T TALKING ABOUT MY ACTUAL BUTT.
I WAS, THOUGH.
I GOT IT.

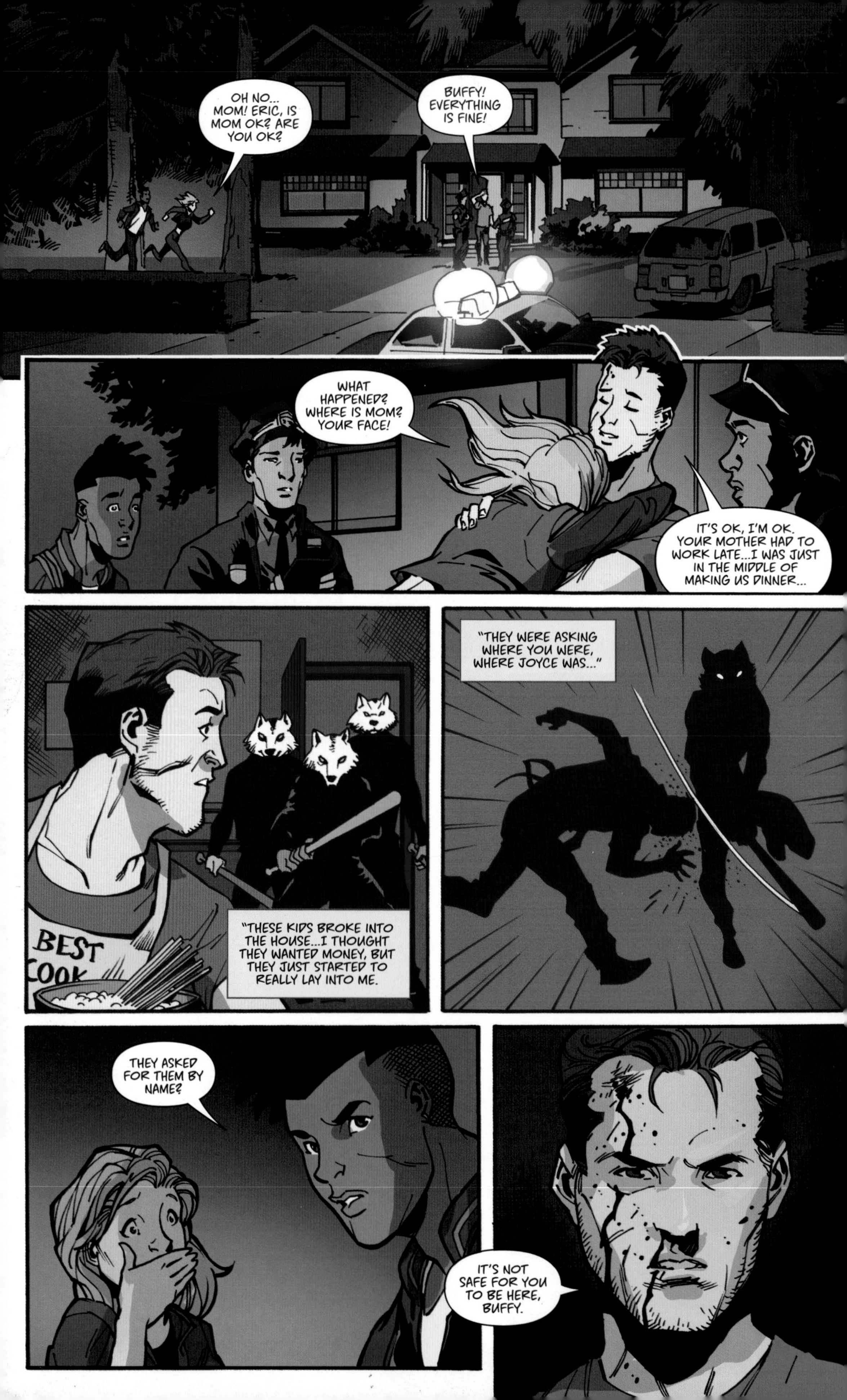
OH NO... MOM! ERIC, IS MOM OK? ARE YOU OK?
BUFFY! EVERYTHING IS FINE!
WHAT HAPPENED? WHERE IS MOM? YOUR FACE!
IT'S OK, I'M OK. YOUR MOTHER HAD TO WORK LATE...I WAS JUST IN THE MIDDLE OF MAKING US DINNER...
"THESE KIDS BROKE INTO THE HOUSE...I THOUGHT THEY WANTED MONEY, BUT THEY JUST STARTED TO REALLY LAY INTO ME.
BEST COOK
"THEY WERE ASKING WHERE YOU WERE, WHERE JOYCE WAS..."
THEY ASKED FOR THEM BY NAME?
IT'S NOT SAFE FOR YOU TO BE HERE, BUFFY.

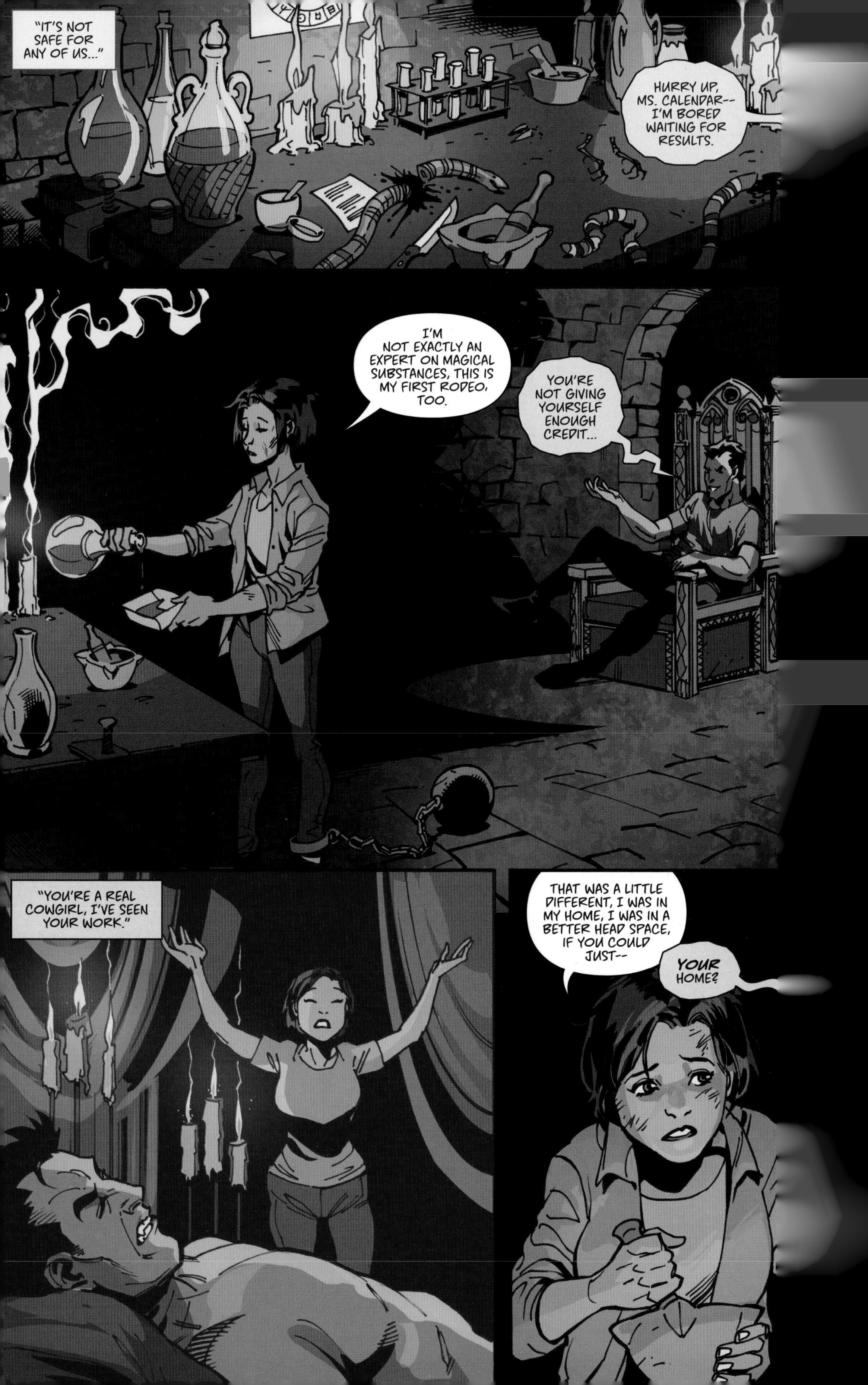
"IT'S NOT SAFE FOR ANY OF US..."
HURRY UP, MS. CALENDAR-- I'M BORED WAITING FOR RESULTS.
I'M NOT EXACTLY AN EXPERT ON MAGICAL SUBSTANCES, THIS IS MY FIRST RODEO, TOO.
YOU'RE NOT GIVING YOURSELF ENOUGH CREDIT...
"YOU'RE A REAL COWGIRL, I'VE SEEN YOUR WORK."
THAT WAS A LITTLE DIFFERENT, I WAS IN MY HOME, I WAS IN A BETTER HEAD SPACE, IF YOU COULD JUST--
YOUR HOME?

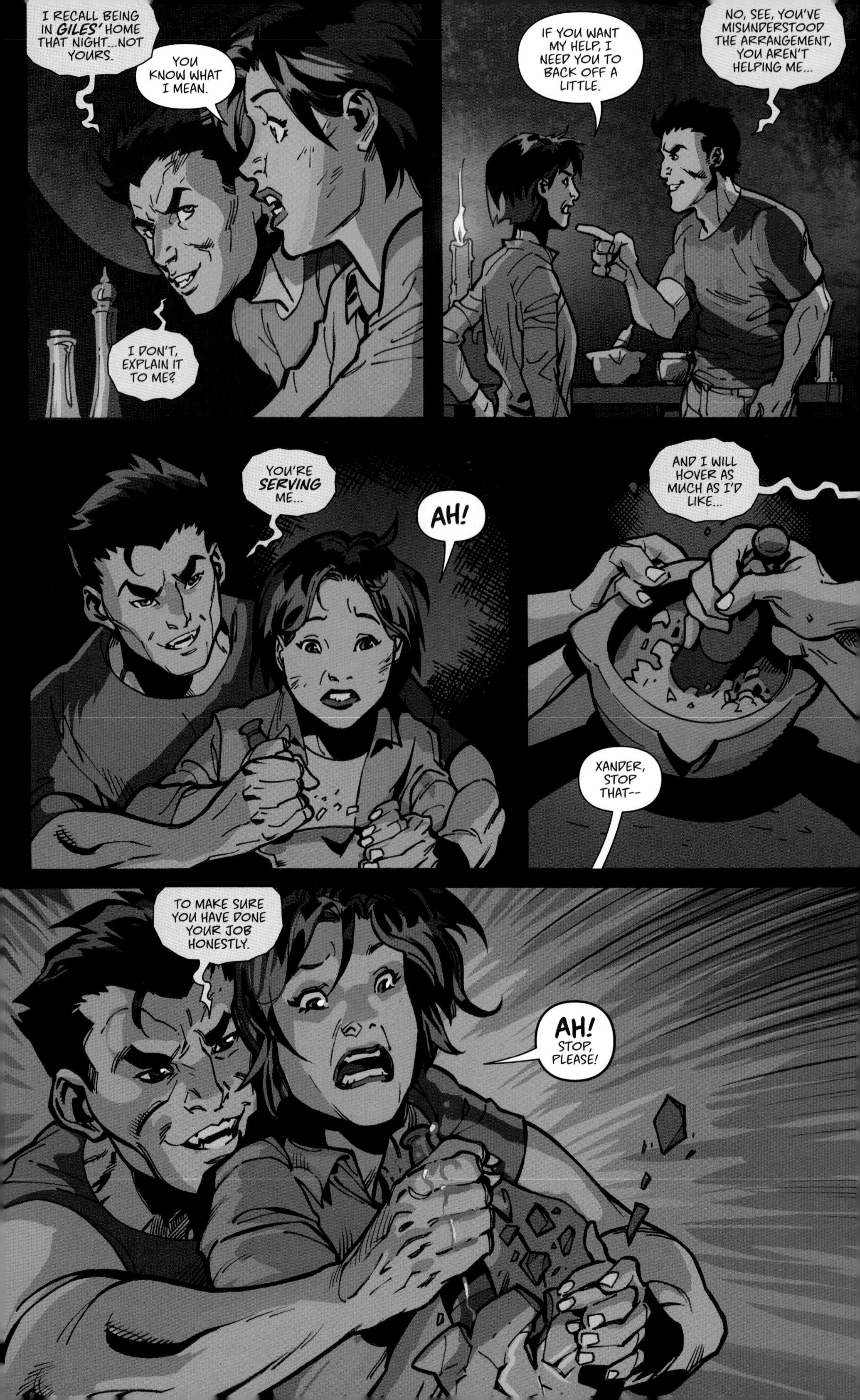
I RECALL BEING IN GILES' HOME THAT NIGHT...NOT YOURS.
YOU KNOW WHAT I MEAN.
I DON'T, EXPLAIN IT TO ME?
IF YOU WANT MY HELP, I NEED YOU TO BACK OFF A LITTLE.
NO, SEE, YOU'VE MISUNDERSTOOD THE ARRANGEMENT, YOU AREN'T HELPING ME...
YOU'RE SERVING ME...
AH!
AND I WILL HOVER AS MUCH AS I'D LIKE...
XANDER, STOP THAT--
TO MAKE SURE YOU HAVE DONE YOUR JOB HONESTLY.
AH! STOP, PLEASE!

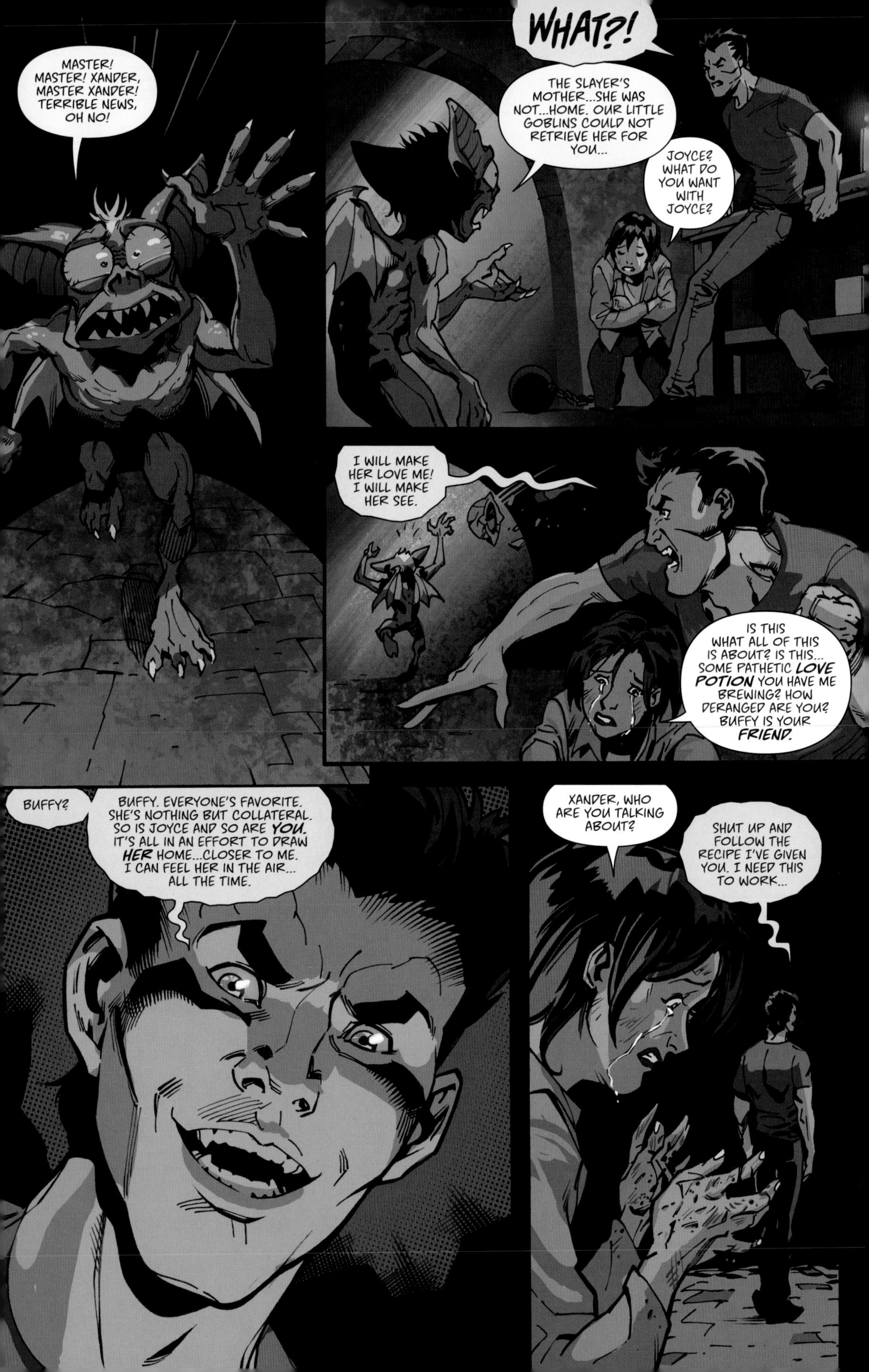
MASTER! MASTER! XANDER, MASTER XANDER! TERRIBLE NEWS, OH NO!
WHAT?!
THE SLAYER'S MOTHER...SHE WAS NOT...HOME. OUR LITTLE GOBLINS COULD NOT RETRIEVE HER FOR YOU...
JOYCE? WHAT DO YOU WANT WITH JOYCE?
I WILL MAKE HER LOVE ME! I WILL MAKE HER SEE.
IS THIS WHAT ALL OF THIS IS ABOUT? IS THIS... SOME PATHETIC LOVE POTION YOU HAVE ME BREWING? HOW DERANGED ARE YOU? BUFFY IS YOUR FRIEND.
BUFFY?
BUFFY. EVERYONE'S FAVORITE. SHE'S NOTHING BUT COLLATERAL. SO IS JOYCE AND SO ARE YOU. IT'S ALL IN AN EFFORT TO DRAW HER HOME...CLOSER TO ME. I CAN FEEL HER IN THE AIR... ALL THE TIME.
XANDER, WHO ARE YOU TALKING ABOUT?
SHUT UP AND FOLLOW THE RECIPE I'VE GIVEN YOU. I NEED THIS TO WORK...

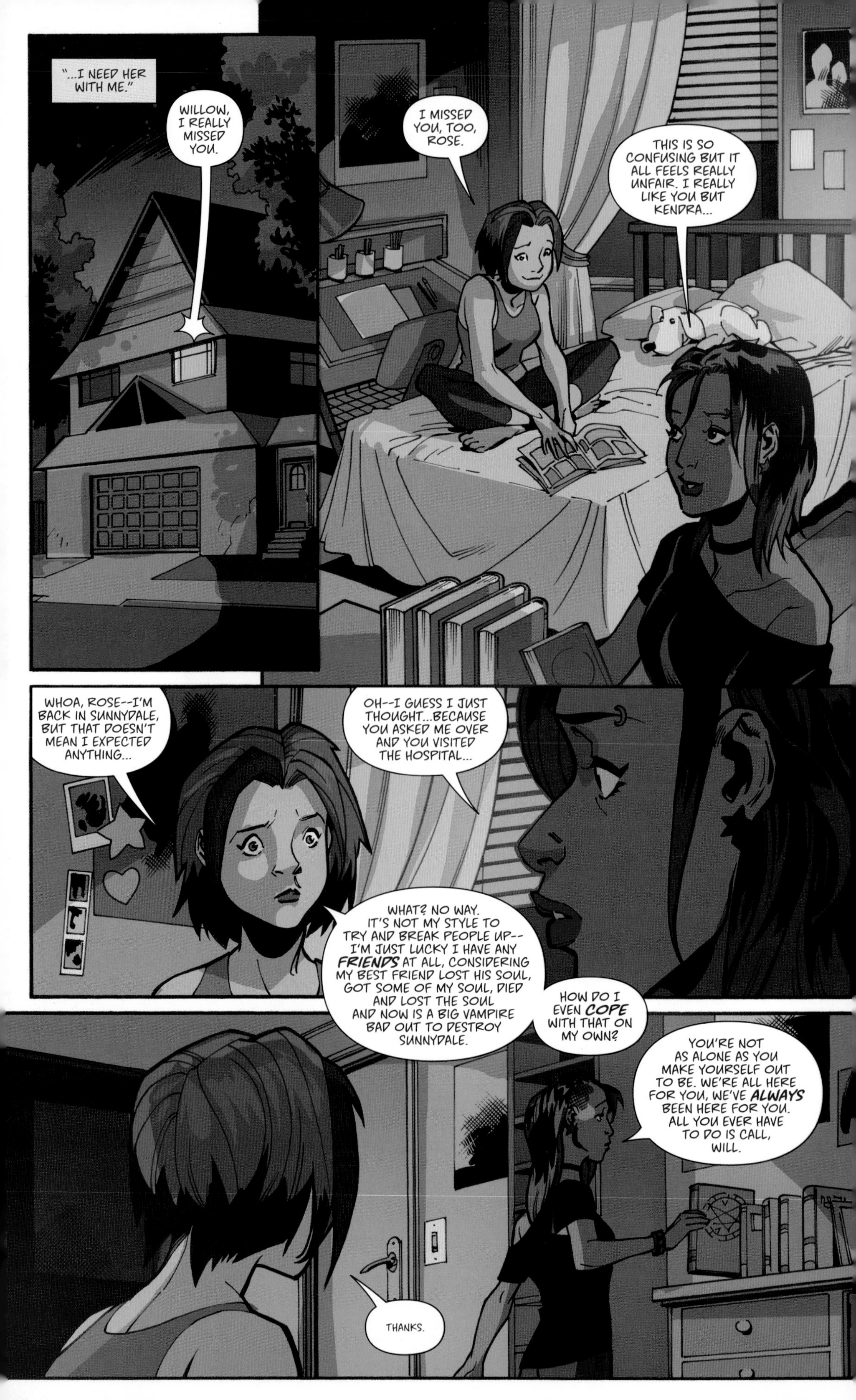
"...I NEED HER WITH ME."
WILLOW, I REALLY MISSED YOU.
I MISSED YOU, TOO, ROSE.
THIS IS SO CONFUSING BUT IT ALL FEELS REALLY UNFAIR. I REALLY LIKE YOU BUT KENDRA...
WHOA, ROSE--I'M BACK IN SUNNYDALE, BUT THAT DOESN'T MEAN I EXPECTED ANYTHING...
OH--I GUESS I JUST THOUGHT...BECAUSE YOU ASKED ME OVER AND YOU VISITED THE HOSPITAL...
WHAT? NO WAY. IT'S NOT MY STYLE TO TRY AND BREAK PEOPLE UP-- I'M JUST LUCKY I HAVE ANY FRIENDS AT ALL, CONSIDERING MY BEST FRIEND LOST HIS SOUL, GOT SOME OF MY SOUL, DIED AND LOST THE SOUL AND NOW IS A BIG VAMPIRE BAD OUT TO DESTROY SUNNYDALE.
HOW DO I EVEN COPE WITH THAT ON MY OWN?
YOU'RE NOT AS ALONE AS YOU MAKE YOURSELF OUT TO BE. WE'RE ALL HERE FOR YOU, WE'VE ALWAYS BEEN HERE FOR YOU. ALL YOU EVER HAVE TO DO IS CALL, WILL.
THANKS.

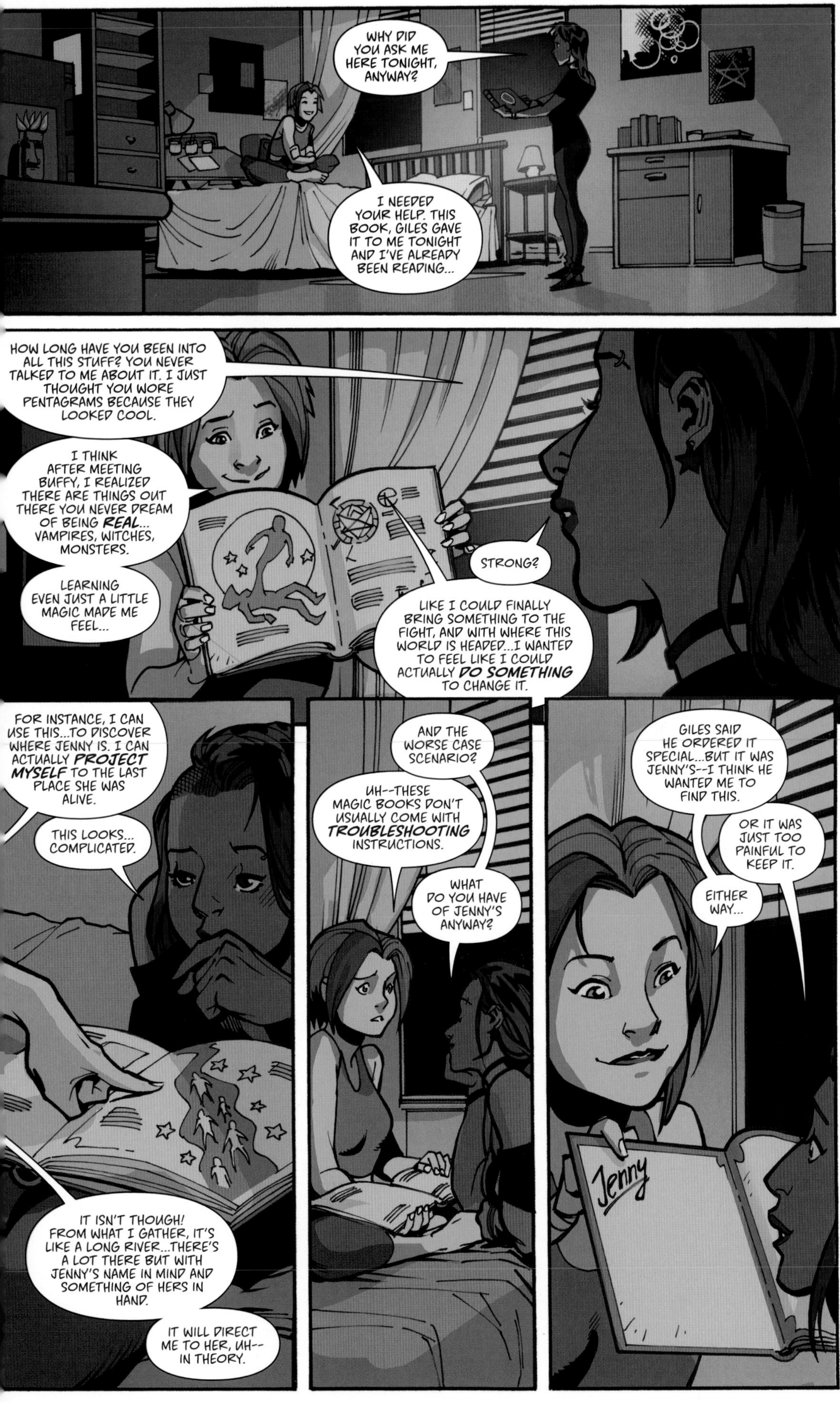

WHY DID YOU ASK ME HERE TONIGHT, ANYWAY?
I NEEDED YOUR HELP. THIS BOOK, GILES GAVE IT TO ME TONIGHT AND I'VE ALREADY BEEN READING...
HOW LONG HAVE YOU BEEN INTO ALL THIS STUFF? YOU NEVER TALKED TO ME ABOUT IT. I JUST THOUGHT YOU WORE PENTAGRAMS BECAUSE THEY LOOKED COOL.
I THINK AFTER MEETING BUFFY, I REALIZED THERE ARE THINGS OUT THERE YOU NEVER DREAM OF BEING REAL... VAMPIRES, WITCHES, MONSTERS.
LEARNING EVEN JUST A LITTLE MAGIC MADE ME FEEL...
STRONG?
LIKE I COULD FINALLY BRING SOMETHING TO THE FIGHT, AND WITH WHERE THIS WORLD IS HEADED...I WANTED TO FEEL LIKE I COULD ACTUALLY DO SOMETHING TO CHANGE IT.
FOR INSTANCE, I CAN USE THIS...TO DISCOVER WHERE JENNY IS. I CAN ACTUALLY PROJECT MYSELF TO THE LAST PLACE SHE WAS ALIVE.
THIS LOOKS... COMPLICATED.
IT ISN'T THOUGH! FROM WHAT I GATHER, IT'S LIKE A LONG RIVER...THERE'S A LOT THERE BUT WITH JENNY'S NAME IN MIND AND SOMETHING OF HERS IN HAND.
IT WILL DIRECT ME TO HER, UH-- IN THEORY.
AND THE WORSE CASE SCENARIO?
UH--THESE MAGIC BOOKS DON'T USUALLY COME WITH TROUBLESHOOTING INSTRUCTIONS.
WHAT DO YOU HAVE OF JENNY'S ANYWAY?
GILES SAID HE ORDERED IT SPECIAL...BUT IT WAS JENNY'S--I THINK HE WANTED ME TO FIND THIS.
OR IT WAS JUST TOO PAINFUL TO KEEP IT.
EITHER WAY...
Jenny

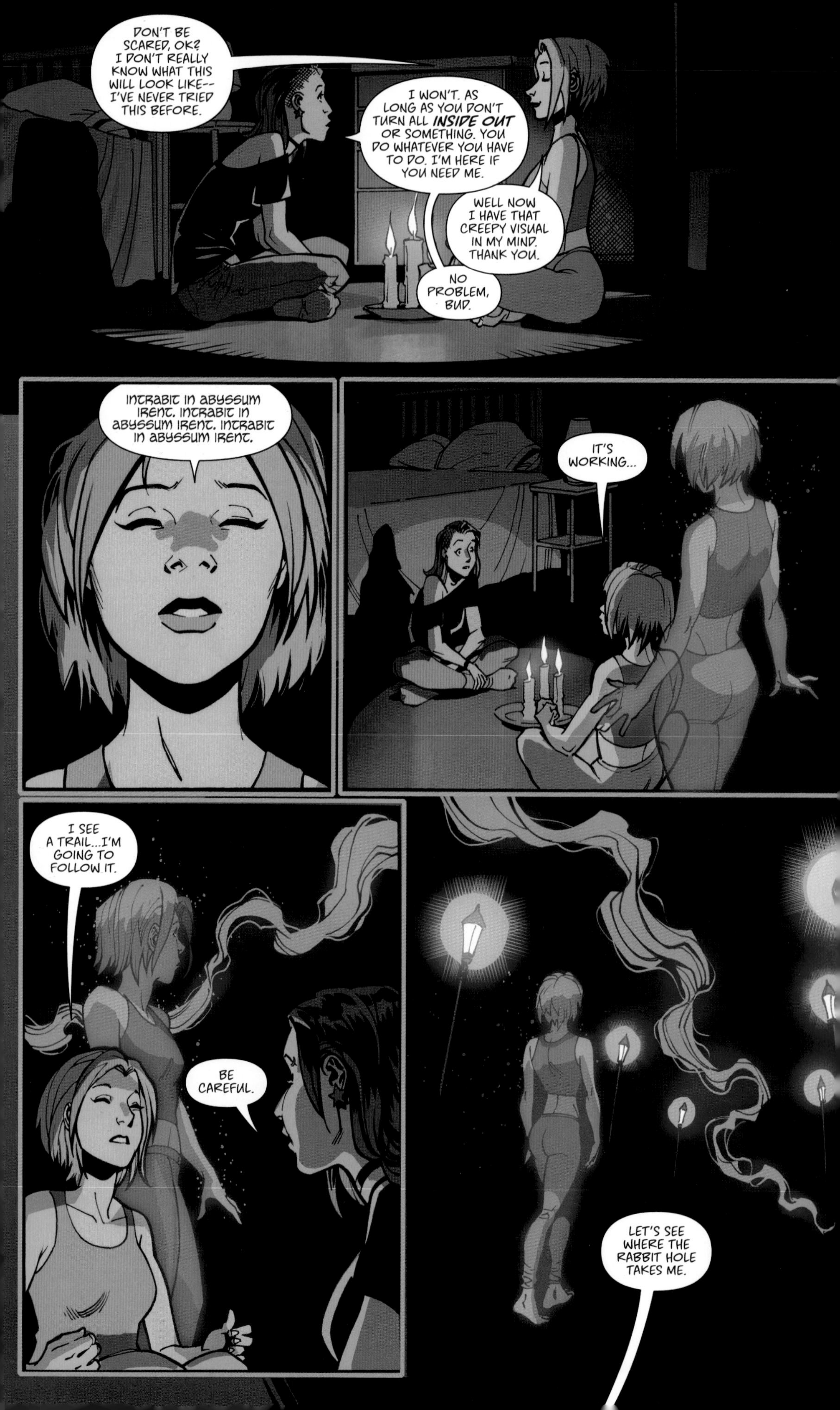
DON'T BE SCARED, OK? I DON'T REALLY KNOW WHAT THIS WILL LOOK LIKE-- I'VE NEVER TRIED THIS BEFORE.
I WON'T. AS LONG AS YOU DON'T TURN ALL ***INSIDE OUT*** OR SOMETHING. YOU DO WHATEVER YOU HAVE TO DO. I'M HERE IF YOU NEED ME.
WELL NOW I HAVE THAT CREEPY VISUAL IN MY MIND. THANK YOU.
NO PROBLEM, BUD.
INTRABIT IN ABYSSUM IRENT. INTRABIT IN ABYSSUM IRENT. INTRABIT IN ABYSSUM IRENT.
IT'S WORKING...
I SEE A TRAIL...I'M GOING TO FOLLOW IT.
BE CAREFUL.
LET'S SEE WHERE THE RABBIT HOLE TAKES ME.

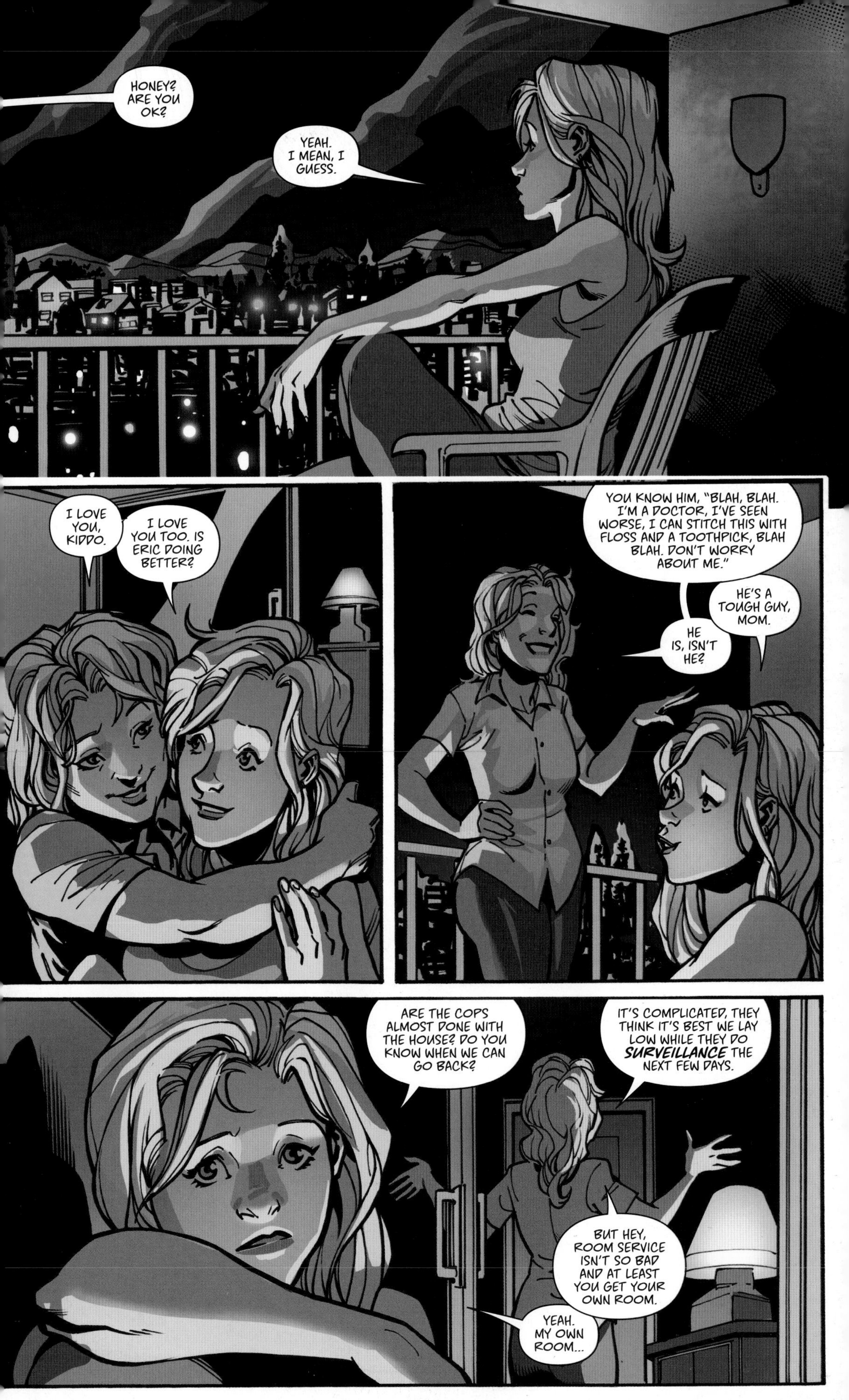
HONEY? ARE YOU OK?
YEAH. I MEAN, I GUESS.
I LOVE YOU, KIDDO.
I LOVE YOU TOO. IS ERIC DOING BETTER?
YOU KNOW HIM, "BLAH, BLAH. I'M A DOCTOR, I'VE SEEN WORSE, I CAN STITCH THIS WITH FLOSS AND A TOOTHPICK, BLAH BLAH. DON'T WORRY ABOUT ME."
HE'S A TOUGH GUY, MOM.
HE IS, ISN'T HE?
ARE THE COPS ALMOST DONE WITH THE HOUSE? DO YOU KNOW WHEN WE CAN GO BACK?
IT'S COMPLICATED, THEY THINK IT'S BEST WE LAY LOW WHILE THEY DO SURVEILLANCE THE NEXT FEW DAYS.
BUT HEY, ROOM SERVICE ISN'T SO BAD AND AT LEAST YOU GET YOUR OWN ROOM.
YEAH. MY OWN ROOM...

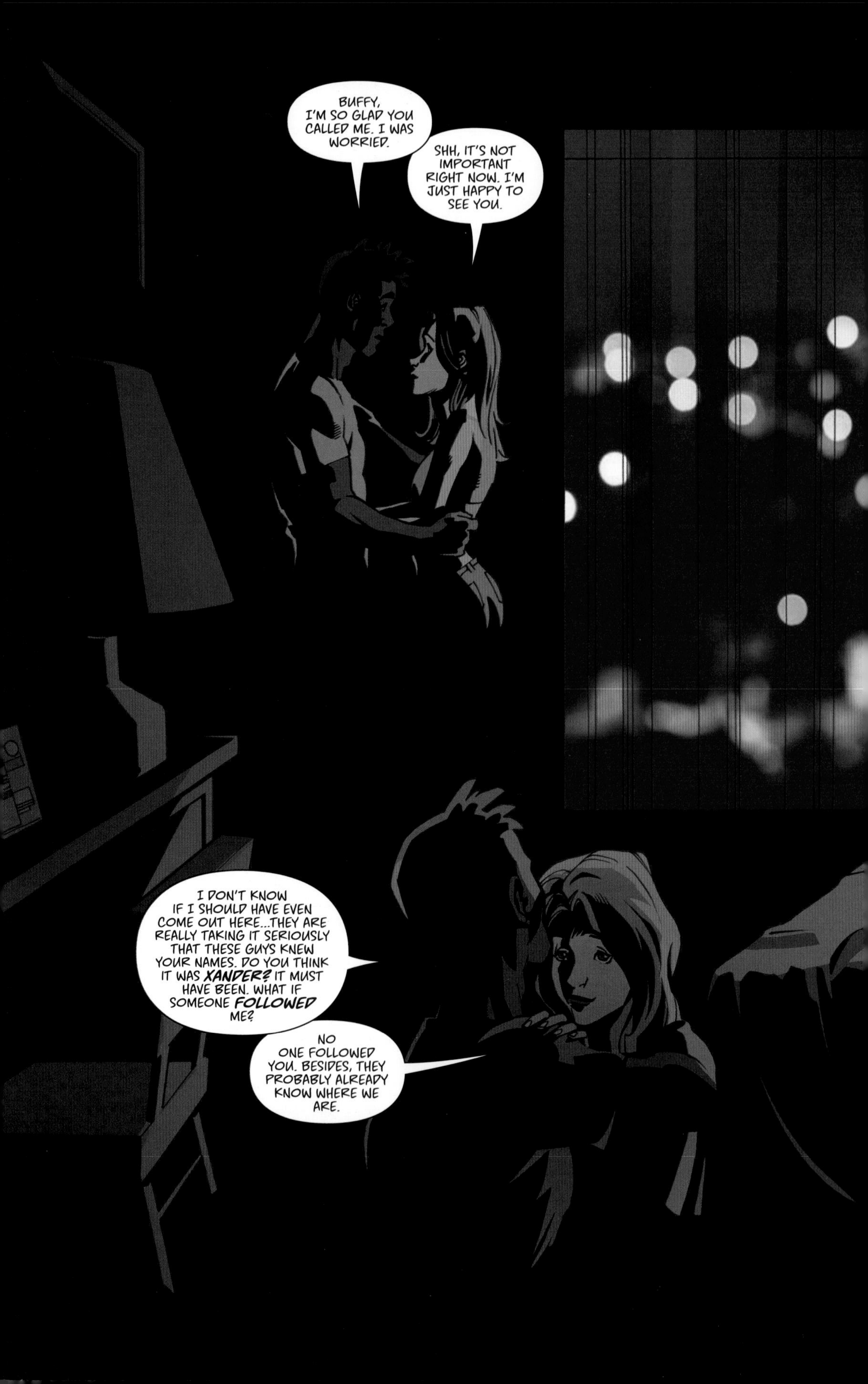
BUFFY, I'M SO GLAD YOU CALLED ME. I WAS WORRIED.
SHH, IT'S NOT IMPORTANT RIGHT NOW. I'M JUST HAPPY TO SEE YOU.
I DON'T KNOW IF I SHOULD HAVE EVEN COME OUT HERE...THEY ARE REALLY TAKING IT SERIOUSLY THAT THESE GUYS KNEW YOUR NAMES. DO YOU THINK IT WAS XANDER? IT MUST HAVE BEEN. WHAT IF SOMEONE FOLLOWED ME?
NO ONE FOLLOWED YOU. BESIDES, THEY PROBABLY ALREADY KNOW WHERE WE ARE.

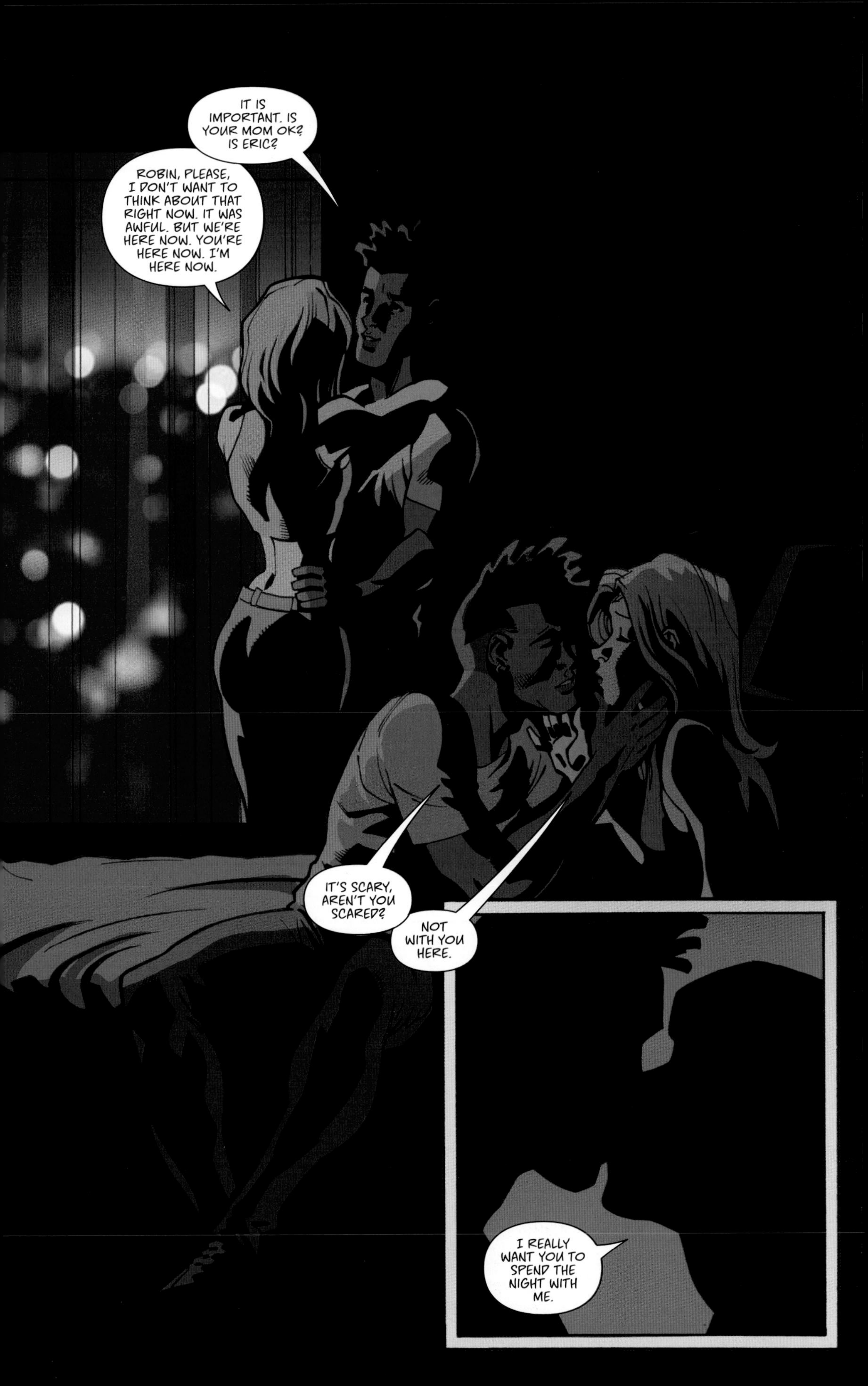
IT IS IMPORTANT. IS YOUR MOM OK? IS ERIC?
ROBIN, PLEASE, I DON'T WANT TO THINK ABOUT THAT RIGHT NOW. IT WAS AWFUL. BUT WE'RE HERE NOW. YOU'RE HERE NOW. I'M HERE NOW.
IT'S SCARY, AREN'T YOU SCARED?
NOT WITH YOU HERE.
I REALLY WANT YOU TO SPEND THE NIGHT WITH ME.

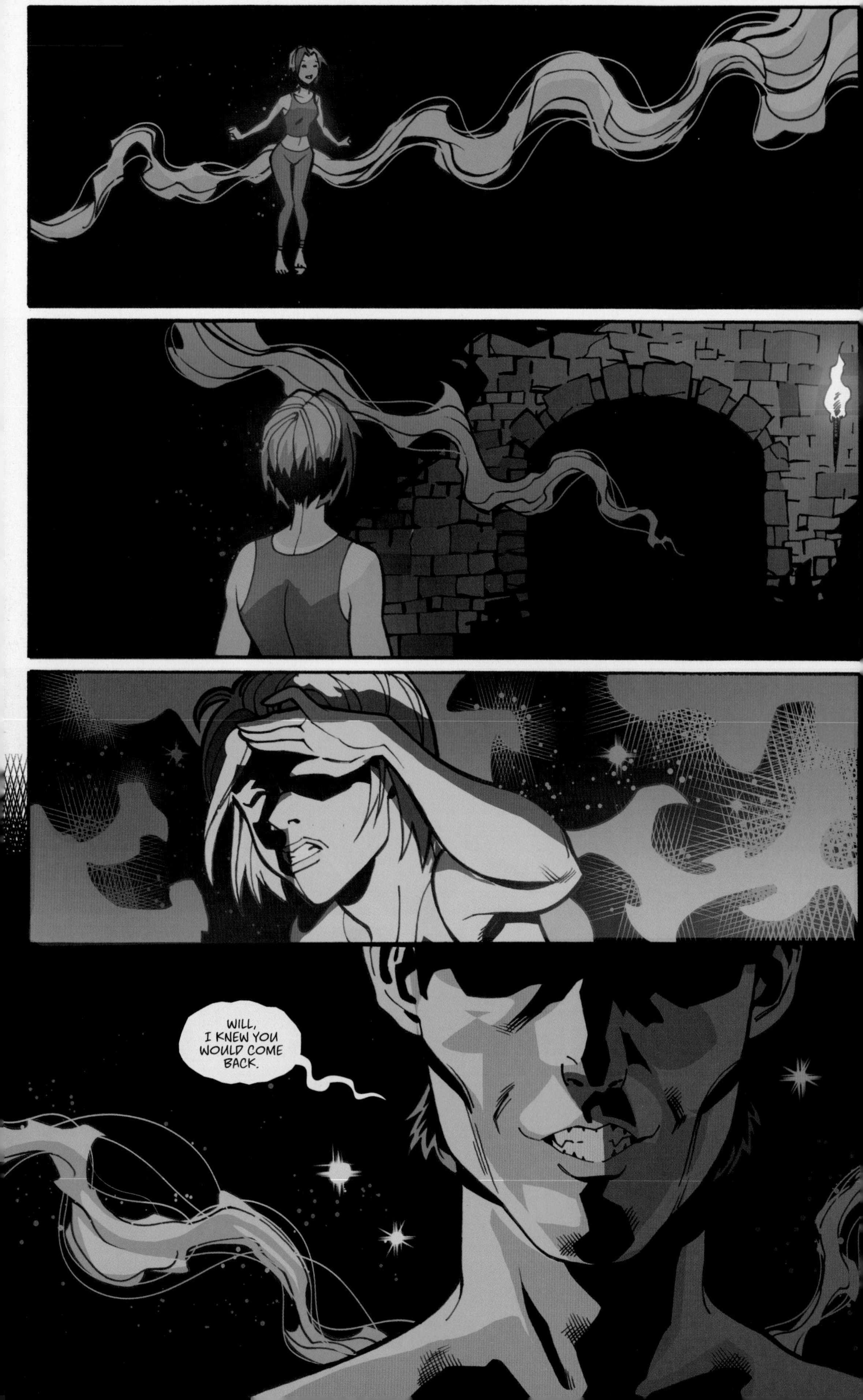
WILL, I KNEW YOU WOULD COME BACK.

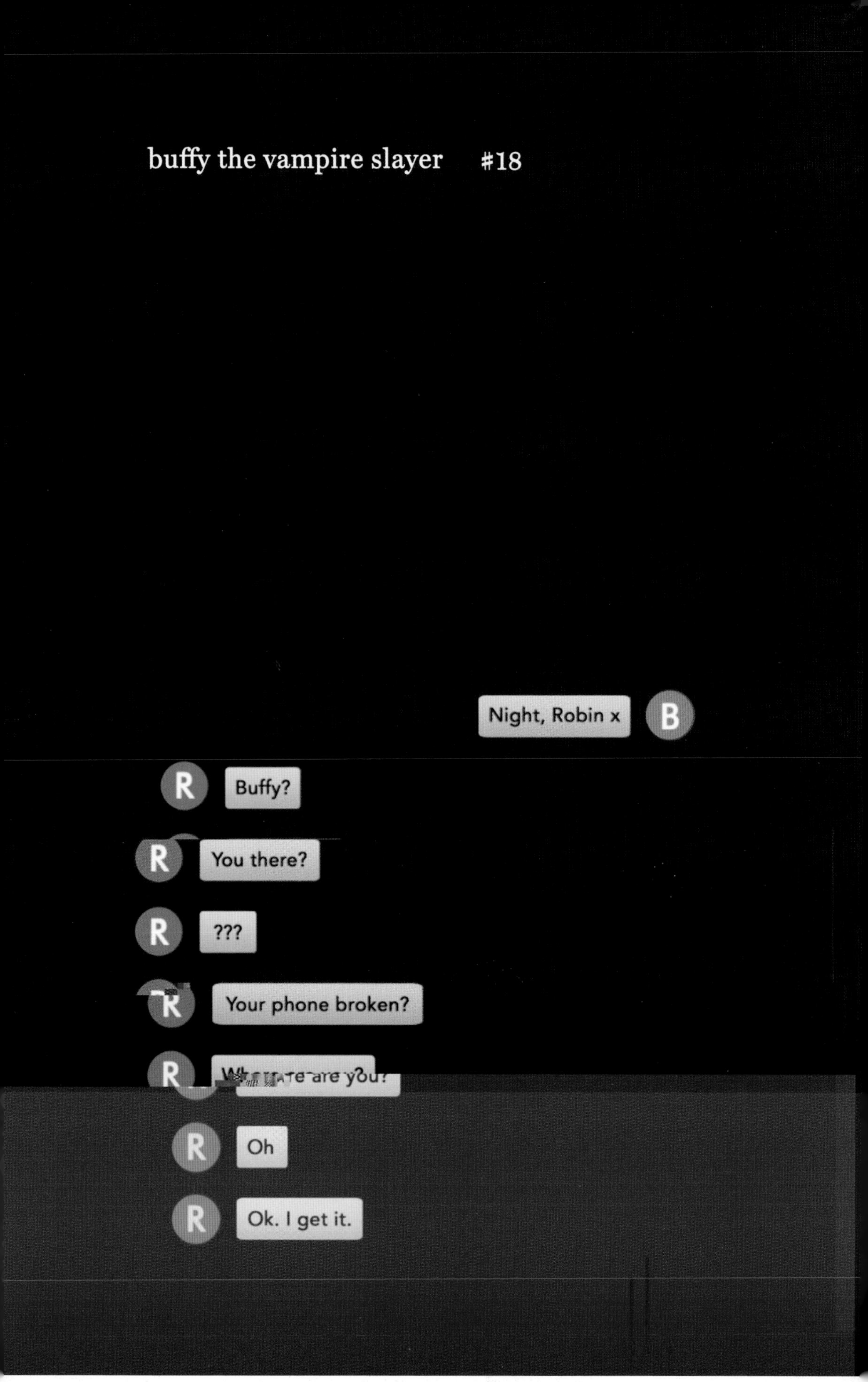
buffy the vampire slayer #18
Night, Robin x
B
R
Buffy?
You there?
???
Your phone broken?
Oh
Ok. I get it.

Issue Eighteen Ring of Fire Cover by **Becca Carey**

CHAPTER NINETEEN

Issue Nineteen Cover by **David López**

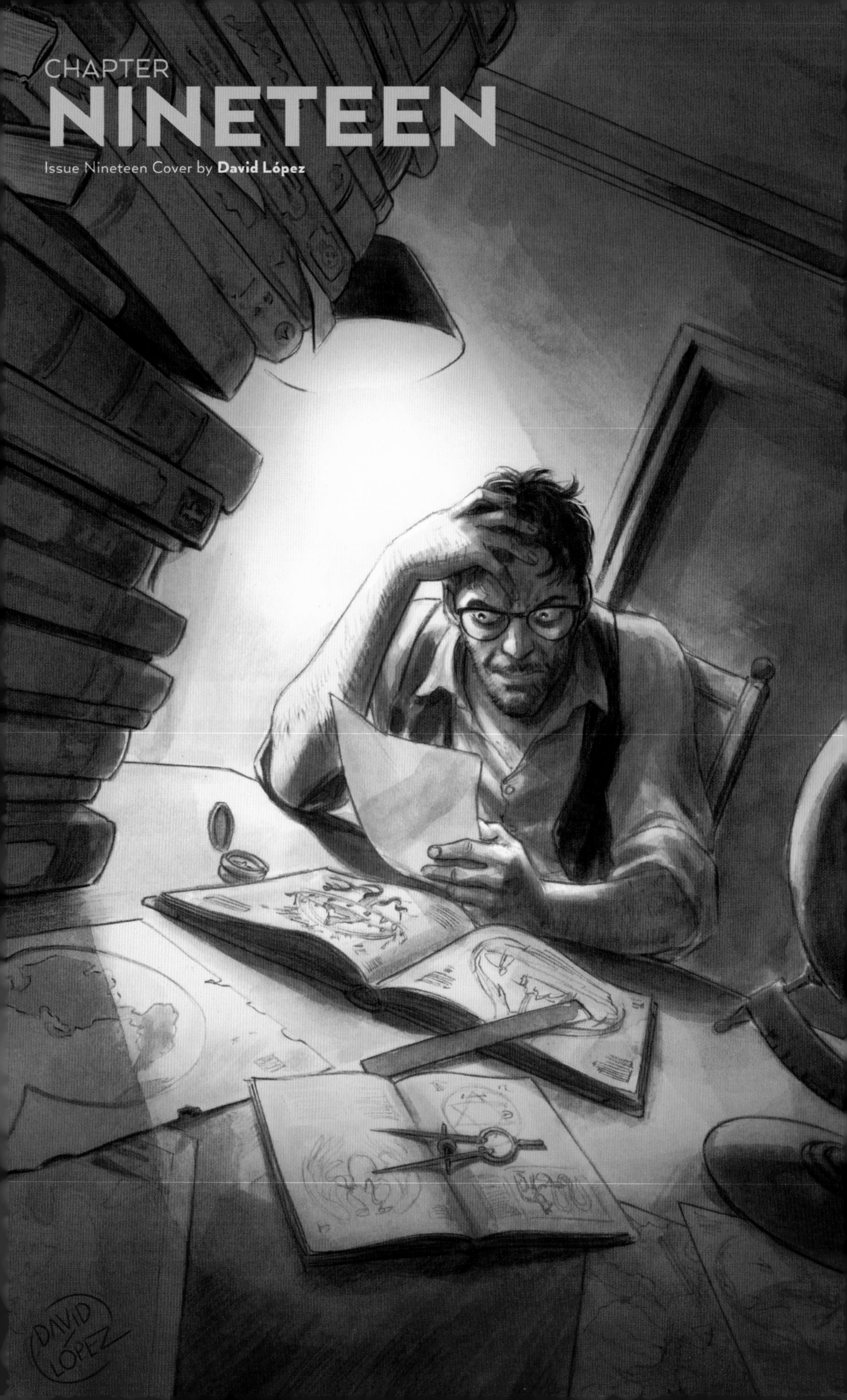
DAVID LOPEZ

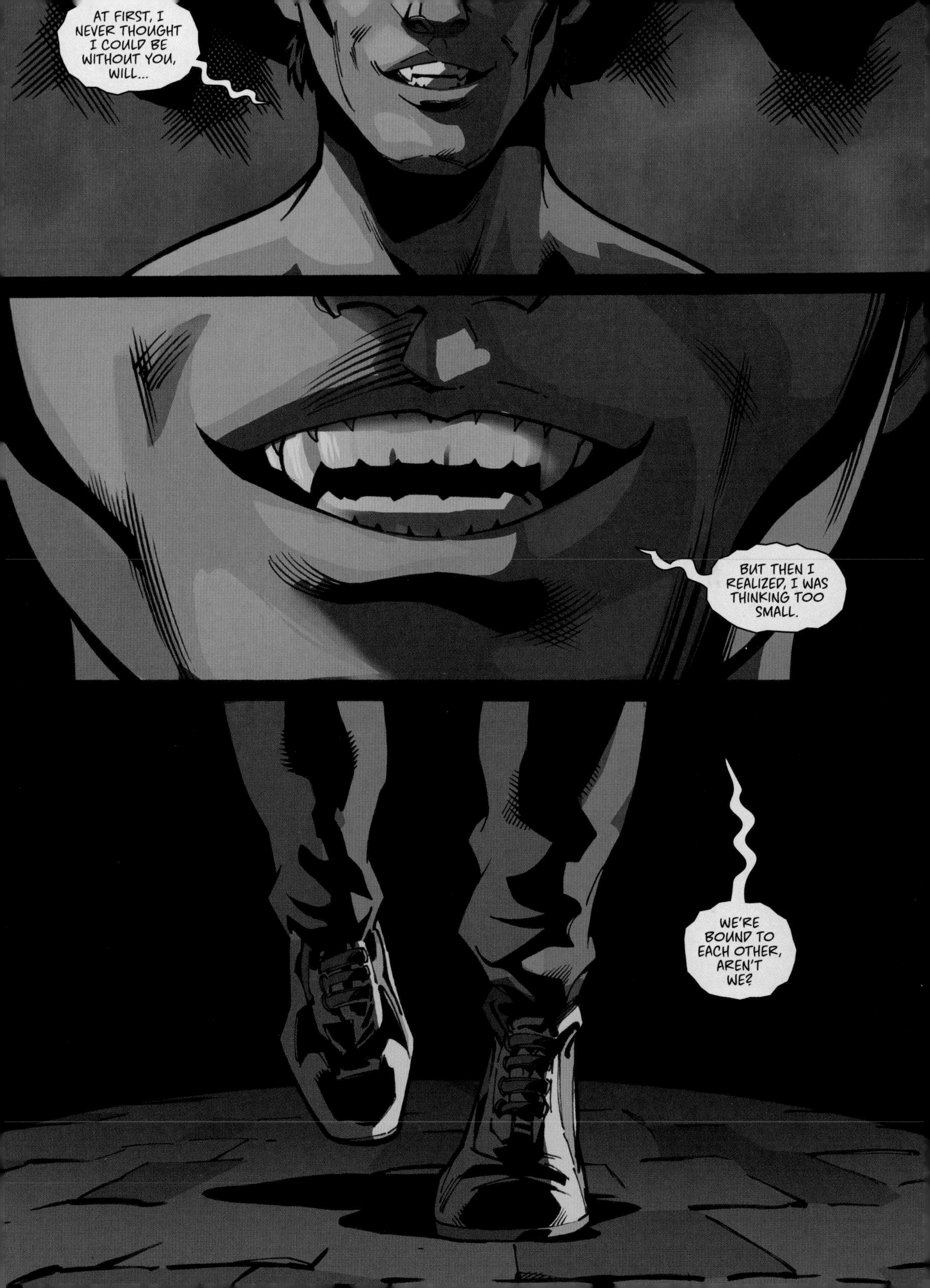
AT FIRST, I NEVER THOUGHT I COULD BE WITHOUT YOU, WILL...
BUT THEN I REALIZED, I WAS THINKING TOO SMALL.
WE'RE BOUND TO EACH OTHER, AREN'T WE?

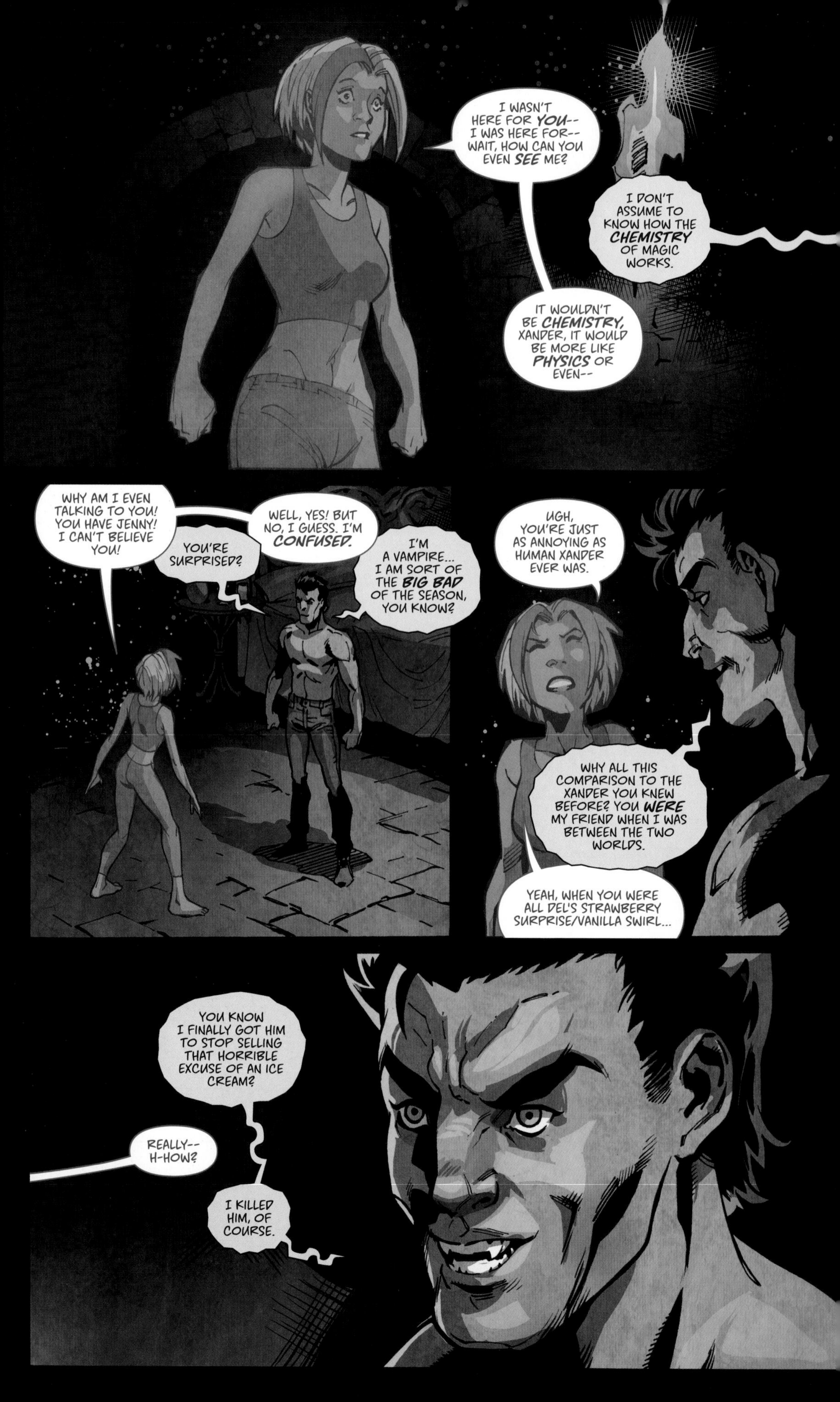
I WASN'T HERE FOR **YOU**-- I WAS HERE FOR-- WAIT, HOW CAN YOU EVEN **SEE** ME?
I DON'T ASSUME TO KNOW HOW THE **CHEMISTRY** OF MAGIC WORKS.
IT WOULDN'T BE **CHEMISTRY,** XANDER, IT WOULD BE MORE LIKE **PHYSICS** OR EVEN--
WHY AM I EVEN TALKING TO YOU! YOU HAVE JENNY! I CAN'T BELIEVE YOU!
YOU'RE SURPRISED?
WELL, YES! BUT NO, I GUESS. I'M **CONFUSED.**
I'M A VAMPIRE... I AM SORT OF THE **BIG BAD** OF THE SEASON, YOU KNOW?
UGH, YOU'RE JUST AS ANNOYING AS HUMAN XANDER EVER WAS.
WHY ALL THIS COMPARISON TO THE XANDER YOU KNEW BEFORE? YOU **WERE** MY FRIEND WHEN I WAS BETWEEN THE TWO WORLDS.
YEAH, WHEN YOU WERE ALL DEL'S STRAWBERRY SURPRISE/VANILLA SWIRL...
YOU KNOW I FINALLY GOT HIM TO STOP SELLING THAT HORRIBLE EXCUSE OF AN ICE CREAM?
REALLY-- H-HOW?
I KILLED HIM, OF COURSE.

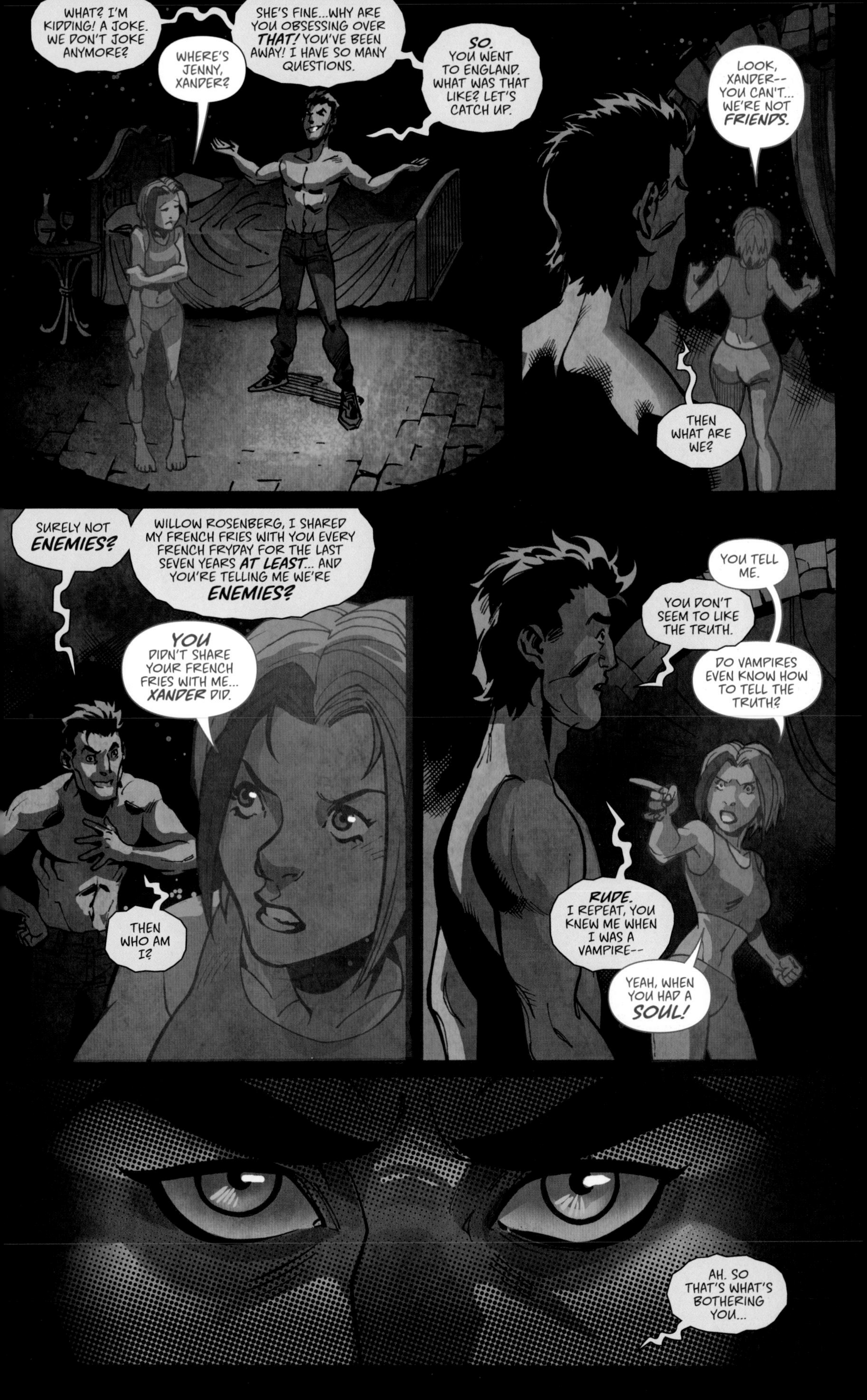
WHAT? I'M KIDDING! A JOKE. WE DON'T JOKE ANYMORE?
WHERE'S JENNY, XANDER?
SHE'S FINE...WHY ARE YOU OBSESSING OVER THAT! YOU'VE BEEN AWAY! I HAVE SO MANY QUESTIONS.
SO. YOU WENT TO ENGLAND. WHAT WAS THAT LIKE? LET'S CATCH UP.
LOOK, XANDER-- YOU CAN'T... WE'RE NOT FRIENDS.
THEN WHAT ARE WE?
SURELY NOT ENEMIES?
WILLOW ROSENBERG, I SHARED MY FRENCH FRIES WITH YOU EVERY FRENCH FRYDAY FOR THE LAST SEVEN YEARS AT LEAST... AND YOU'RE TELLING ME WE'RE ENEMIES?
YOU DIDN'T SHARE YOUR FRENCH FRIES WITH ME... XANDER DID.
THEN WHO AM I?
YOU TELL ME.
YOU DON'T SEEM TO LIKE THE TRUTH.
DO VAMPIRES EVEN KNOW HOW TO TELL THE TRUTH?
RUDE. I REPEAT, YOU KNEW ME WHEN I WAS A VAMPIRE--
YEAH, WHEN YOU HAD A SOUL!
AH. SO THAT'S WHAT'S BOTHERING YOU...

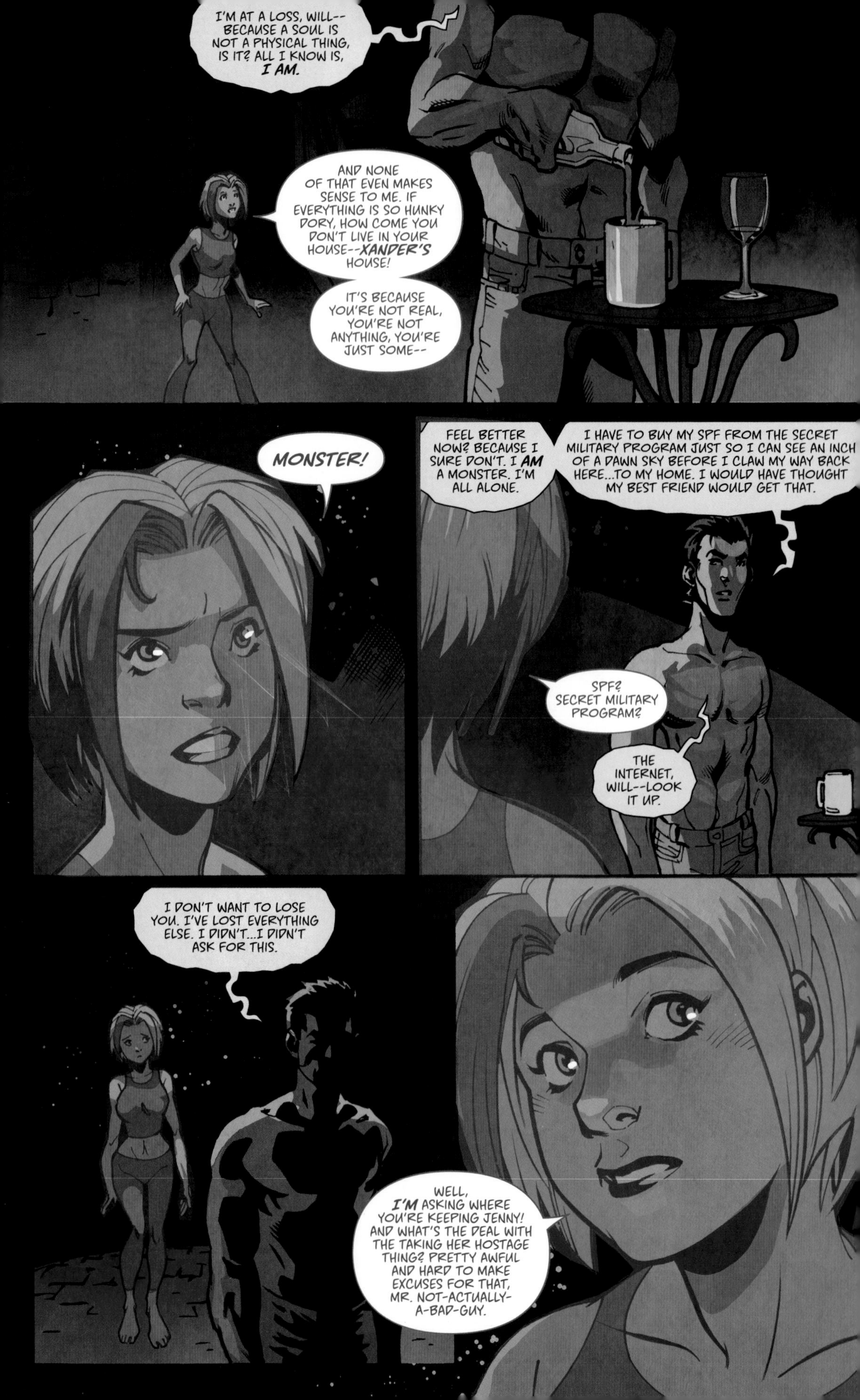

I'M AT A LOSS, WILL--BECAUSE A SOUL IS NOT A PHYSICAL THING, IS IT? ALL I KNOW IS, I AM.
AND NONE OF THAT EVEN MAKES SENSE TO ME. IF EVERYTHING IS SO HUNKY DORY, HOW COME YOU DON'T LIVE IN YOUR HOUSE--XANDER'S HOUSE!
IT'S BECAUSE YOU'RE NOT REAL, YOU'RE NOT ANYTHING, YOU'RE JUST SOME--
MONSTER!
FEEL BETTER NOW? BECAUSE I SURE DON'T. I AM A MONSTER. I'M ALL ALONE.
I HAVE TO BUY MY SPF FROM THE SECRET MILITARY PROGRAM JUST SO I CAN SEE AN INCH OF A DAWN SKY BEFORE I CLAW MY WAY BACK HERE...TO MY HOME. I WOULD HAVE THOUGHT MY BEST FRIEND WOULD GET THAT.
SPF? SECRET MILITARY PROGRAM?
THE INTERNET, WILL--LOOK IT UP.
I DON'T WANT TO LOSE YOU. I'VE LOST EVERYTHING ELSE. I DIDN'T...I DIDN'T ASK FOR THIS.
WELL, I'M ASKING WHERE YOU'RE KEEPING JENNY! AND WHAT'S THE DEAL WITH THE TAKING HER HOSTAGE THING? PRETTY AWFUL AND HARD TO MAKE EXCUSES FOR THAT, MR. NOT-ACTUALLY-A-BAD-GUY.

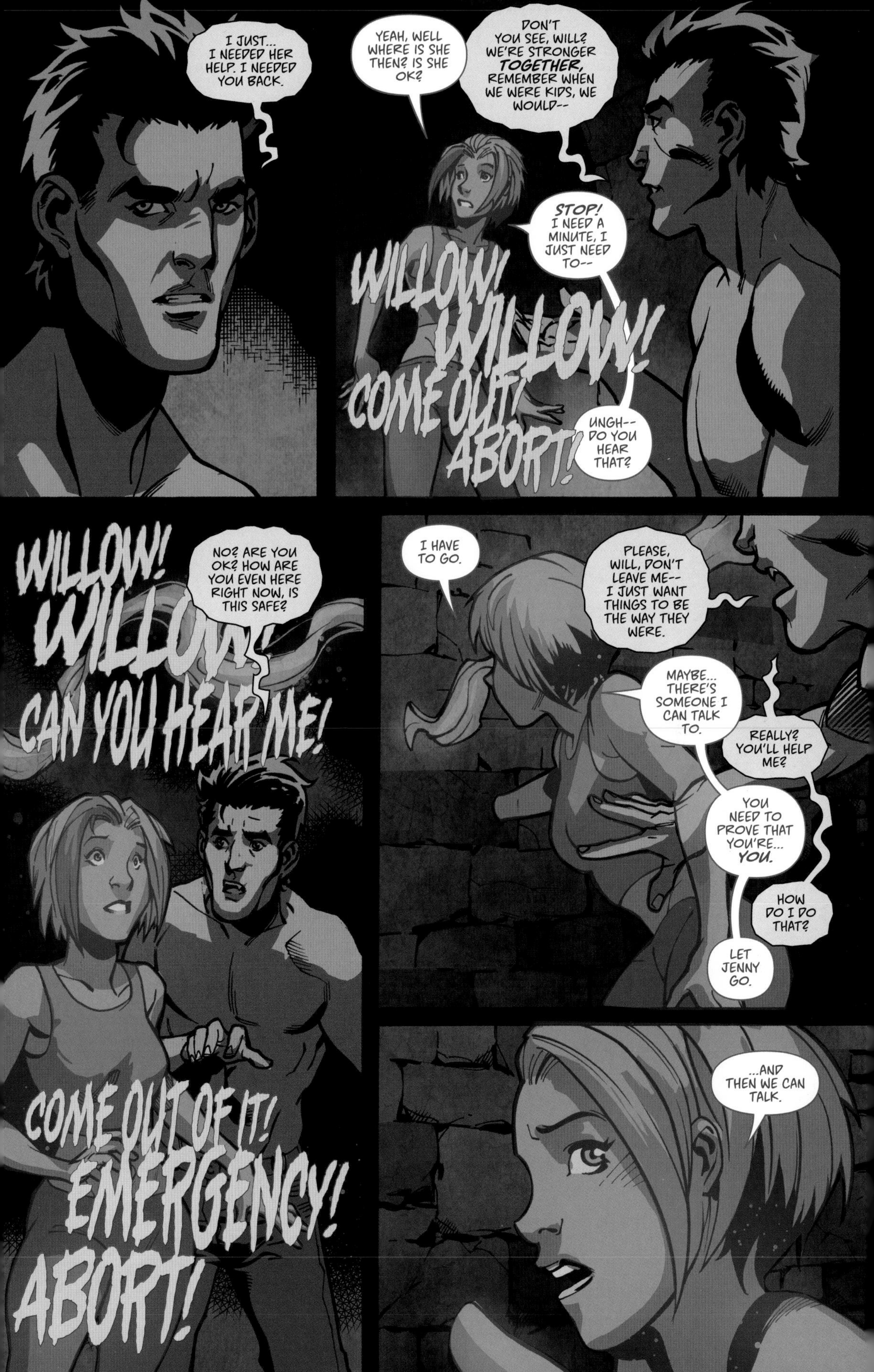
I JUST... I NEEDED HER HELP. I NEEDED YOU BACK.
YEAH, WELL WHERE IS SHE THEN? IS SHE OK?
DON'T YOU SEE, WILL? WE'RE STRONGER *TOGETHER*, REMEMBER WHEN WE WERE KIDS, WE WOULD--
STOP! I NEED A MINUTE, I JUST NEED TO--
WILLOW! WILLOW! COME OUT! ABORT!
UNGH-- DO YOU HEAR THAT?
WILLOW! WILLOW! CAN YOU HEAR ME!
NO? ARE YOU OK? HOW ARE YOU EVEN HERE RIGHT NOW, IS THIS SAFE?
COME OUT OF IT! EMERGENCY! ABORT!
I HAVE TO GO.
PLEASE, WILL, DON'T LEAVE ME-- I JUST WANT THINGS TO BE THE WAY THEY WERE.
MAYBE... THERE'S SOMEONE I CAN TALK TO.
REALLY? YOU'LL HELP ME?
YOU NEED TO PROVE THAT YOU'RE... *YOU.*
HOW DO I DO THAT?
LET JENNY GO.
...AND THEN WE CAN TALK.

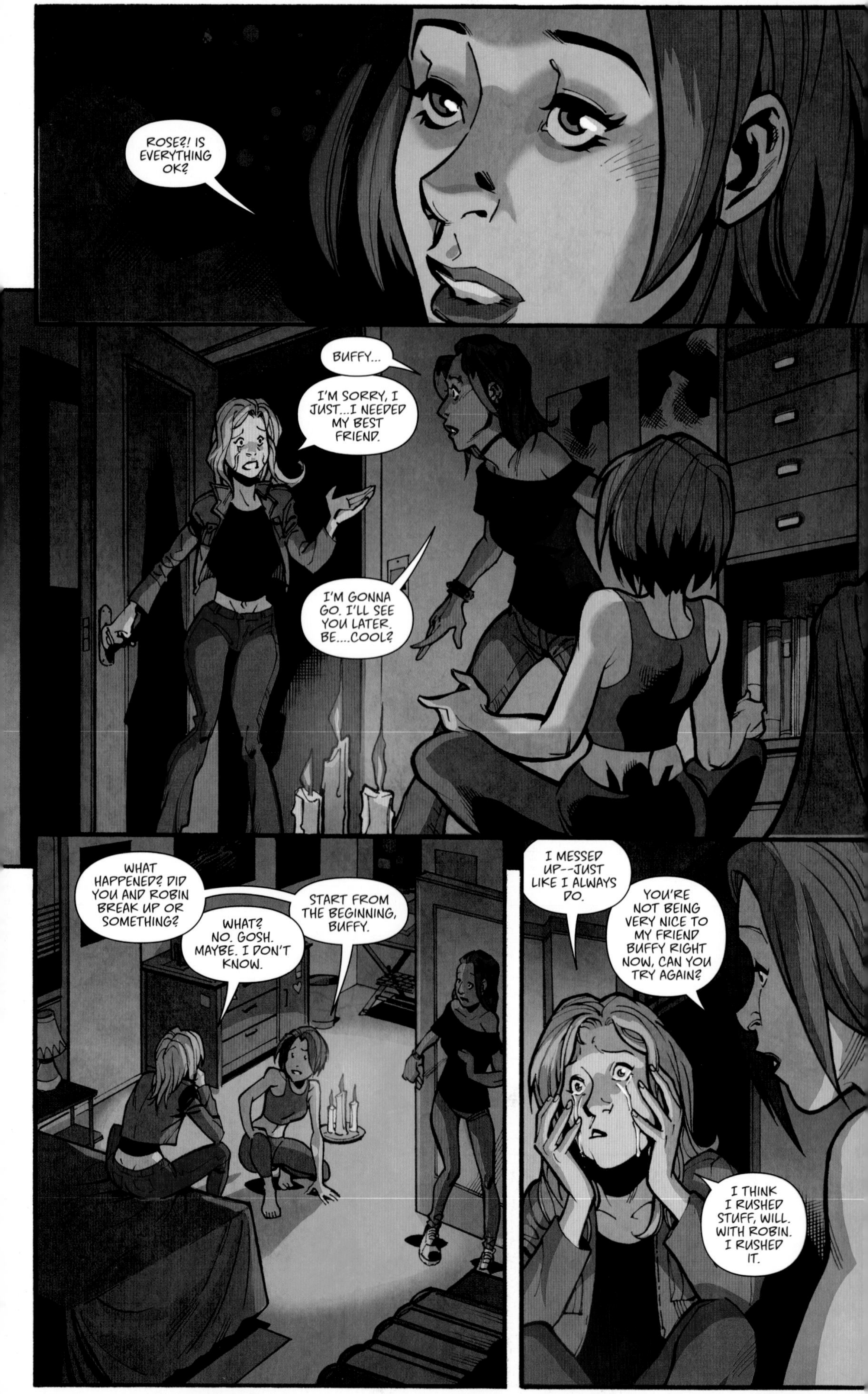
ROSE?! IS EVERYTHING OK?
BUFFY...
I'M SORRY, I JUST...I NEEDED MY BEST FRIEND.
I'M GONNA GO. I'LL SEE YOU LATER. BE....COOL?
WHAT HAPPENED? DID YOU AND ROBIN BREAK UP OR SOMETHING?
WHAT? NO. GOSH. MAYBE. I DON'T KNOW.
START FROM THE BEGINNING, BUFFY.
I MESSED UP--JUST LIKE I ALWAYS DO.
YOU'RE NOT BEING VERY NICE TO MY FRIEND BUFFY RIGHT NOW, CAN YOU TRY AGAIN?
I THINK I RUSHED STUFF, WILL. WITH ROBIN. I RUSHED IT.

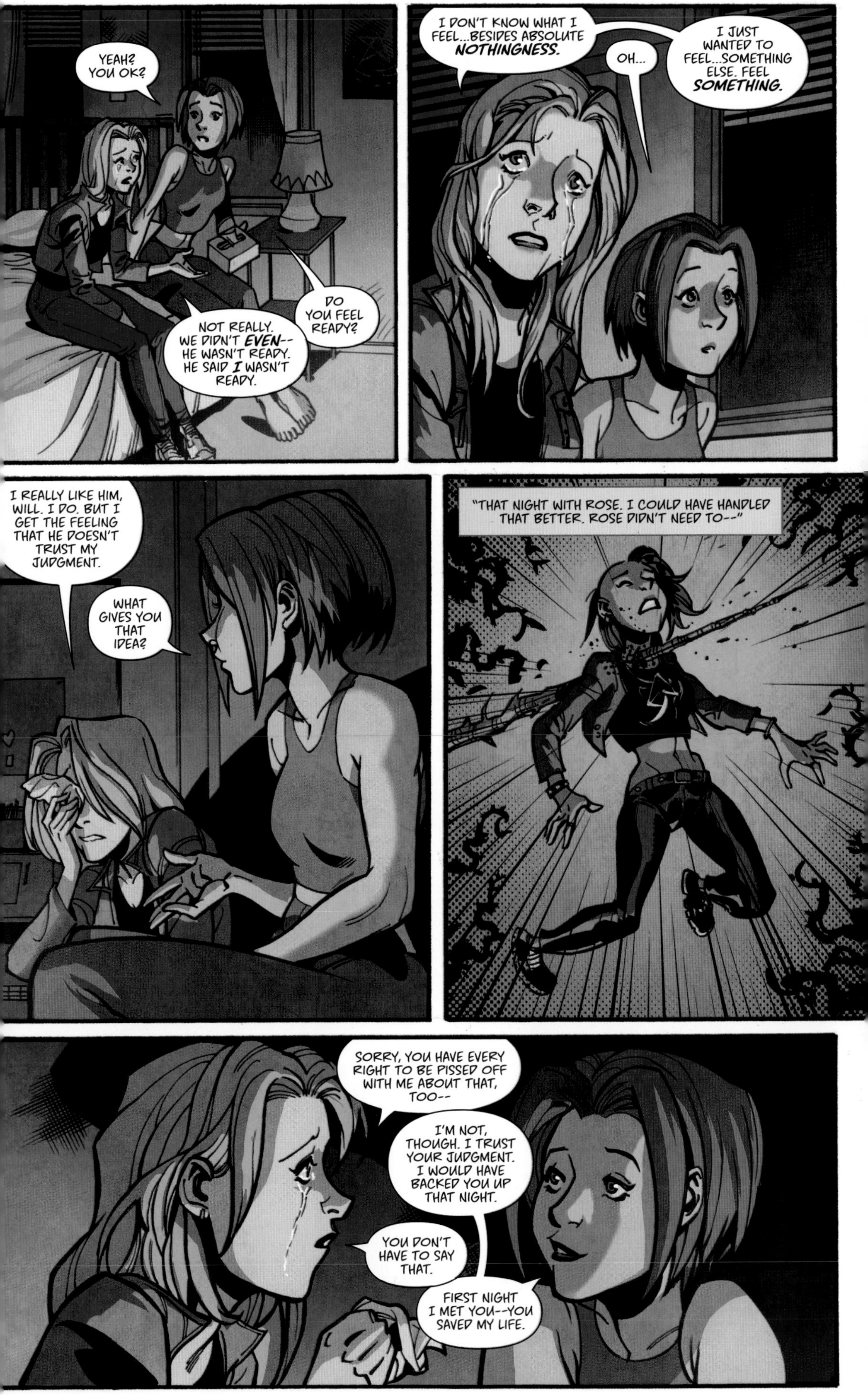

YEAH? YOU OK?
NOT REALLY. WE DIDN'T **EVEN**-- HE WASN'T READY. HE SAID **I** WASN'T READY.
DO YOU FEEL READY?
I DON'T KNOW WHAT I FEEL...BESIDES ABSOLUTE **NOTHINGNESS.**
OH...
I JUST WANTED TO FEEL...SOMETHING ELSE. FEEL **SOMETHING.**
I REALLY LIKE HIM, WILL. I DO. BUT I GET THE FEELING THAT HE DOESN'T TRUST MY JUDGMENT.
WHAT GIVES YOU THAT IDEA?
"THAT NIGHT WITH ROSE. I COULD HAVE HANDLED THAT BETTER. ROSE DIDN'T NEED TO--"
SORRY, YOU HAVE EVERY RIGHT TO BE PISSED OFF WITH ME ABOUT THAT, TOO--
I'M NOT, THOUGH. I TRUST YOUR JUDGMENT. I WOULD HAVE BACKED YOU UP THAT NIGHT.
YOU DON'T HAVE TO SAY THAT.
FIRST NIGHT I MET YOU--YOU SAVED MY LIFE.

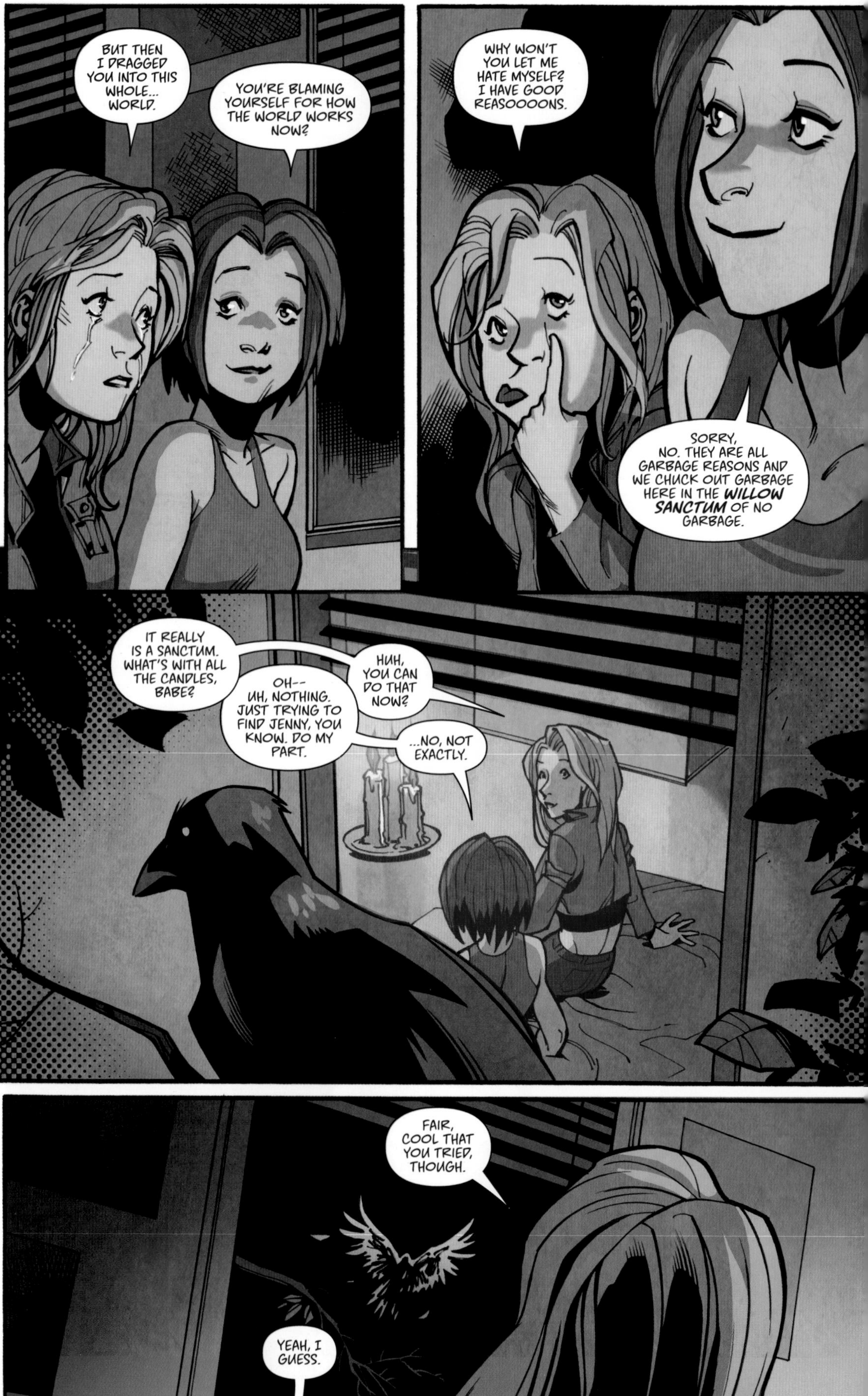
BUT THEN I DRAGGED YOU INTO THIS WHOLE... WORLD.
YOU'RE BLAMING YOURSELF FOR HOW THE WORLD WORKS NOW?
WHY WON'T YOU LET ME HATE MYSELF? I HAVE GOOD REASOOOONS.
SORRY, NO. THEY ARE ALL GARBAGE REASONS AND WE CHUCK OUT GARBAGE HERE IN THE WILLOW SANCTUM OF NO GARBAGE.
IT REALLY IS A SANCTUM. WHAT'S WITH ALL THE CANDLES, BABE?
OH-- UH, NOTHING. JUST TRYING TO FIND JENNY, YOU KNOW. DO MY PART.
HUH, YOU CAN DO THAT NOW?
...NO, NOT EXACTLY.
FAIR, COOL THAT YOU TRIED, THOUGH.
YEAH, I GUESS.

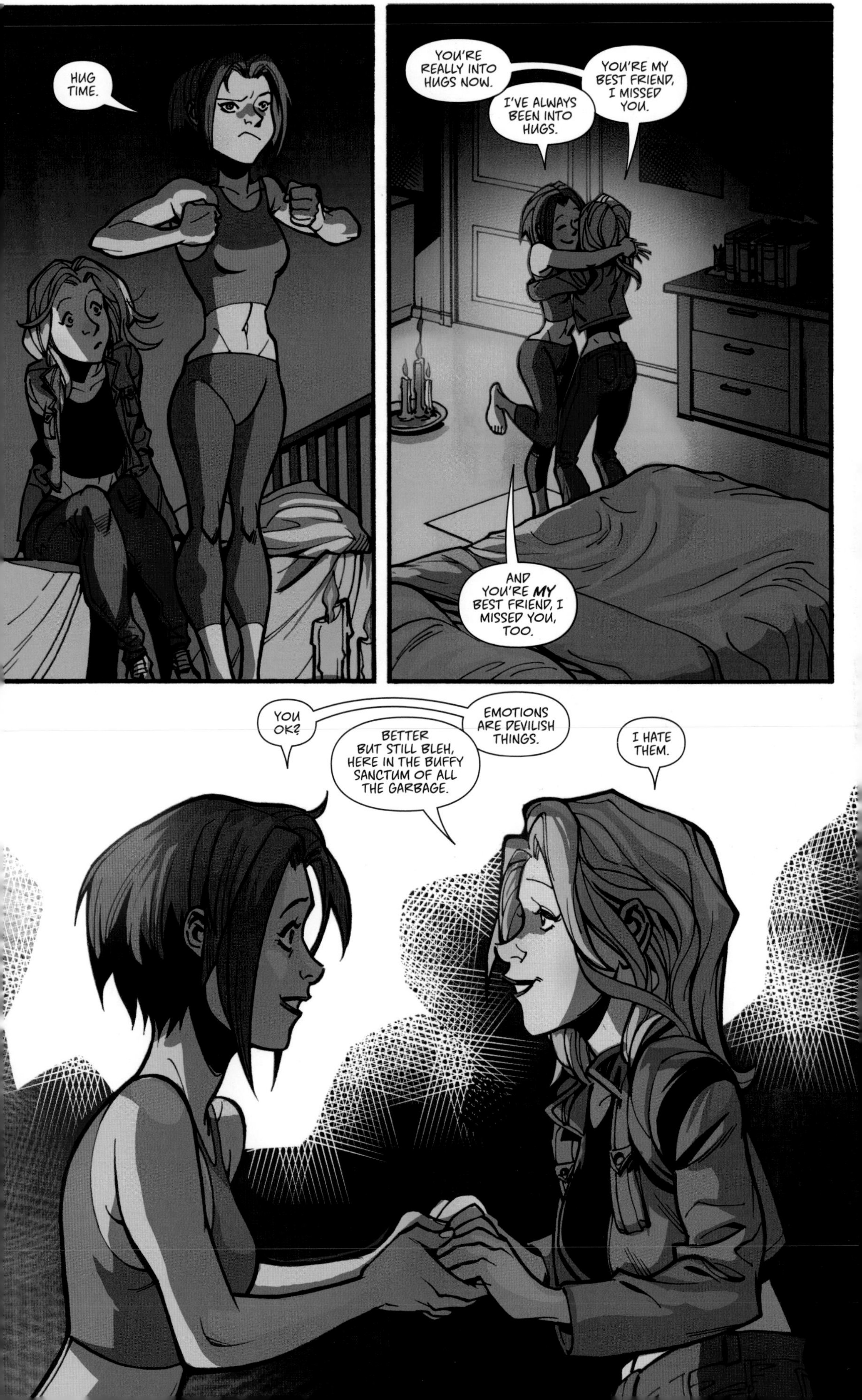
HUG TIME.
YOU'RE REALLY INTO HUGS NOW.
I'VE ALWAYS BEEN INTO HUGS.
YOU'RE MY BEST FRIEND, I MISSED YOU.
AND YOU'RE MY BEST FRIEND, I MISSED YOU, TOO.
YOU OK?
BETTER BUT STILL BLEH, HERE IN THE BUFFY SANCTUM OF ALL THE GARBAGE.
EMOTIONS ARE DEVILISH THINGS.
I HATE THEM.

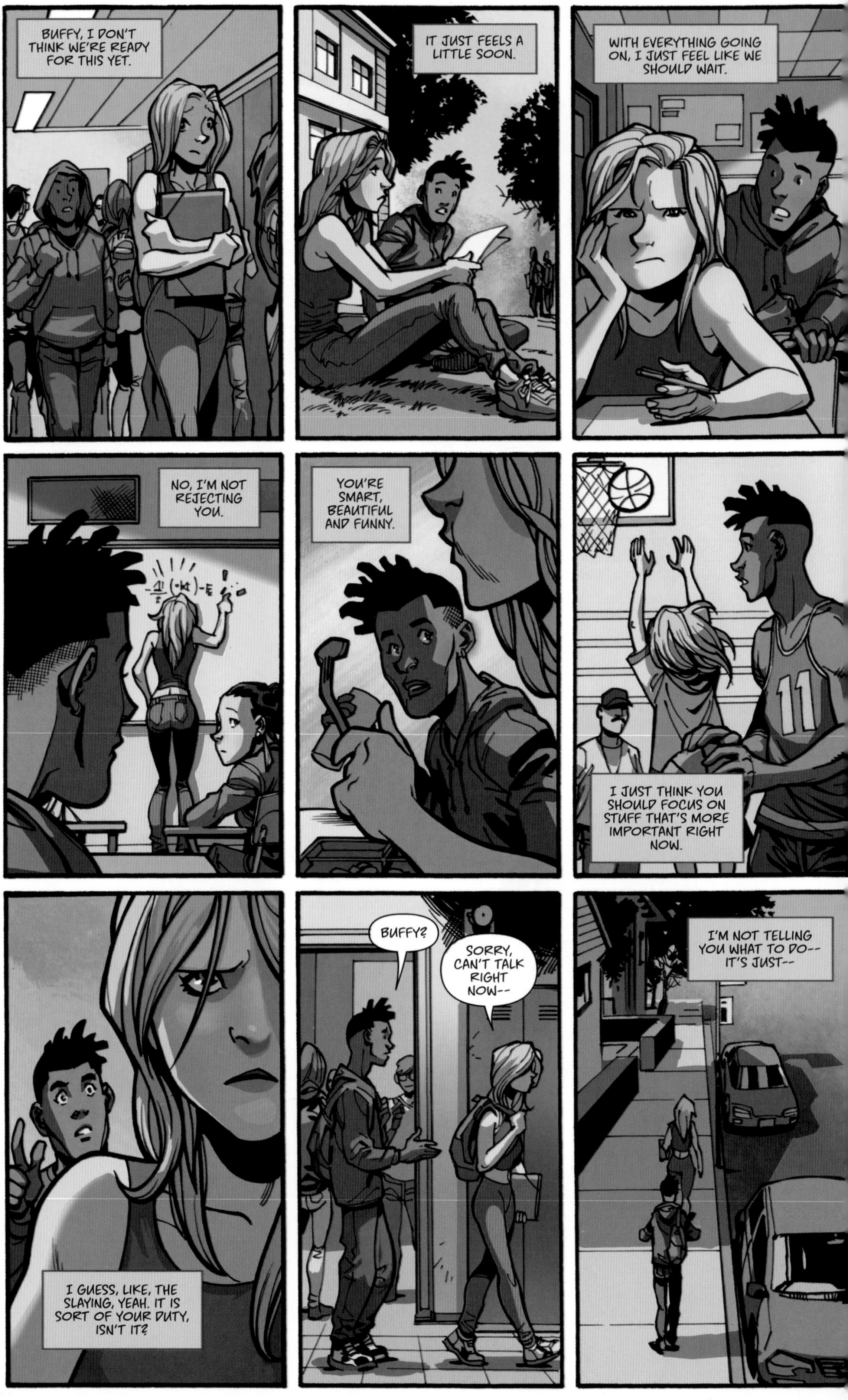
BUFFY, I DON'T THINK WE'RE READY FOR THIS YET.
IT JUST FEELS A LITTLE SOON.
WITH EVERYTHING GOING ON, I JUST FEEL LIKE WE SHOULD WAIT.
NO, I'M NOT REJECTING YOU.
YOU'RE SMART, BEAUTIFUL AND FUNNY.
I JUST THINK YOU SHOULD FOCUS ON STUFF THAT'S MORE IMPORTANT RIGHT NOW.
I GUESS, LIKE, THE SLAYING, YEAH. IT IS SORT OF YOUR DUTY, ISN'T IT?
BUFFY?
SORRY, CAN'T TALK RIGHT NOW--
I'M NOT TELLING YOU WHAT TO DO-- IT'S JUST--

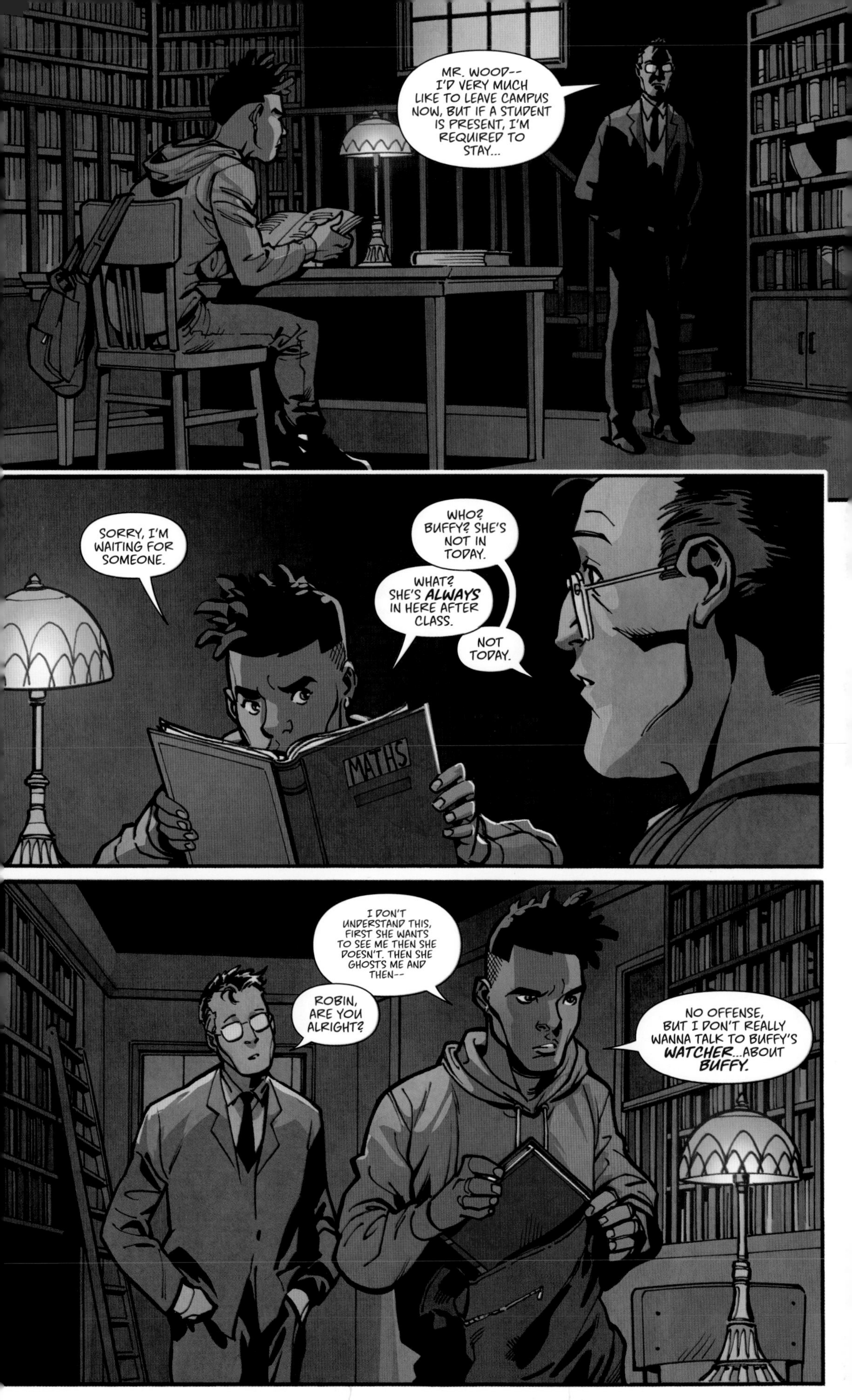
MR. WOOD-- I'D VERY MUCH LIKE TO LEAVE CAMPUS NOW, BUT IF A STUDENT IS PRESENT, I'M REQUIRED TO STAY...
SORRY, I'M WAITING FOR SOMEONE.
WHO? BUFFY? SHE'S NOT IN TODAY.
WHAT? SHE'S ALWAYS IN HERE AFTER CLASS.
NOT TODAY.
MATHS
I DON'T UNDERSTAND THIS, FIRST SHE WANTS TO SEE ME THEN SHE DOESN'T. THEN SHE GHOSTS ME AND THEN--
ROBIN, ARE YOU ALRIGHT?
NO OFFENSE, BUT I DON'T REALLY WANNA TALK TO BUFFY'S WATCHER...ABOUT BUFFY.

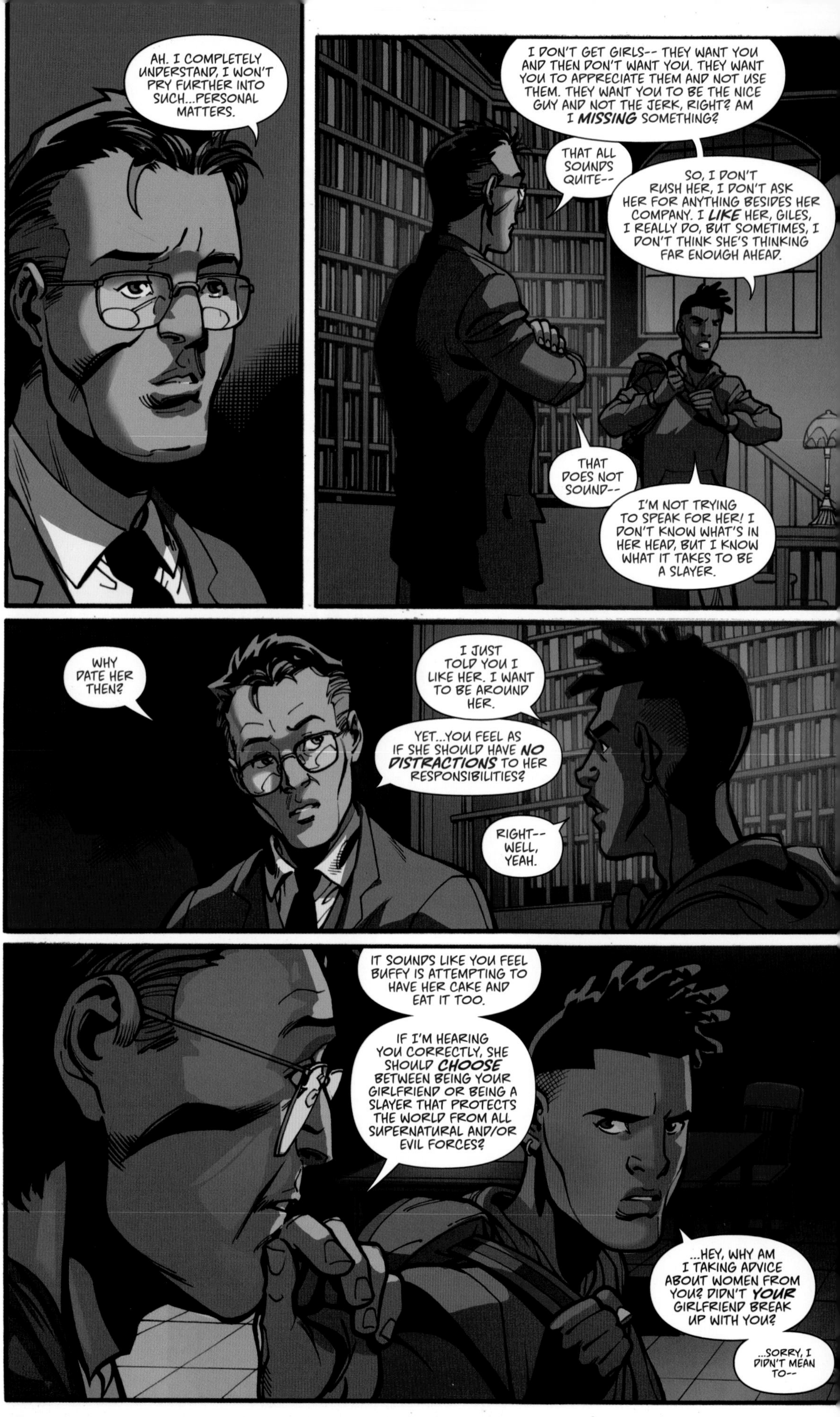

AH. I COMPLETELY UNDERSTAND, I WON'T PRY FURTHER INTO SUCH...PERSONAL MATTERS.
I DON'T GET GIRLS-- THEY WANT YOU AND THEN DON'T WANT YOU. THEY WANT YOU TO APPRECIATE THEM AND NOT USE THEM. THEY WANT YOU TO BE THE NICE GUY AND NOT THE JERK, RIGHT? AM I MISSING SOMETHING?
THAT ALL SOUNDS QUITE--
SO, I DON'T RUSH HER, I DON'T ASK HER FOR ANYTHING BESIDES HER COMPANY. I LIKE HER, GILES, I REALLY DO, BUT SOMETIMES, I DON'T THINK SHE'S THINKING FAR ENOUGH AHEAD.
THAT DOES NOT SOUND--
I'M NOT TRYING TO SPEAK FOR HER! I DON'T KNOW WHAT'S IN HER HEAD, BUT I KNOW WHAT IT TAKES TO BE A SLAYER.
WHY DATE HER THEN?
I JUST TOLD YOU I LIKE HER. I WANT TO BE AROUND HER.
YET...YOU FEEL AS IF SHE SHOULD HAVE NO DISTRACTIONS TO HER RESPONSIBILITIES?
RIGHT-- WELL, YEAH.
IT SOUNDS LIKE YOU FEEL BUFFY IS ATTEMPTING TO HAVE HER CAKE AND EAT IT TOO.
IF I'M HEARING YOU CORRECTLY, SHE SHOULD CHOOSE BETWEEN BEING YOUR GIRLFRIEND OR BEING A SLAYER THAT PROTECTS THE WORLD FROM ALL SUPERNATURAL AND/OR EVIL FORCES?
...HEY, WHY AM I TAKING ADVICE ABOUT WOMEN FROM YOU? DIDN'T YOUR GIRLFRIEND BREAK UP WITH YOU?
...SORRY, I DIDN'T MEAN TO--

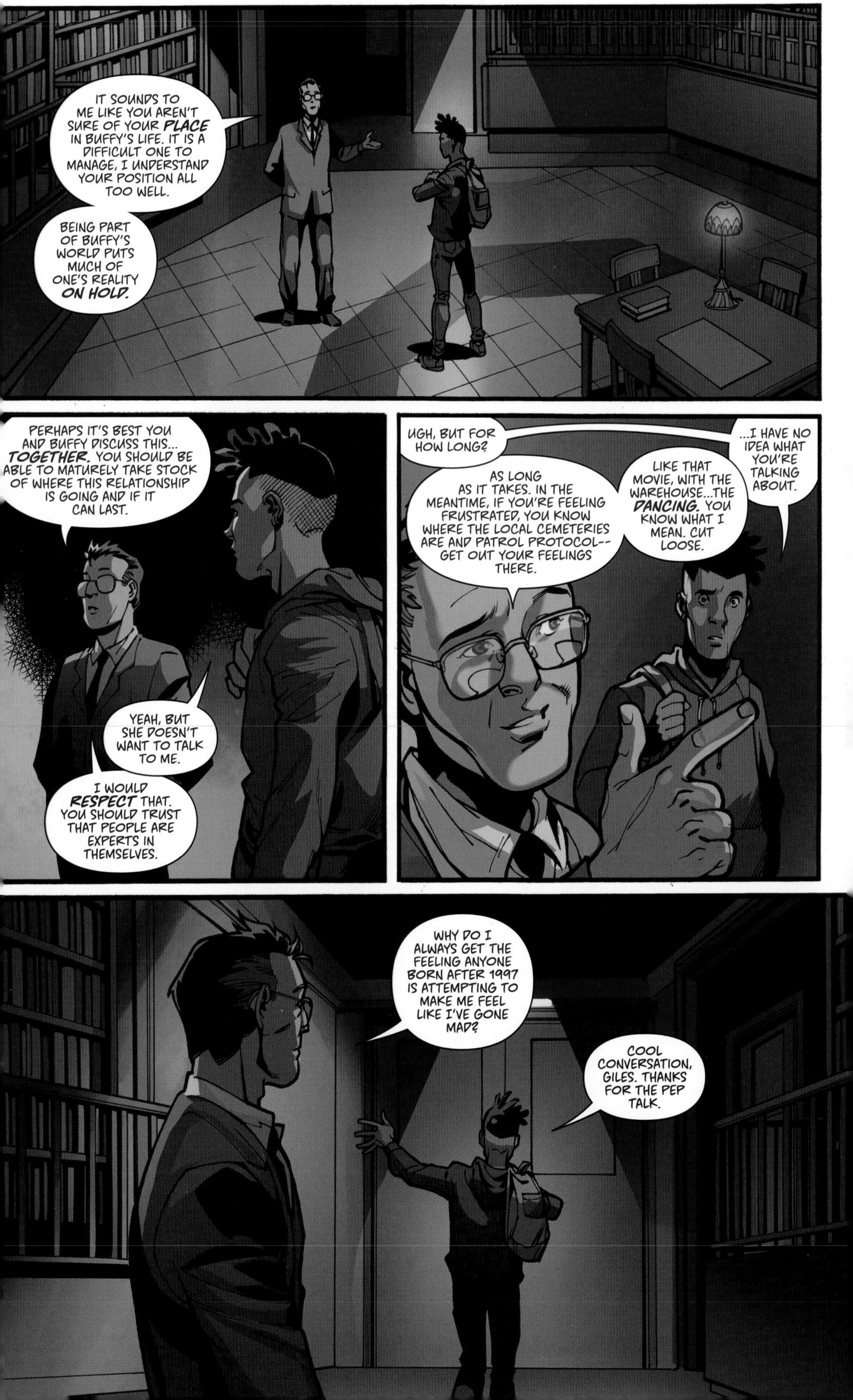
IT SOUNDS TO ME LIKE YOU AREN'T SURE OF YOUR PLACE IN BUFFY'S LIFE. IT IS A DIFFICULT ONE TO MANAGE, I UNDERSTAND YOUR POSITION ALL TOO WELL.
BEING PART OF BUFFY'S WORLD PUTS MUCH OF ONE'S REALITY ON HOLD.
PERHAPS IT'S BEST YOU AND BUFFY DISCUSS THIS... TOGETHER. YOU SHOULD BE ABLE TO MATURELY TAKE STOCK OF WHERE THIS RELATIONSHIP IS GOING AND IF IT CAN LAST.
YEAH, BUT SHE DOESN'T WANT TO TALK TO ME.
I WOULD RESPECT THAT. YOU SHOULD TRUST THAT PEOPLE ARE EXPERTS IN THEMSELVES.
UGH, BUT FOR HOW LONG?
AS LONG AS IT TAKES. IN THE MEANTIME, IF YOU'RE FEELING FRUSTRATED, YOU KNOW WHERE THE LOCAL CEMETERIES ARE AND PATROL PROTOCOL-- GET OUT YOUR FEELINGS THERE.
LIKE THAT MOVIE, WITH THE WAREHOUSE...THE DANCING. YOU KNOW WHAT I MEAN. CUT LOOSE.
...I HAVE NO IDEA WHAT YOU'RE TALKING ABOUT.
COOL CONVERSATION, GILES. THANKS FOR THE PEP TALK.
WHY DO I ALWAYS GET THE FEELING ANYONE BORN AFTER 1997 IS ATTEMPTING TO MAKE ME FEEL LIKE I'VE GONE MAD?

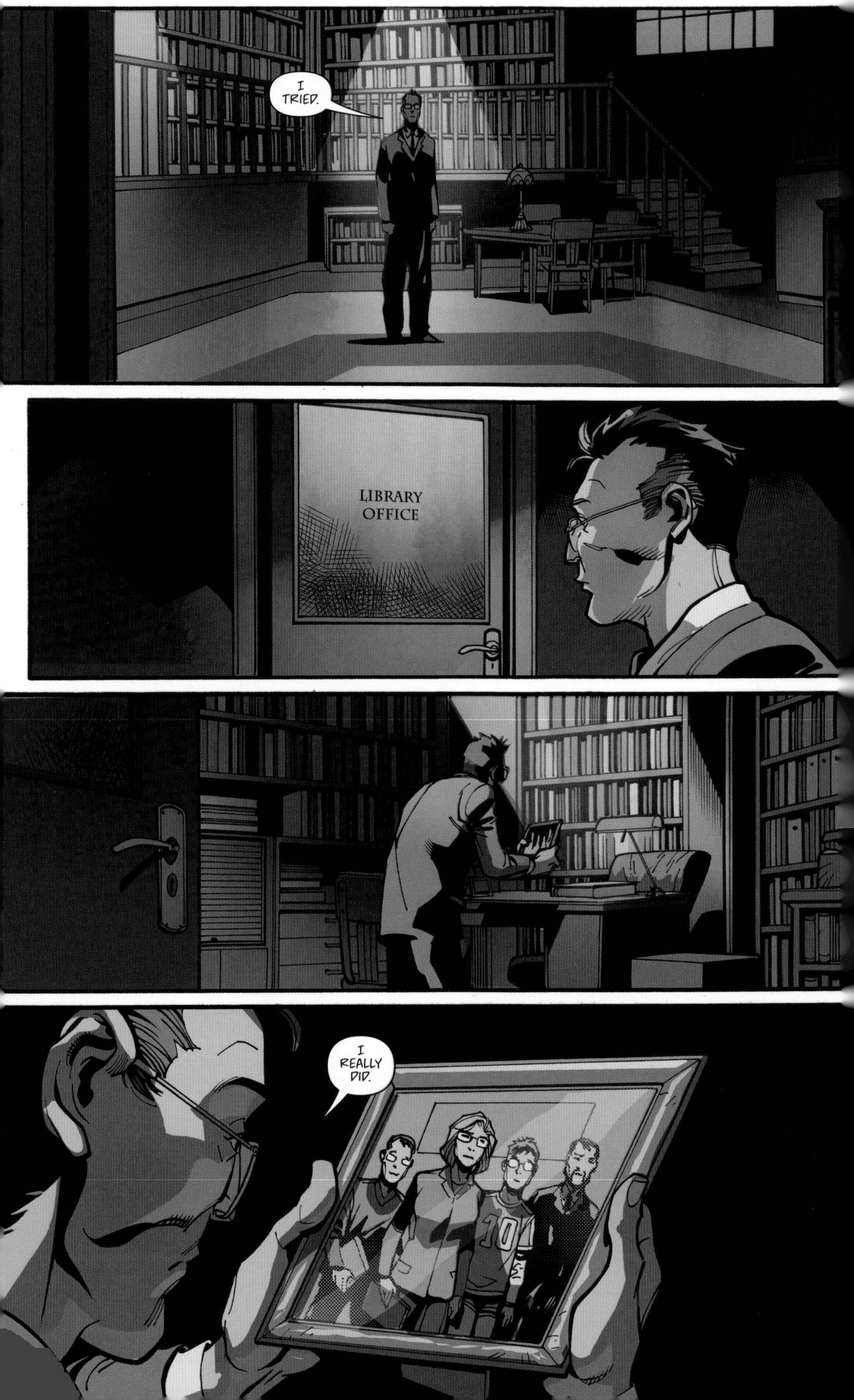
I TRIED.
LIBRARY OFFICE
I REALLY DID.

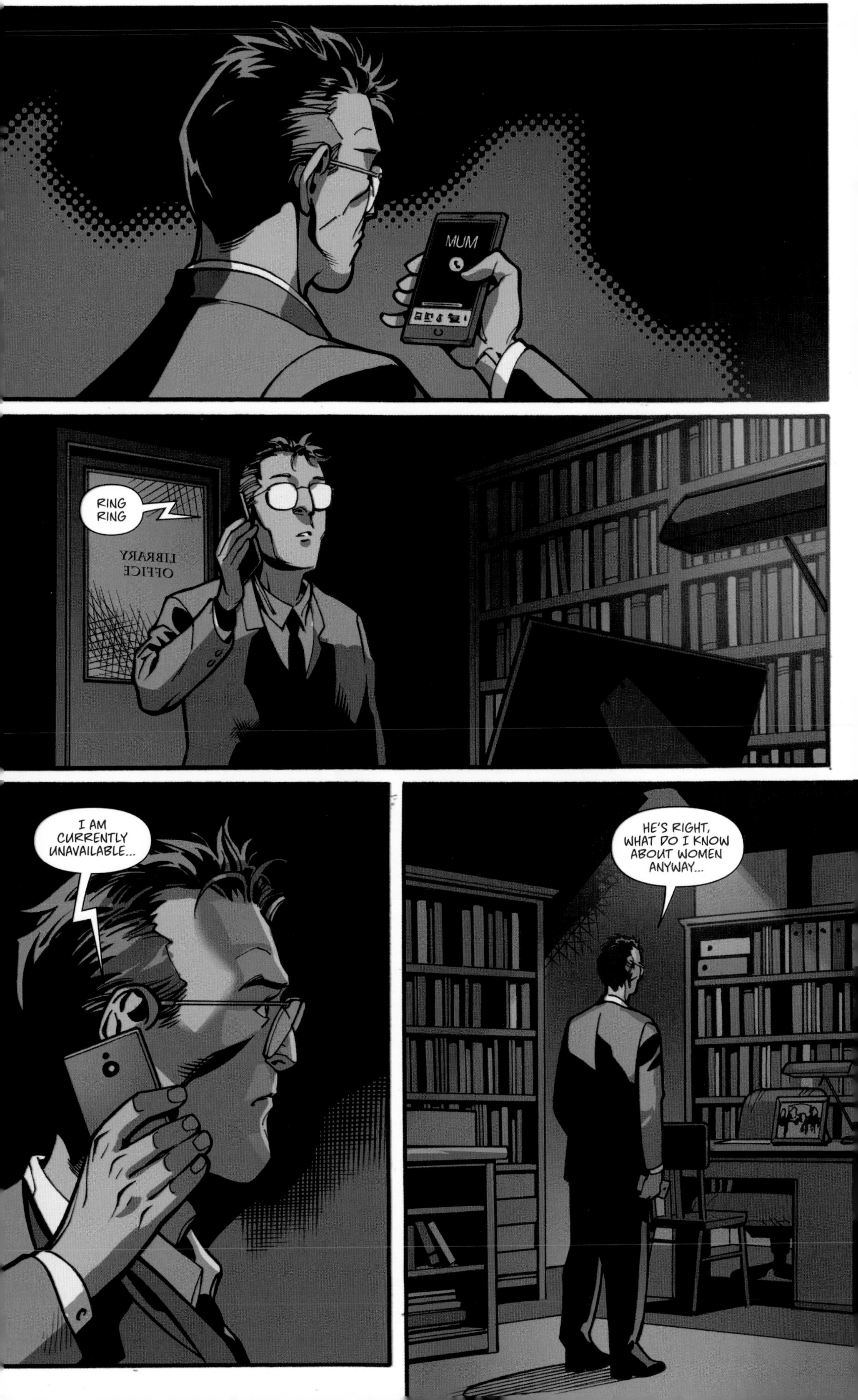
MUM
RING RING
LIBRARY OFFICE
I AM CURRENTLY UNAVAILABLE...
HE'S RIGHT, WHAT DO I KNOW ABOUT WOMEN ANYWAY...

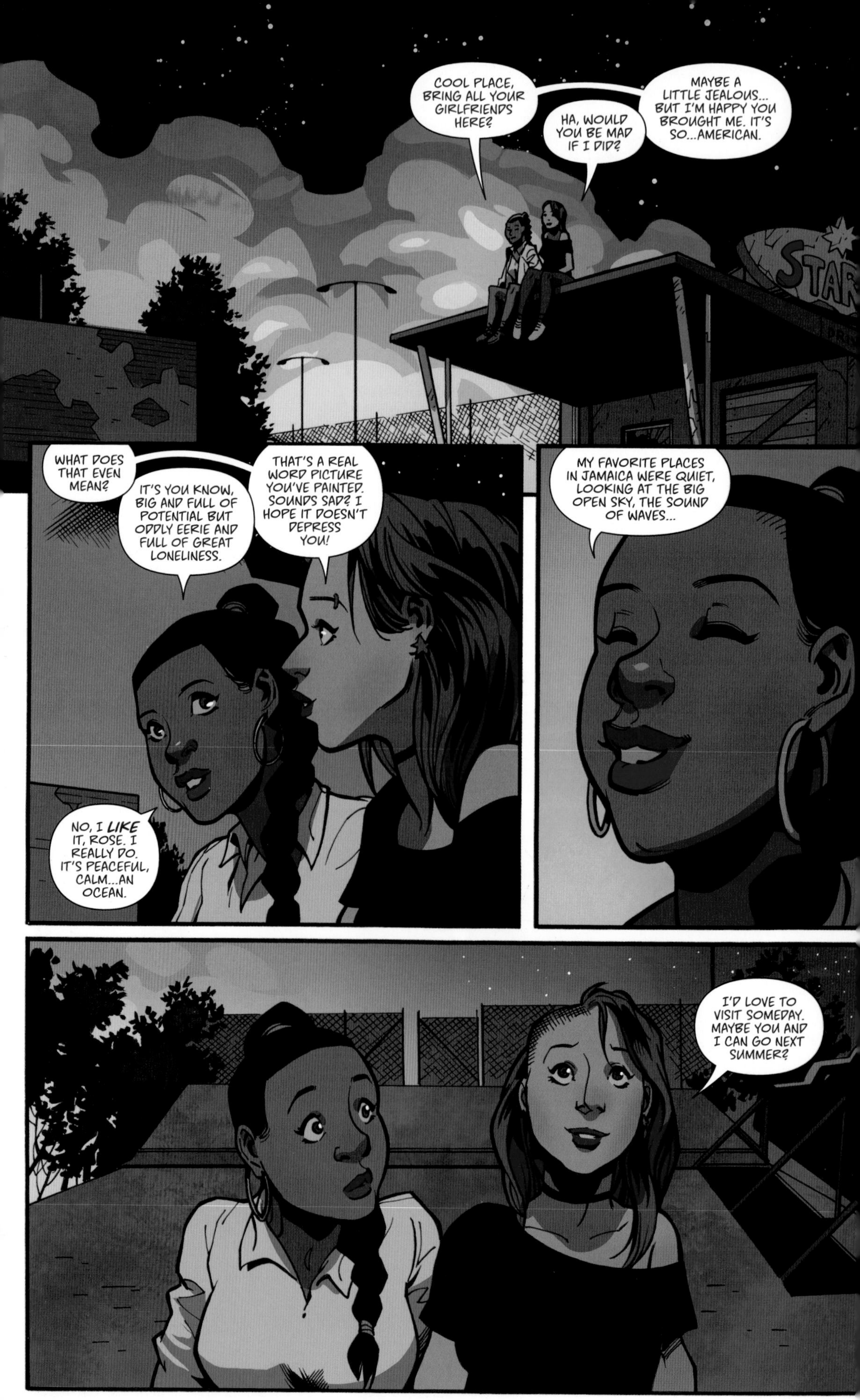
COOL PLACE, BRING ALL YOUR GIRLFRIENDS HERE?
HA, WOULD YOU BE MAD IF I DID?
MAYBE A LITTLE JEALOUS... BUT I'M HAPPY YOU BROUGHT ME. IT'S SO...AMERICAN.
STAR
WHAT DOES THAT EVEN MEAN?
IT'S YOU KNOW, BIG AND FULL OF POTENTIAL BUT ODDLY EERIE AND FULL OF GREAT LONELINESS.
THAT'S A REAL WORD PICTURE YOU'VE PAINTED. SOUNDS SAD? I HOPE IT DOESN'T DEPRESS YOU!
NO, I *LIKE* IT, ROSE. I REALLY DO. IT'S PEACEFUL, CALM...AN OCEAN.
MY FAVORITE PLACES IN JAMAICA WERE QUIET, LOOKING AT THE BIG OPEN SKY, THE SOUND OF WAVES...
I'D LOVE TO VISIT SOMEDAY. MAYBE YOU AND I CAN GO NEXT SUMMER?

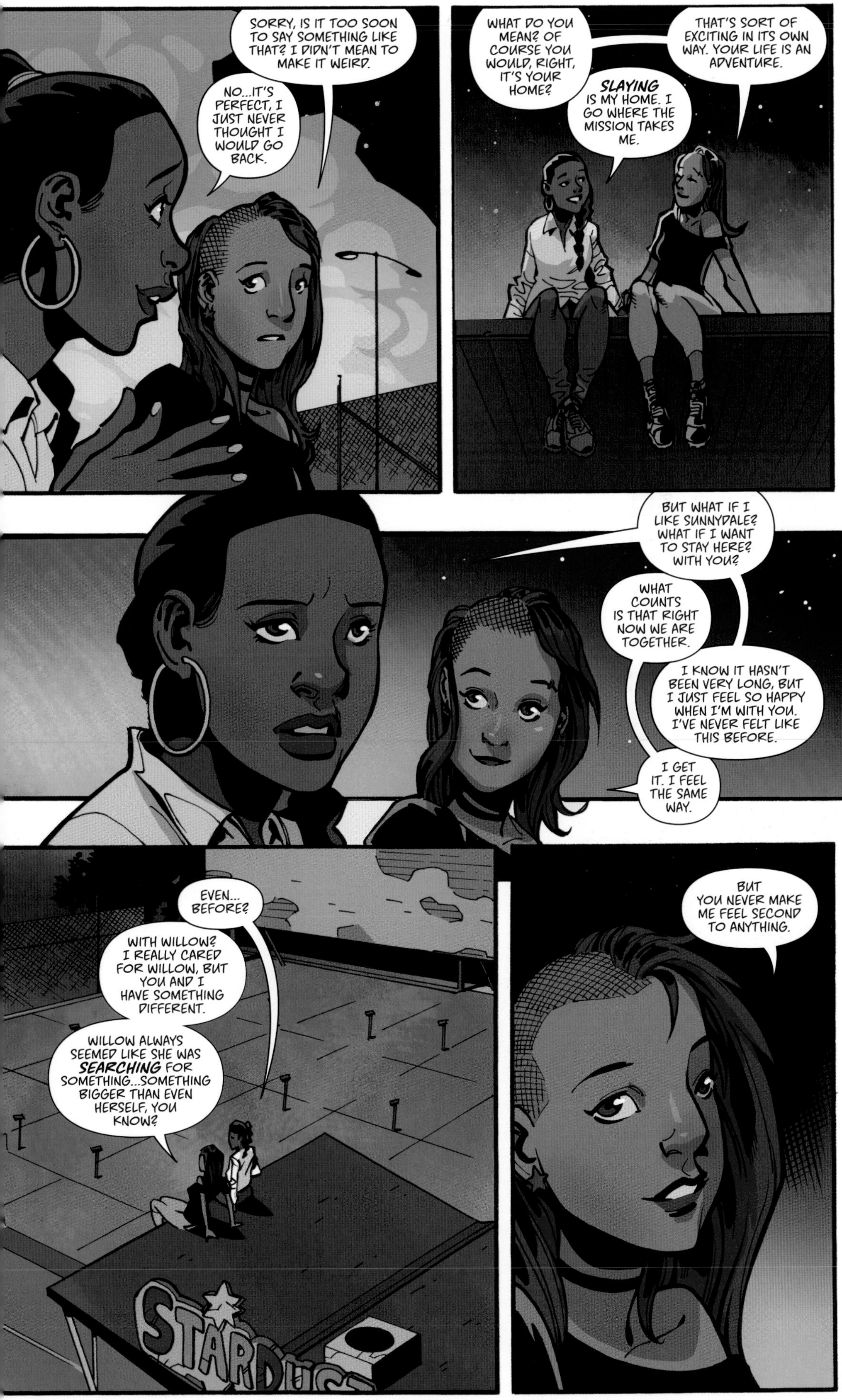
SORRY, IS IT TOO SOON TO SAY SOMETHING LIKE THAT? I DIDN'T MEAN TO MAKE IT WEIRD.
NO...IT'S PERFECT, I JUST NEVER THOUGHT I WOULD GO BACK.
WHAT DO YOU MEAN? OF COURSE YOU WOULD, RIGHT, IT'S YOUR HOME?
SLAYING IS MY HOME. I GO WHERE THE MISSION TAKES ME.
THAT'S SORT OF EXCITING IN ITS OWN WAY. YOUR LIFE IS AN ADVENTURE.
BUT WHAT IF I LIKE SUNNYDALE? WHAT IF I WANT TO STAY HERE? WITH YOU?
WHAT COUNTS IS THAT RIGHT NOW WE ARE TOGETHER.
I KNOW IT HASN'T BEEN VERY LONG, BUT I JUST FEEL SO HAPPY WHEN I'M WITH YOU. I'VE NEVER FELT LIKE THIS BEFORE.
I GET IT. I FEEL THE SAME WAY.
EVEN... BEFORE?
WITH WILLOW? I REALLY CARED FOR WILLOW, BUT YOU AND I HAVE SOMETHING DIFFERENT.
WILLOW ALWAYS SEEMED LIKE SHE WAS SEARCHING FOR SOMETHING...SOMETHING BIGGER THAN EVEN HERSELF, YOU KNOW?
STARDUST
BUT YOU NEVER MAKE ME FEEL SECOND TO ANYTHING.

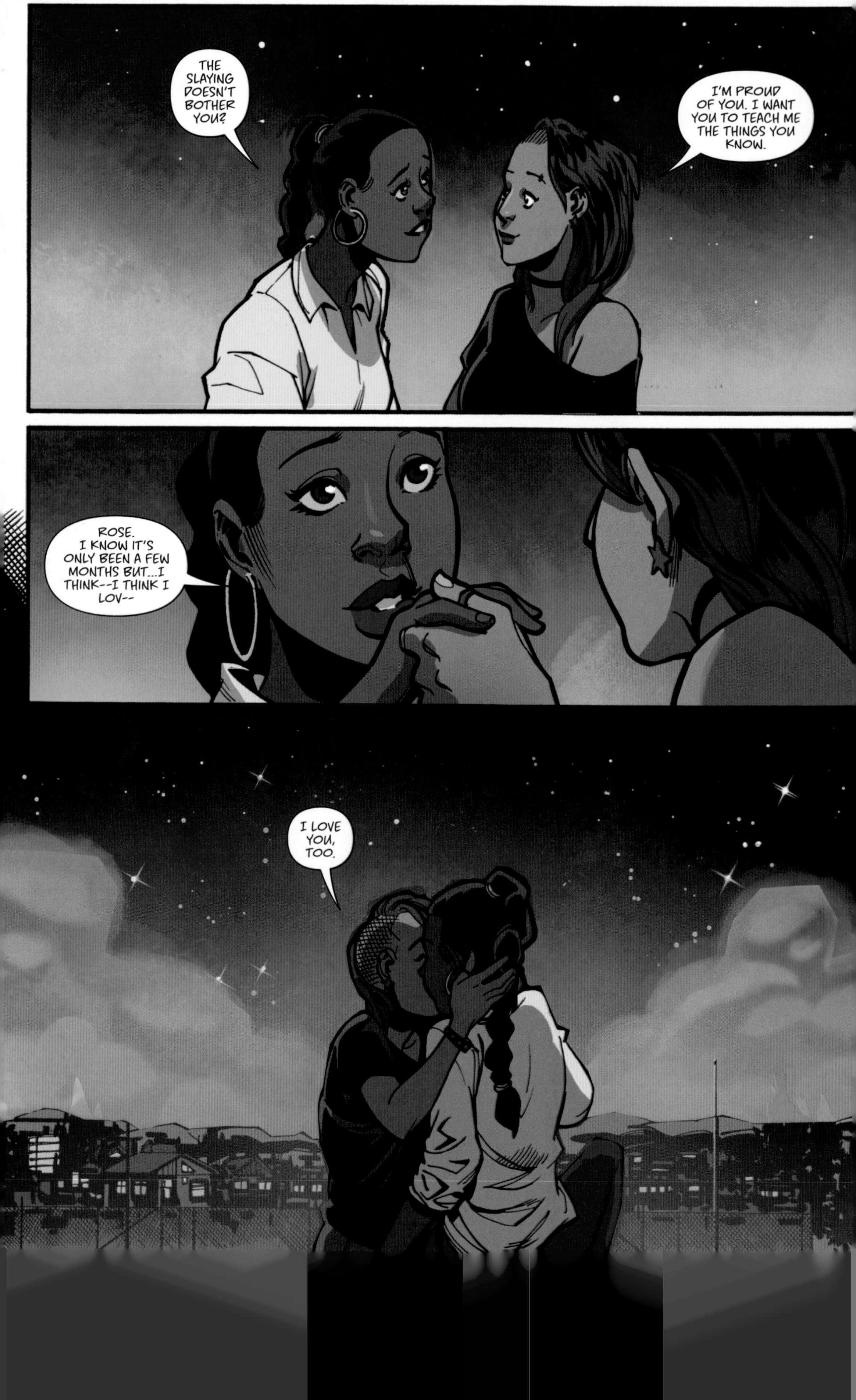

THE SLAYING DOESN'T BOTHER YOU?
I'M PROUD OF YOU. I WANT YOU TO TEACH ME THE THINGS YOU KNOW.
ROSE. I KNOW IT'S ONLY BEEN A FEW MONTHS BUT...I THINK--I THINK I LOV--
I LOVE YOU, TOO.

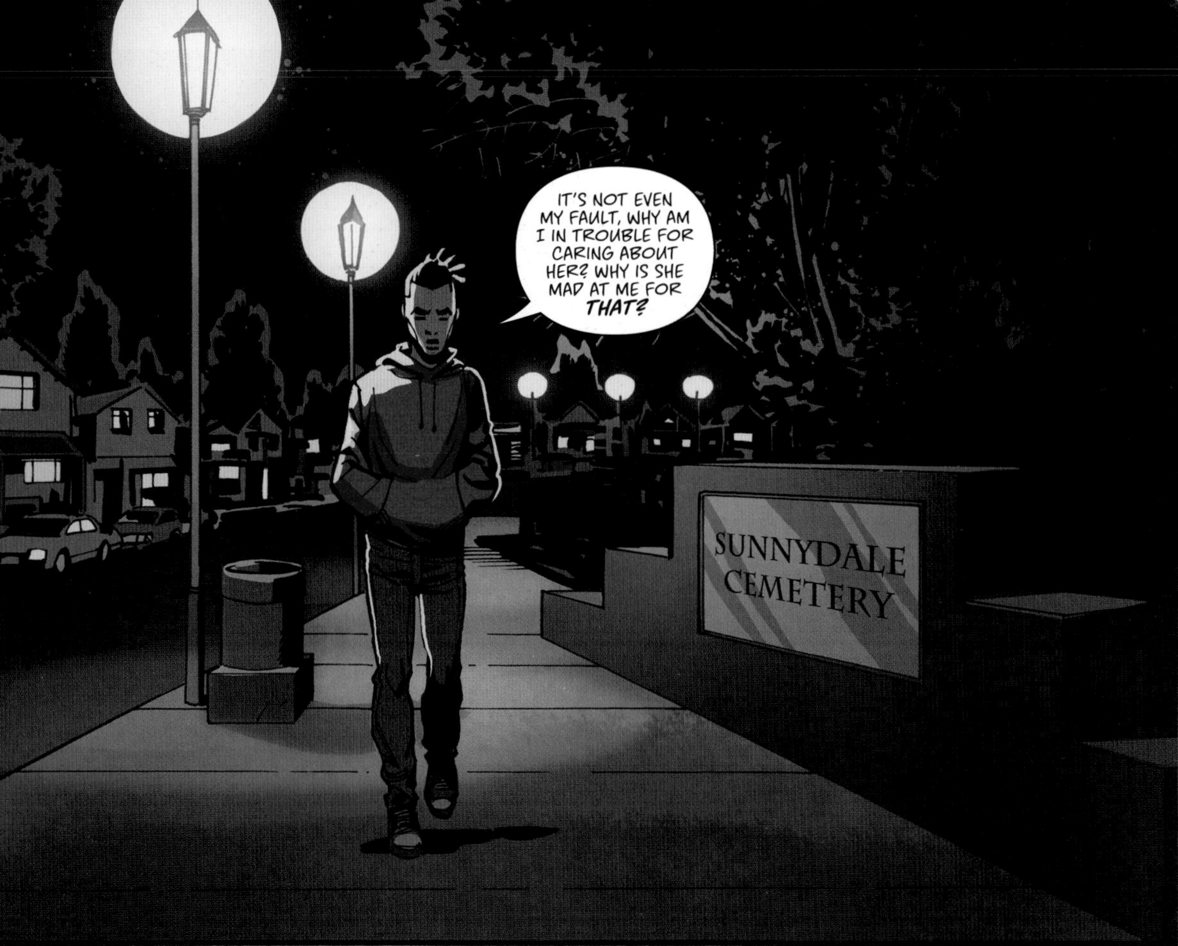
IT'S NOT EVEN MY FAULT, WHY AM I IN TROUBLE FOR CARING ABOUT HER? WHY IS SHE MAD AT ME FOR THAT?
SUNNYDALE CEMETERY

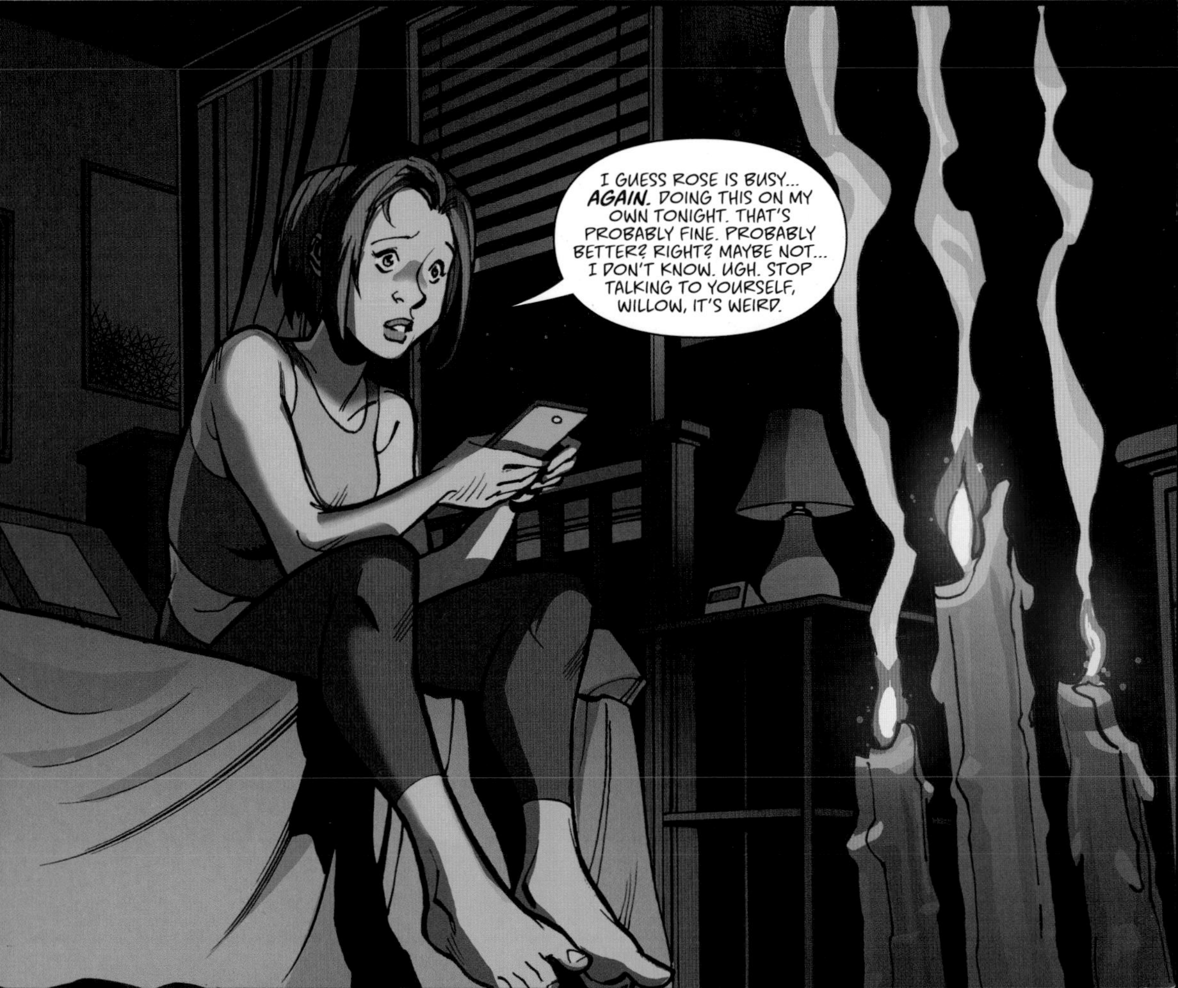
I GUESS ROSE IS BUSY... AGAIN. DOING THIS ON MY OWN TONIGHT. THAT'S PROBABLY FINE. PROBABLY BETTER? RIGHT? MAYBE NOT... I DON'T KNOW. UGH. STOP TALKING TO YOURSELF, WILLOW, IT'S WEIRD.

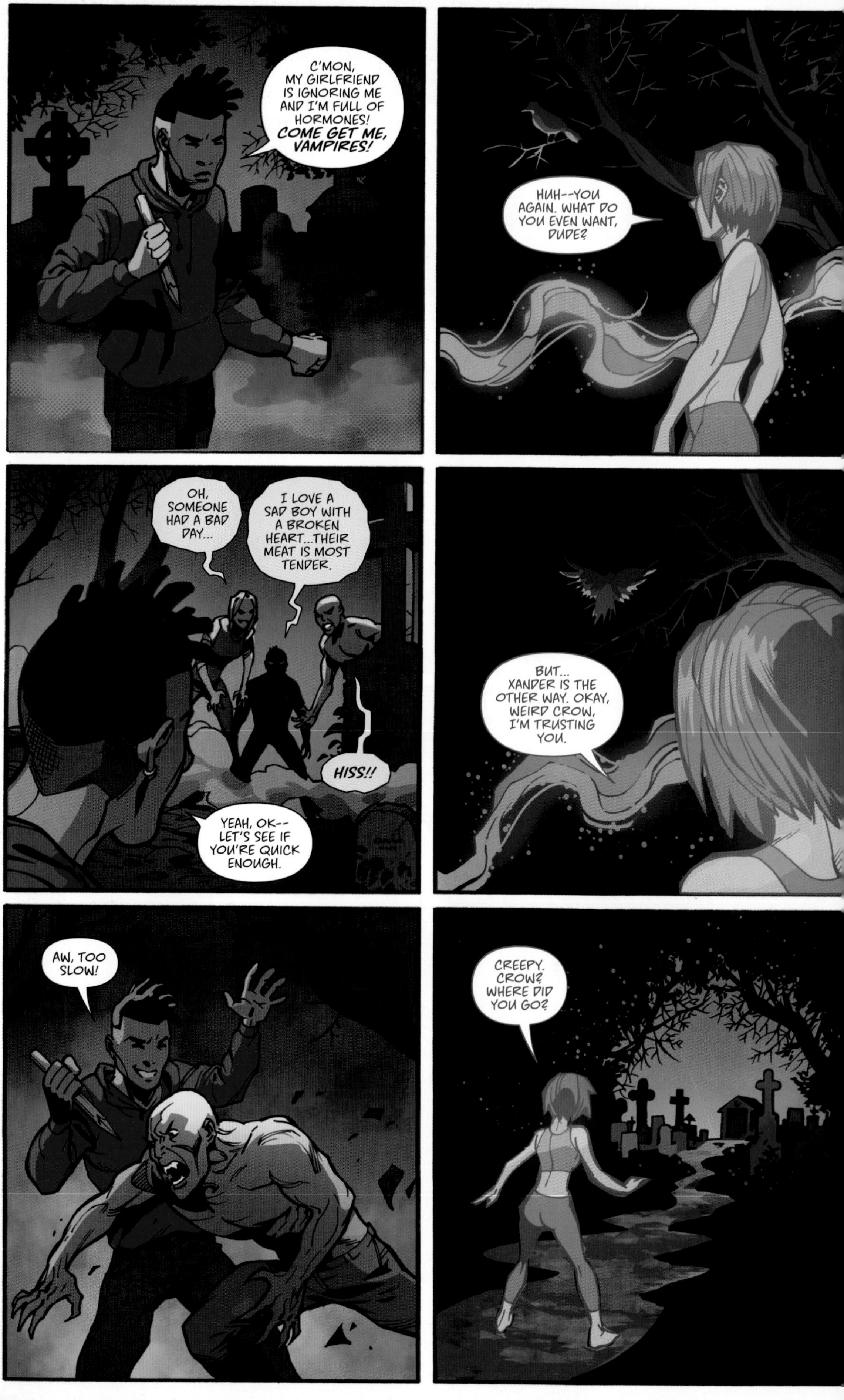
C'MON, MY GIRLFRIEND IS IGNORING ME AND I'M FULL OF HORMONES! COME GET ME, VAMPIRES!
HUH--YOU AGAIN. WHAT DO YOU EVEN WANT, DUDE?
OH, SOMEONE HAD A BAD DAY...
I LOVE A SAD BOY WITH A BROKEN HEART...THEIR MEAT IS MOST TENDER.
HISS!!
YEAH, OK--LET'S SEE IF YOU'RE QUICK ENOUGH.
BUT... XANDER IS THE OTHER WAY. OKAY, WEIRD CROW, I'M TRUSTING YOU.
AW, TOO SLOW!
CREEPY. CROW? WHERE DID YOU GO?

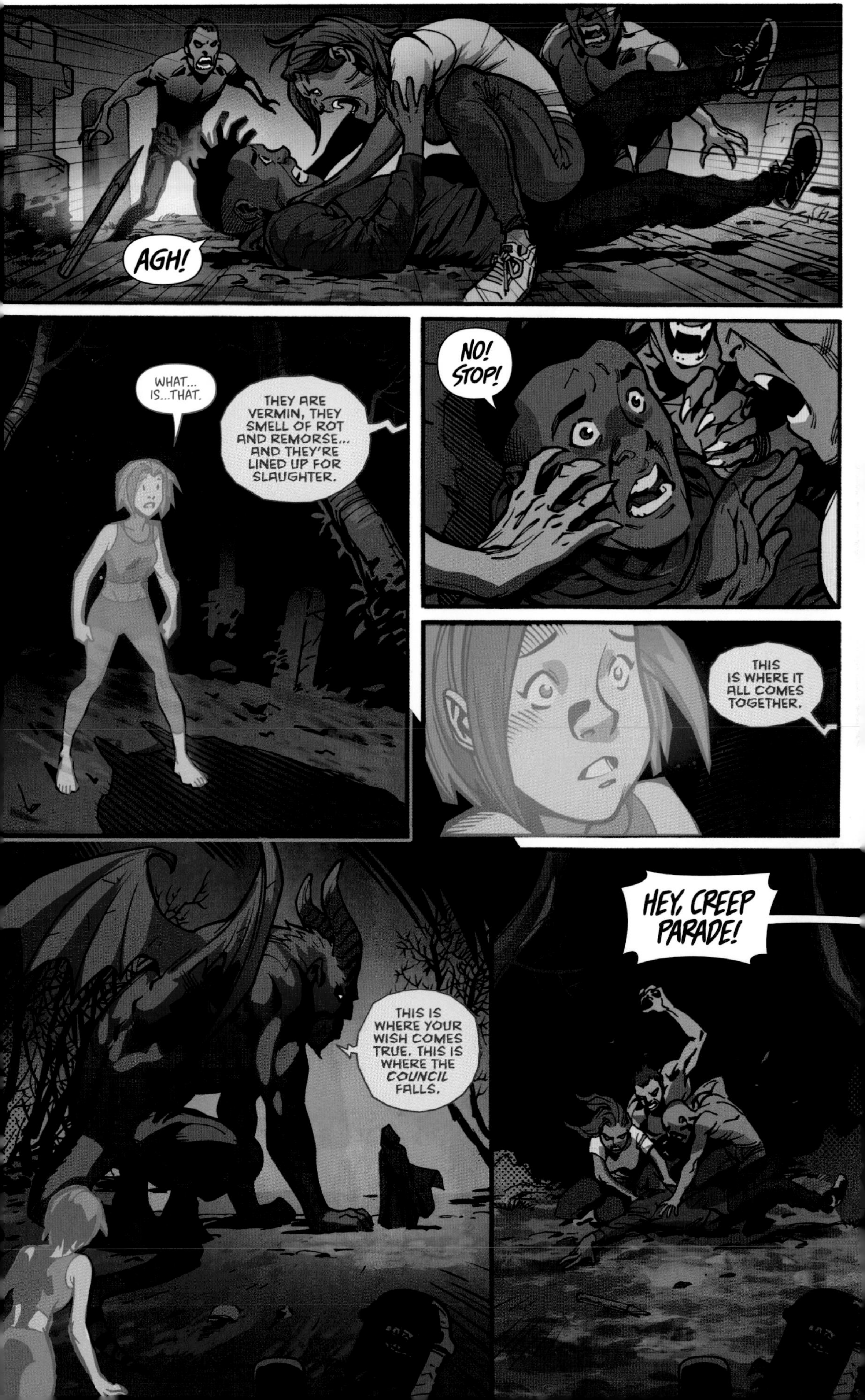
AGH!
WHAT... IS...THAT.
THEY ARE VERMIN, THEY SMELL OF ROT AND REMORSE... AND THEY'RE LINED UP FOR SLAUGHTER.
NO! STOP!
THIS IS WHERE IT ALL COMES TOGETHER.
THIS IS WHERE YOUR WISH COMES TRUE. THIS IS WHERE THE COUNCIL FALLS.
HEY, CREEP PARADE!

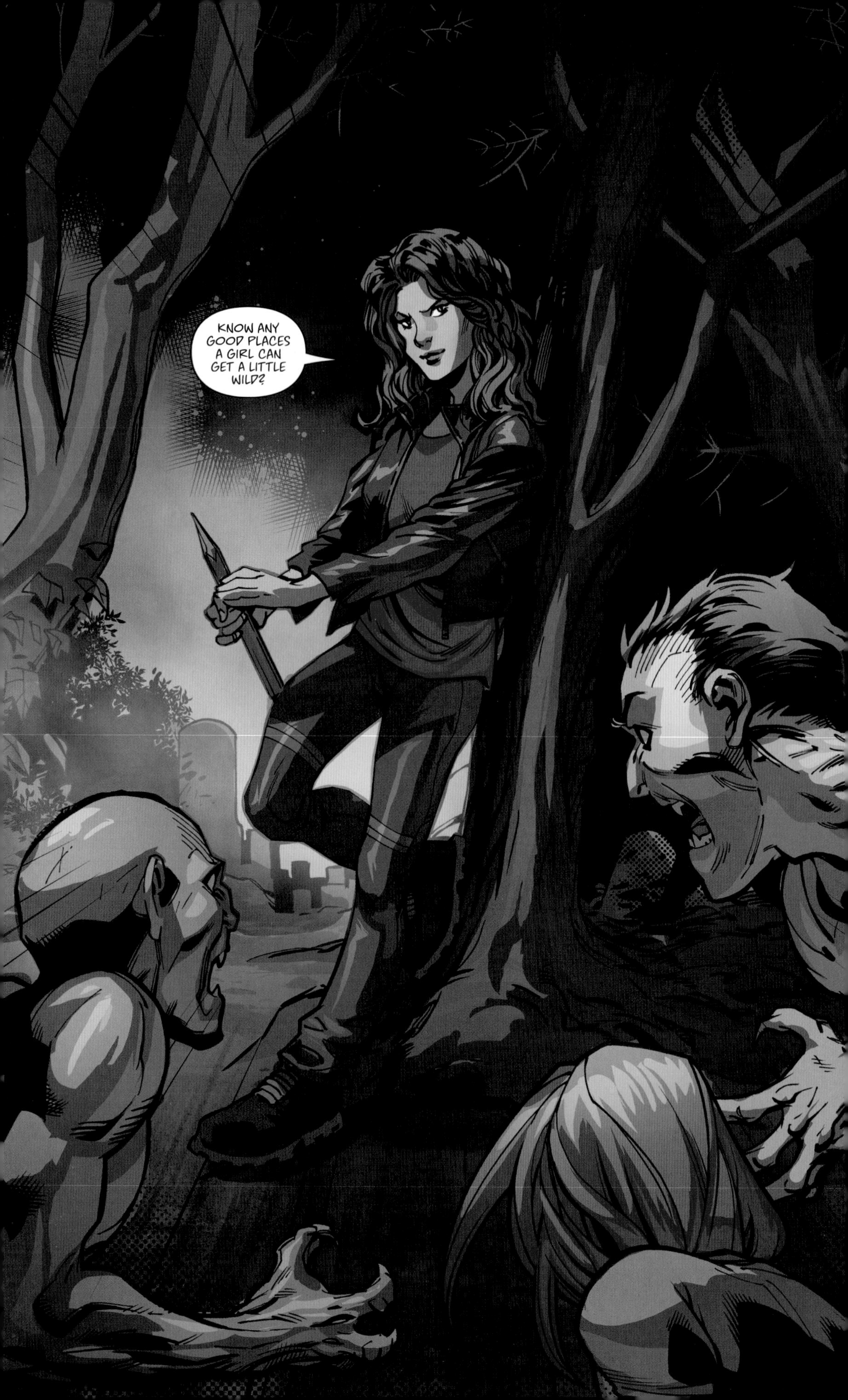
KNOW ANY GOOD PLACES A GIRL CAN GET A LITTLE WILD?

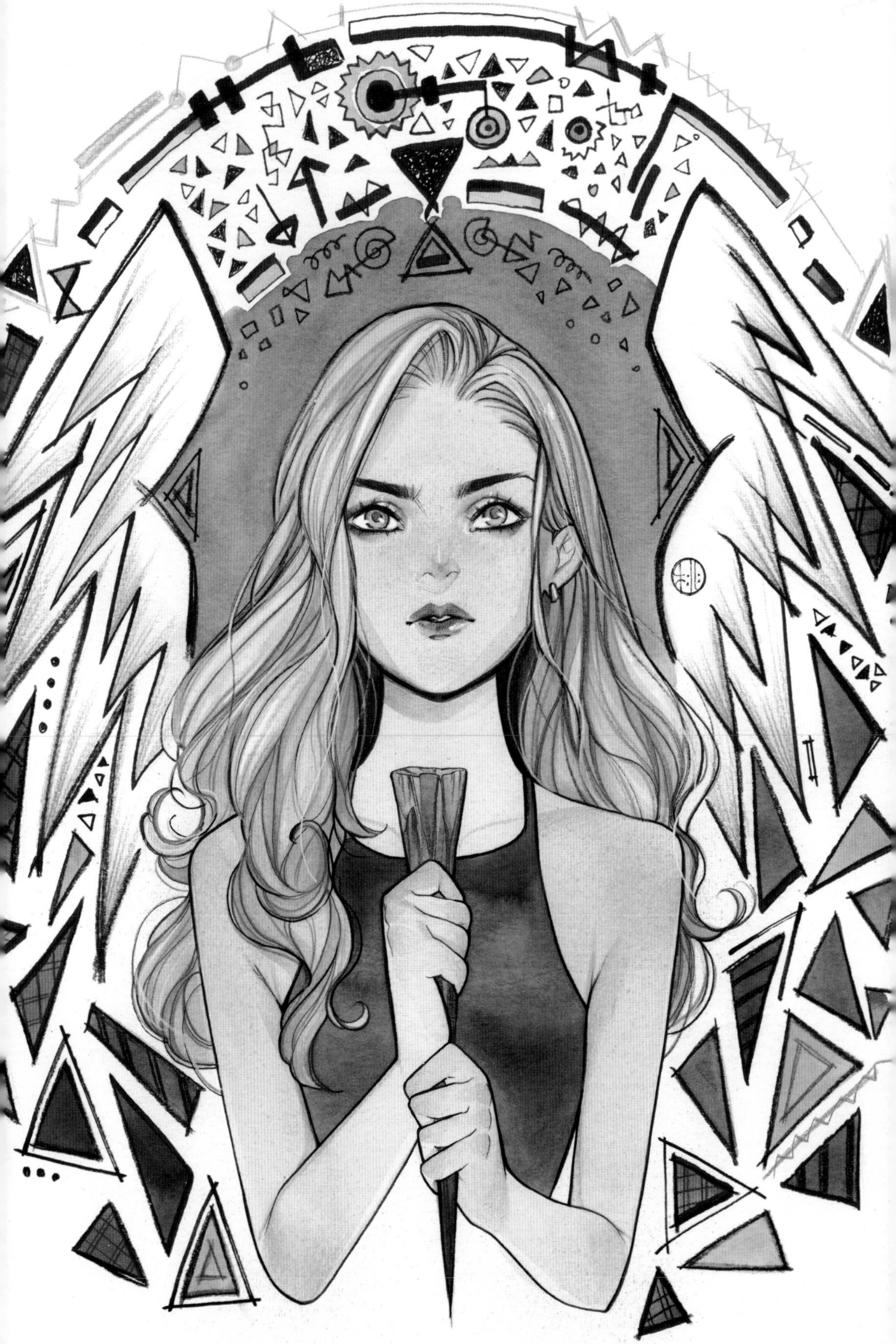

Issue Nineteen Variant Cover by **Peach Momoko**

CHAPTER
TWENTY

Issue Twenty Cover by **David López**

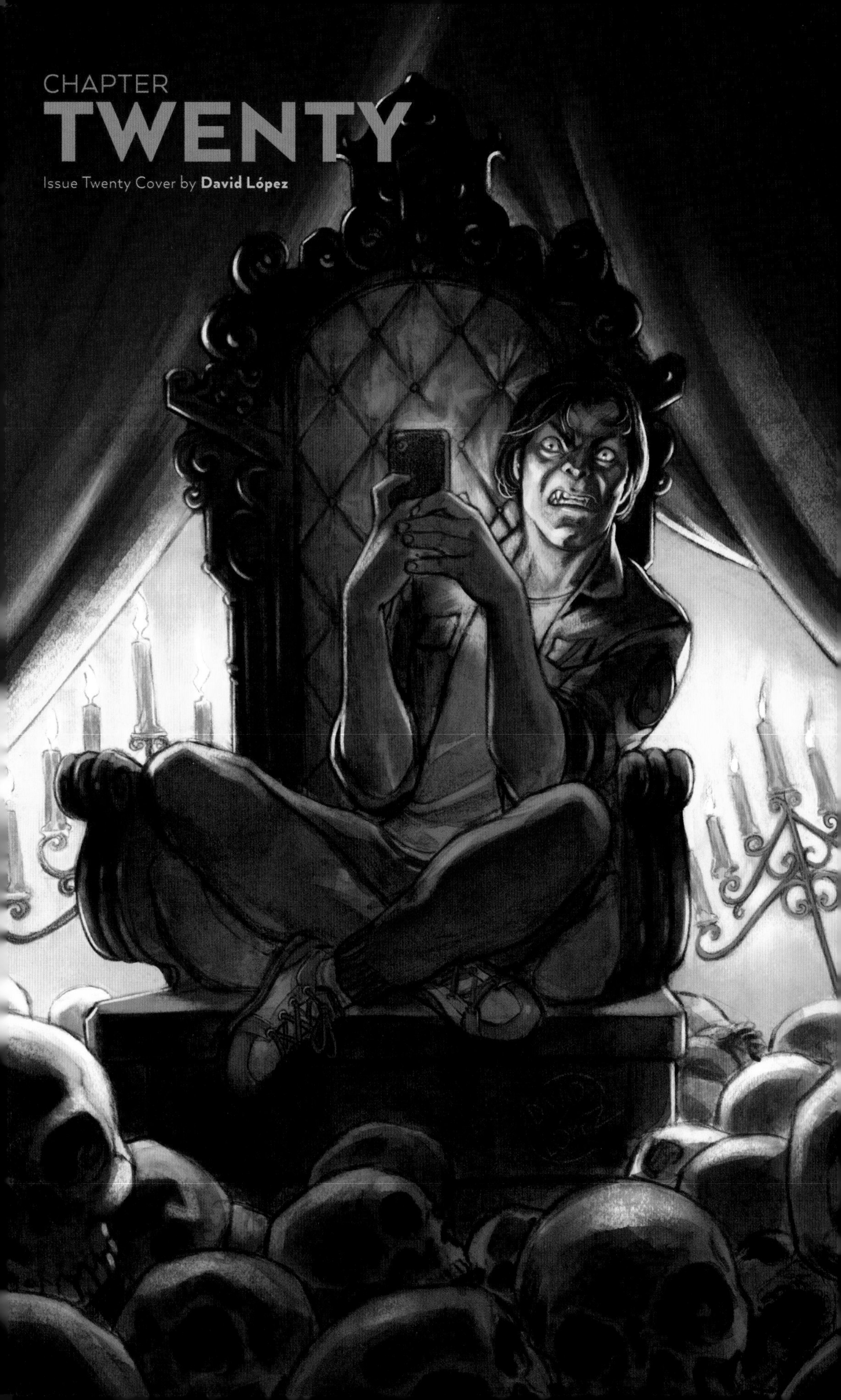

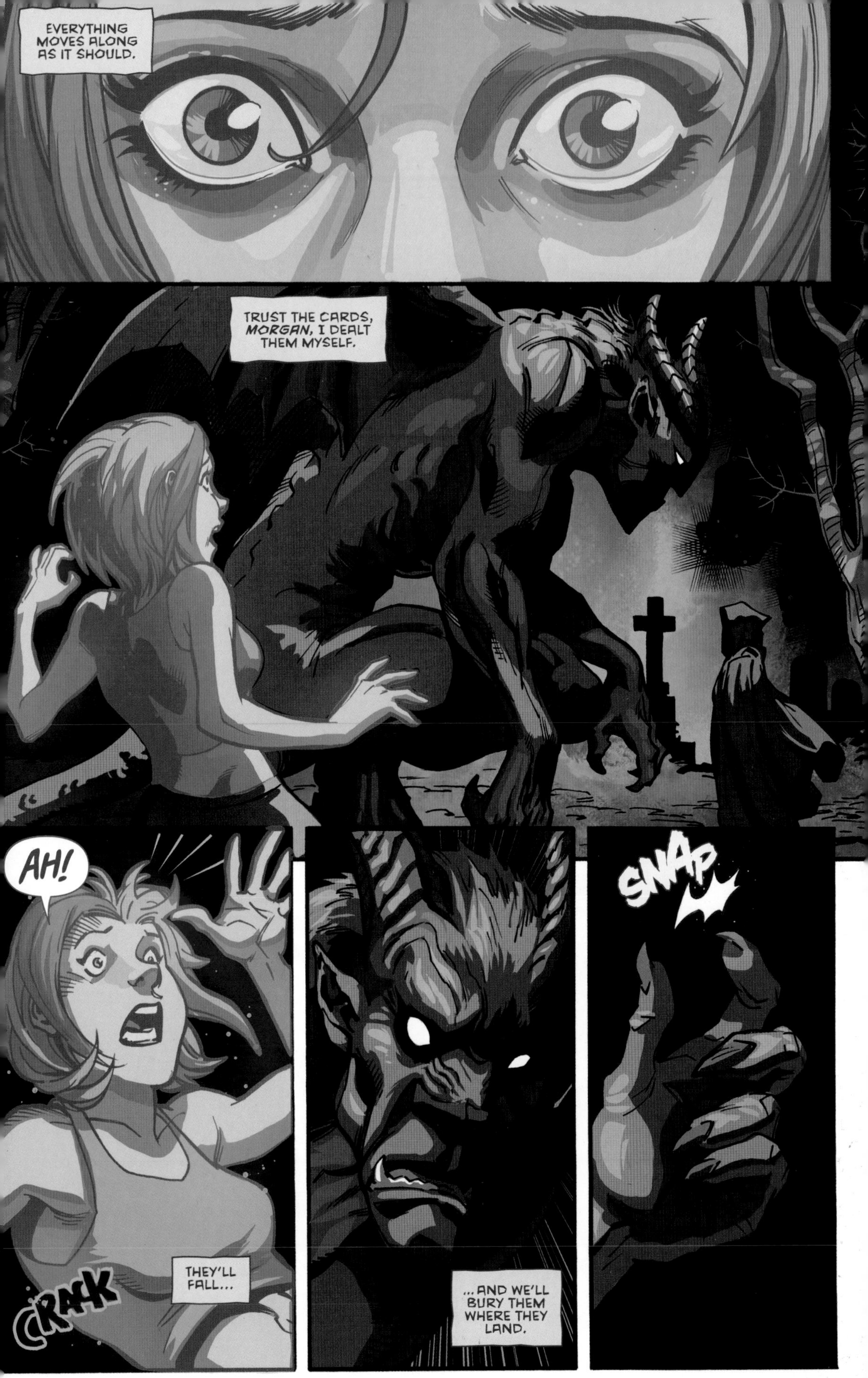
EVERYTHING MOVES ALONG AS IT SHOULD.
TRUST THE CARDS, *MORGAN*, I DEALT THEM MYSELF.
AH!
CRACK
THEY'LL FALL...
...AND WE'LL BURY THEM WHERE THEY LAND.
SNAP

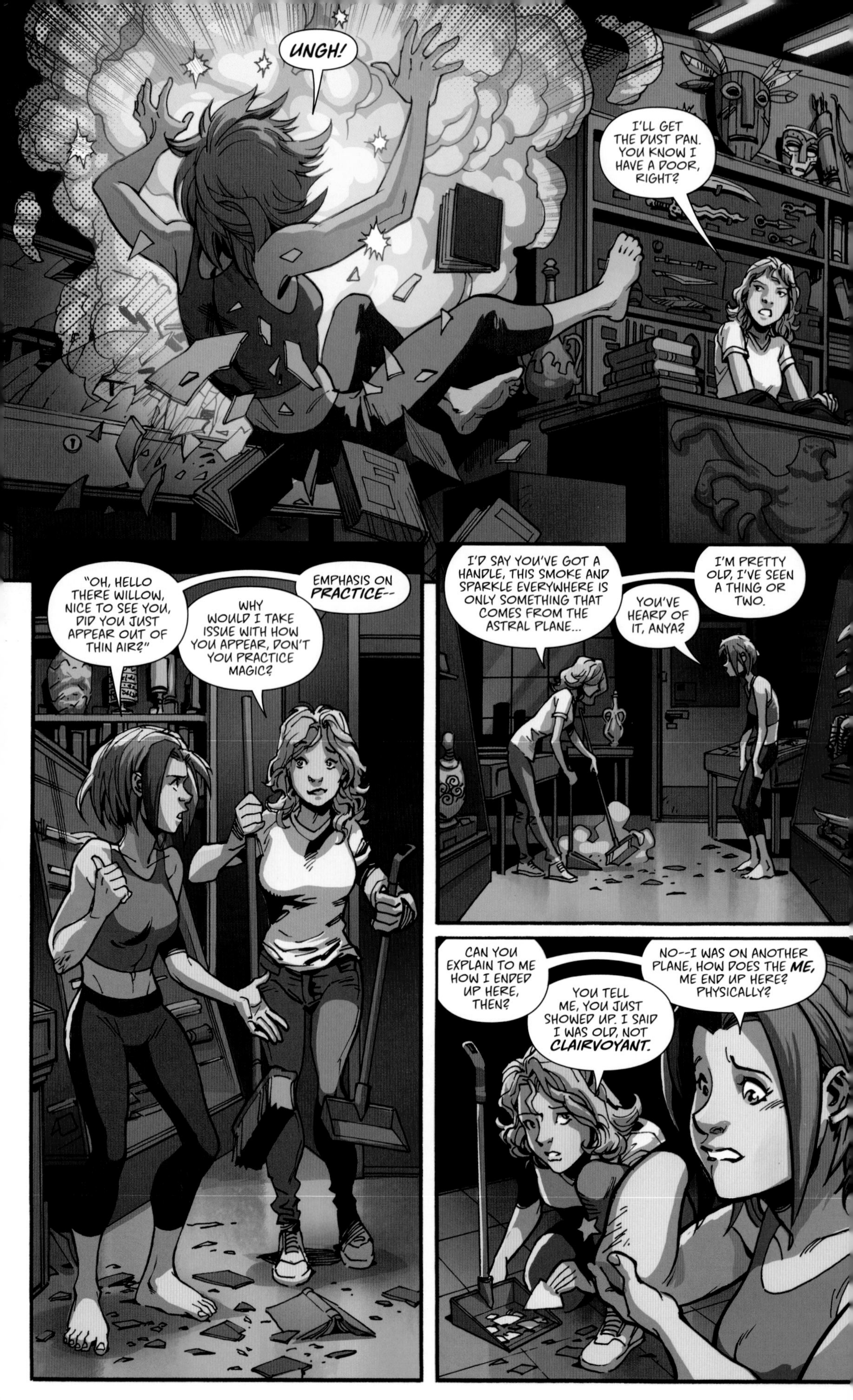
UNGH!
I'LL GET THE DUST PAN. YOU KNOW I HAVE A DOOR, RIGHT?
"OH, HELLO THERE WILLOW, NICE TO SEE YOU, DID YOU JUST APPEAR OUT OF THIN AIR?"
WHY WOULD I TAKE ISSUE WITH HOW YOU APPEAR, DON'T YOU PRACTICE MAGIC?
EMPHASIS ON ***PRACTICE***--
I'D SAY YOU'VE GOT A HANDLE, THIS SMOKE AND SPARKLE EVERYWHERE IS ONLY SOMETHING THAT COMES FROM THE ASTRAL PLANE...
YOU'VE HEARD OF IT, ANYA?
I'M PRETTY OLD, I'VE SEEN A THING OR TWO.
CAN YOU EXPLAIN TO ME HOW I ENDED UP HERE, THEN?
YOU TELL ME, YOU JUST SHOWED UP. I SAID I WAS OLD, NOT ***CLAIRVOYANT.***
NO--I WAS ON ANOTHER PLANE, HOW DOES THE ***ME,*** ME END UP HERE? PHYSICALLY?

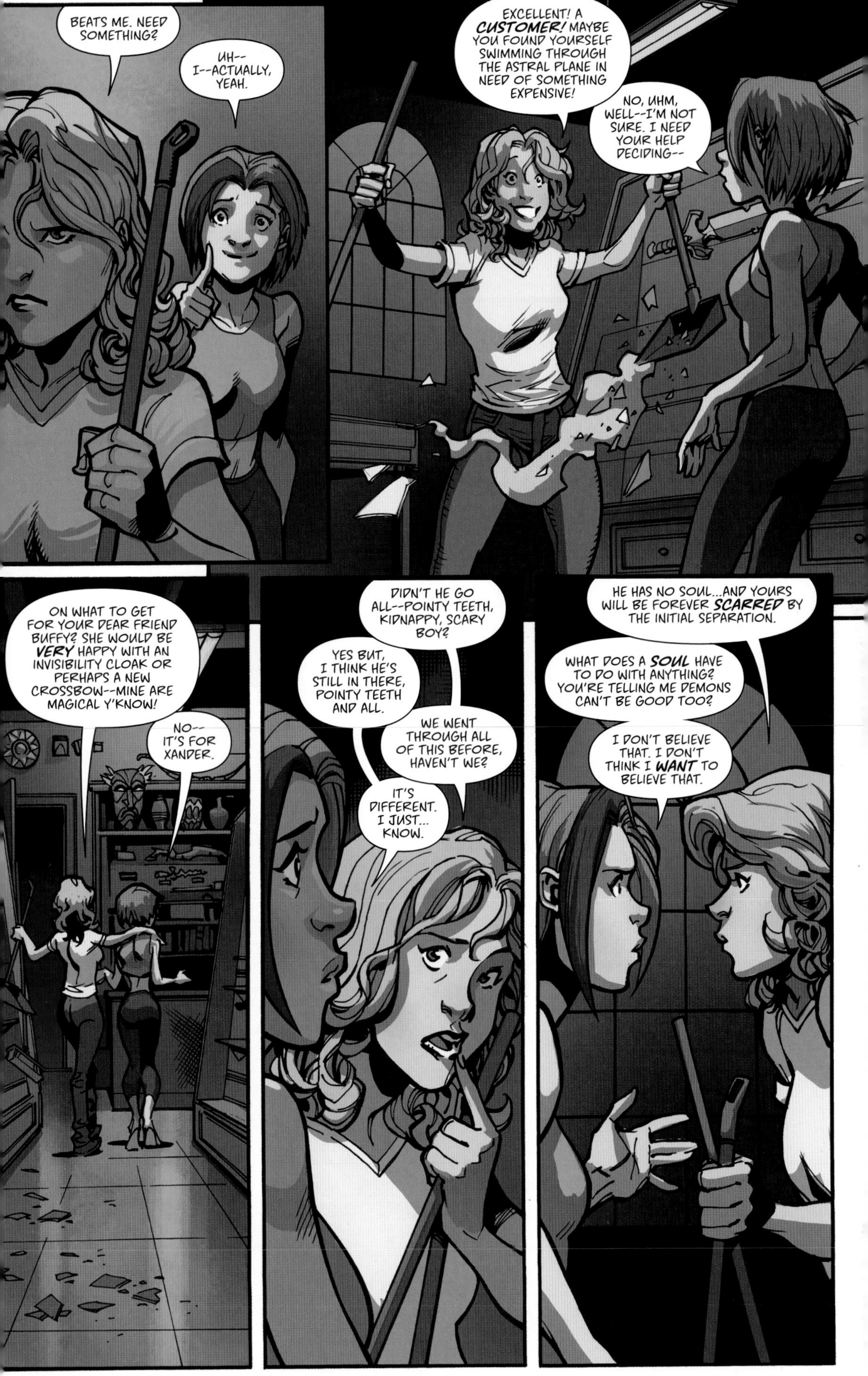
BEATS ME. NEED SOMETHING?
UH-- I--ACTUALLY, YEAH.
EXCELLENT! A CUSTOMER! MAYBE YOU FOUND YOURSELF SWIMMING THROUGH THE ASTRAL PLANE IN NEED OF SOMETHING EXPENSIVE!
NO, UHM, WELL--I'M NOT SURE. I NEED YOUR HELP DECIDING--
ON WHAT TO GET FOR YOUR DEAR FRIEND BUFFY? SHE WOULD BE VERY HAPPY WITH AN INVISIBILITY CLOAK OR PERHAPS A NEW CROSSBOW--MINE ARE MAGICAL Y'KNOW!
NO-- IT'S FOR XANDER.
DIDN'T HE GO ALL--POINTY TEETH, KIDNAPPY, SCARY BOY?
YES BUT, I THINK HE'S STILL IN THERE, POINTY TEETH AND ALL.
WE WENT THROUGH ALL OF THIS BEFORE, HAVEN'T WE?
IT'S DIFFERENT. I JUST... KNOW.
HE HAS NO SOUL...AND YOURS WILL BE FOREVER SCARRED BY THE INITIAL SEPARATION.
WHAT DOES A SOUL HAVE TO DO WITH ANYTHING? YOU'RE TELLING ME DEMONS CAN'T BE GOOD TOO?
I DON'T BELIEVE THAT. I DON'T THINK I WANT TO BELIEVE THAT.

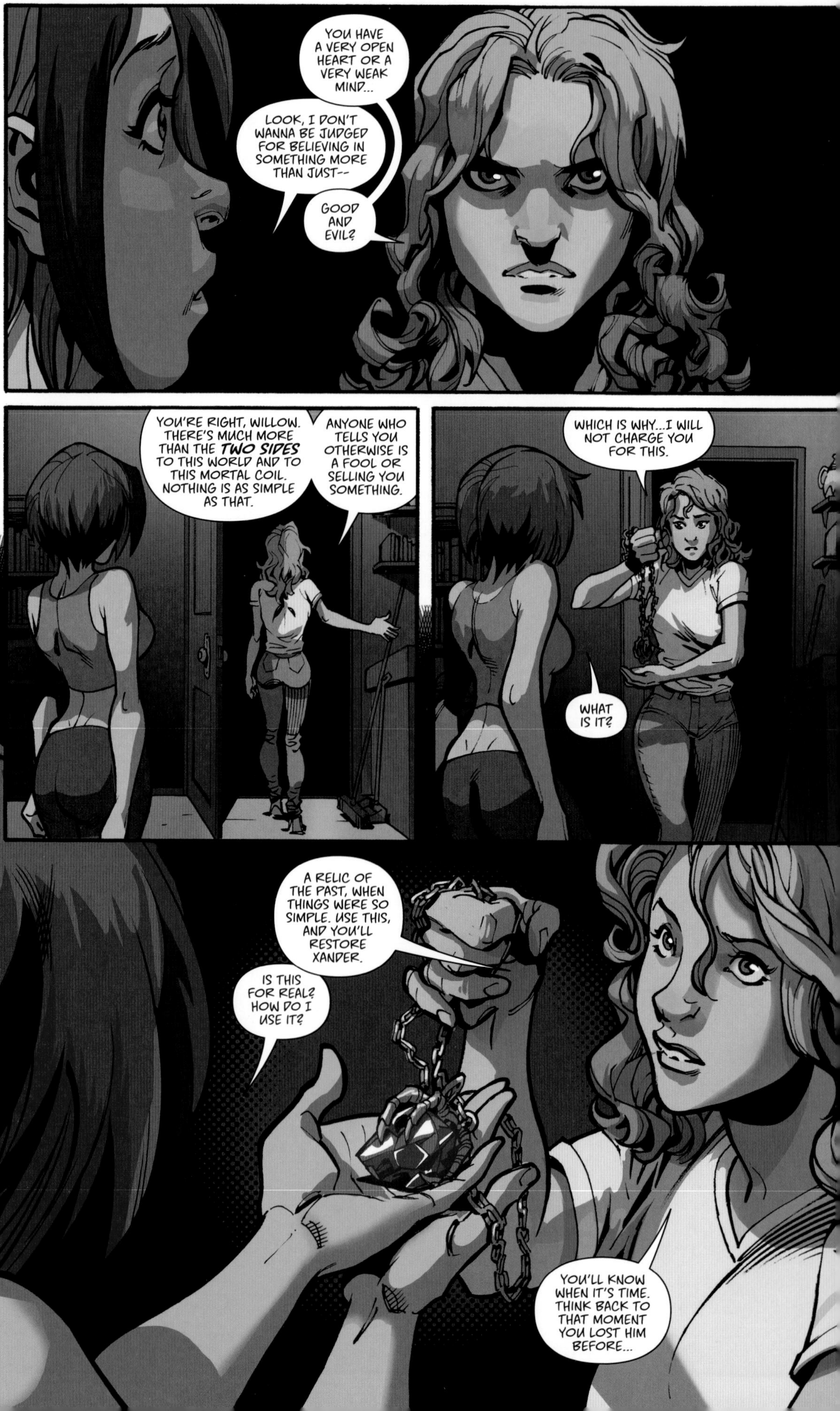
YOU HAVE A VERY OPEN HEART OR A VERY WEAK MIND...
LOOK, I DON'T WANNA BE JUDGED FOR BELIEVING IN SOMETHING MORE THAN JUST--
GOOD AND EVIL?
YOU'RE RIGHT, WILLOW. THERE'S MUCH MORE THAN THE TWO SIDES TO THIS WORLD AND TO THIS MORTAL COIL. NOTHING IS AS SIMPLE AS THAT.
ANYONE WHO TELLS YOU OTHERWISE IS A FOOL OR SELLING YOU SOMETHING.
WHICH IS WHY...I WILL NOT CHARGE YOU FOR THIS.
WHAT IS IT?
A RELIC OF THE PAST, WHEN THINGS WERE SO SIMPLE. USE THIS, AND YOU'LL RESTORE XANDER.
IS THIS FOR REAL? HOW DO I USE IT?
YOU'LL KNOW WHEN IT'S TIME. THINK BACK TO THAT MOMENT YOU LOST HIM BEFORE...

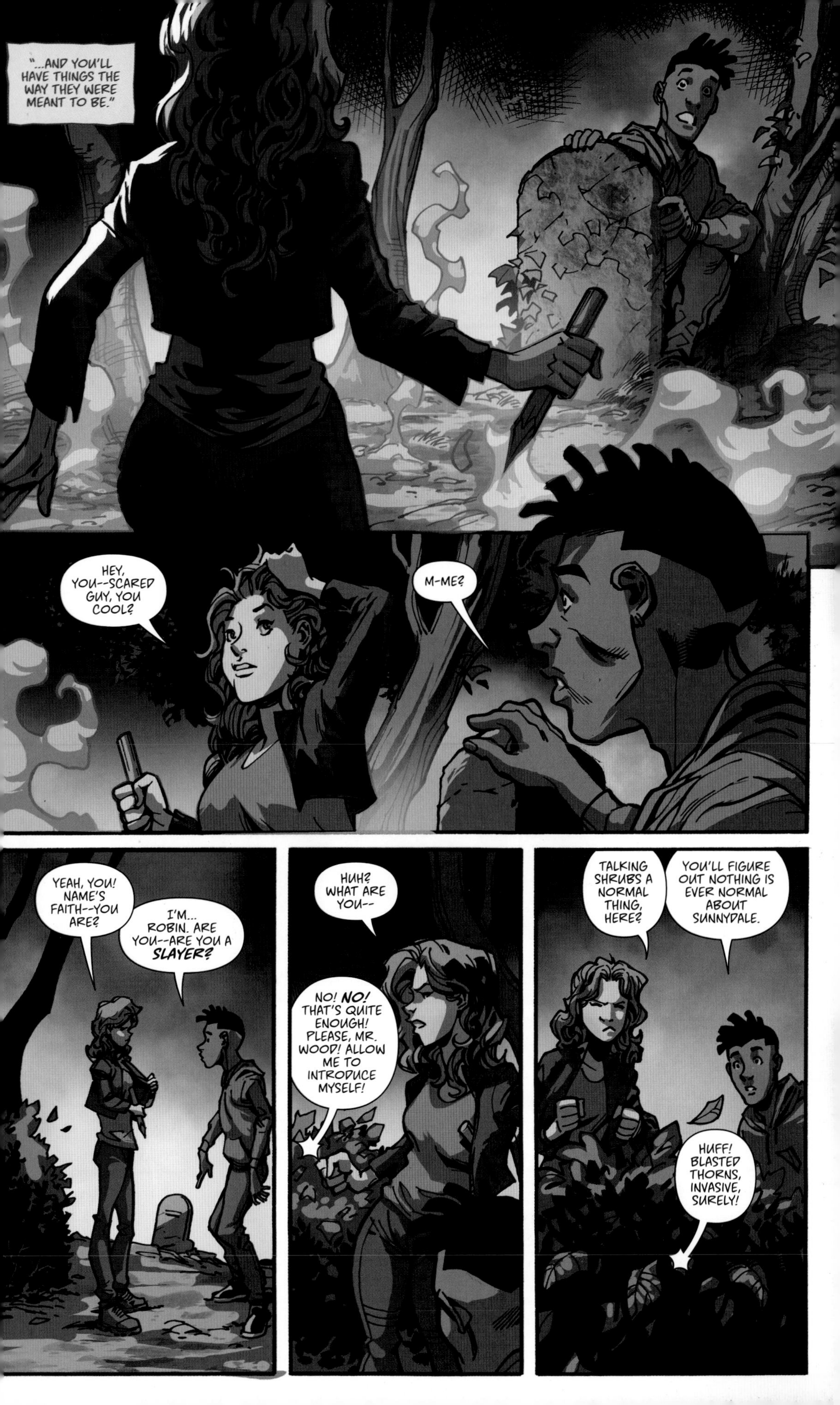

"...AND YOU'LL HAVE THINGS THE WAY THEY WERE MEANT TO BE."
HEY, YOU--SCARED GUY, YOU COOL?
M-ME?
YEAH, YOU! NAME'S FAITH--YOU ARE?
I'M... ROBIN. ARE YOU--ARE YOU A *SLAYER?*
HUH? WHAT ARE YOU--
NO! **NO!** THAT'S QUITE ENOUGH! PLEASE, MR. WOOD! ALLOW ME TO INTRODUCE MYSELF!
TALKING SHRUBS A NORMAL THING, HERE?
YOU'LL FIGURE OUT NOTHING IS EVER NORMAL ABOUT SUNNYDALE.
HUFF! BLASTED THORNS, INVASIVE, SURELY!

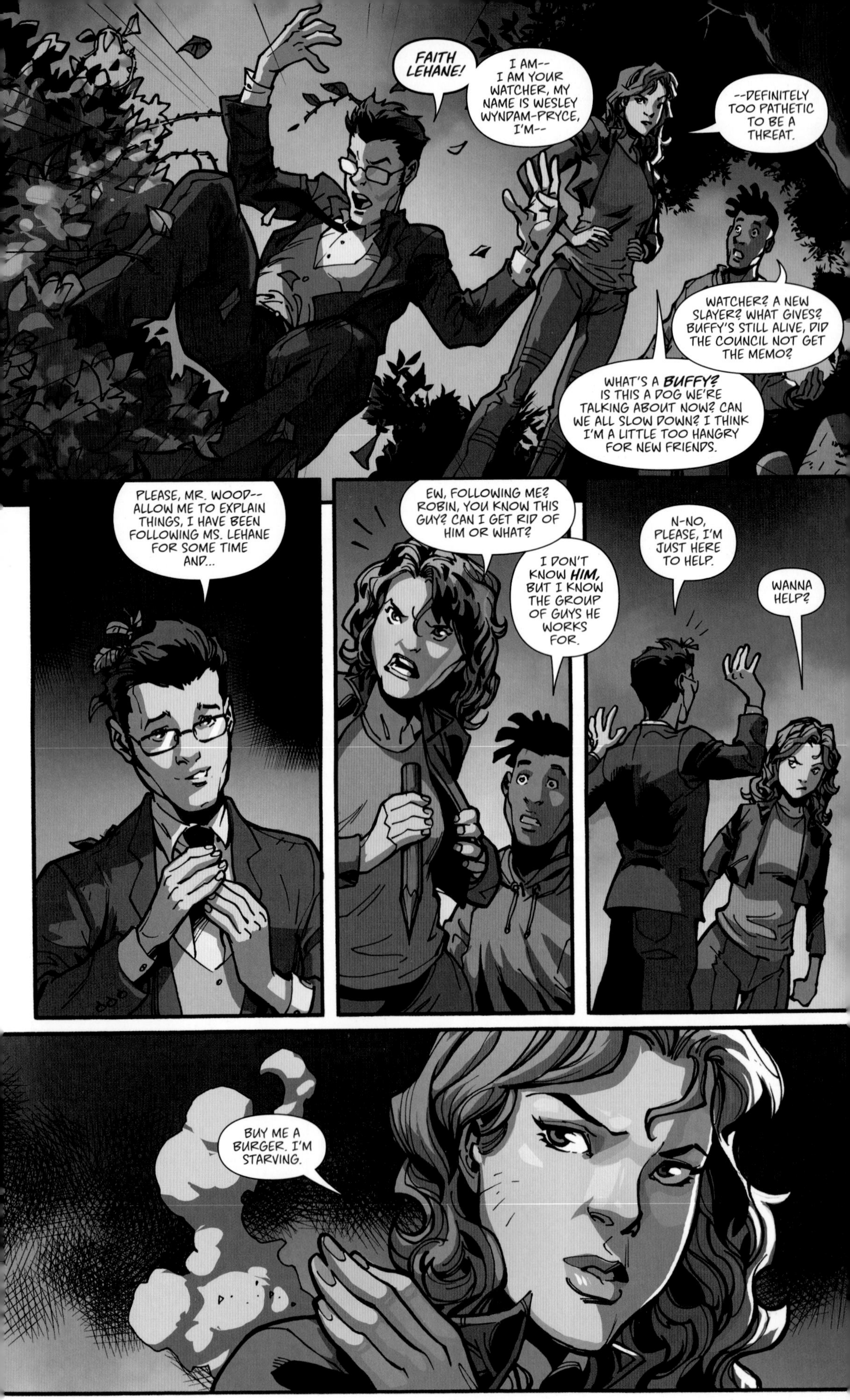

FAITH LEHANE!
I AM-- I AM YOUR WATCHER, MY NAME IS WESLEY WYNDAM-PRYCE, I'M--
--DEFINITELY TOO PATHETIC TO BE A THREAT.
WATCHER? A NEW SLAYER? WHAT GIVES? BUFFY'S STILL ALIVE, DID THE COUNCIL NOT GET THE MEMO?
WHAT'S A BUFFY? IS THIS A DOG WE'RE TALKING ABOUT NOW? CAN WE ALL SLOW DOWN? I THINK I'M A LITTLE TOO HANGRY FOR NEW FRIENDS.
PLEASE, MR. WOOD-- ALLOW ME TO EXPLAIN THINGS, I HAVE BEEN FOLLOWING MS. LEHANE FOR SOME TIME AND...
EW, FOLLOWING ME? ROBIN, YOU KNOW THIS GUY? CAN I GET RID OF HIM OR WHAT?
I DON'T KNOW HIM, BUT I KNOW THE GROUP OF GUYS HE WORKS FOR.
N-NO, PLEASE, I'M JUST HERE TO HELP.
WANNA HELP?
BUY ME A BURGER. I'M STARVING.

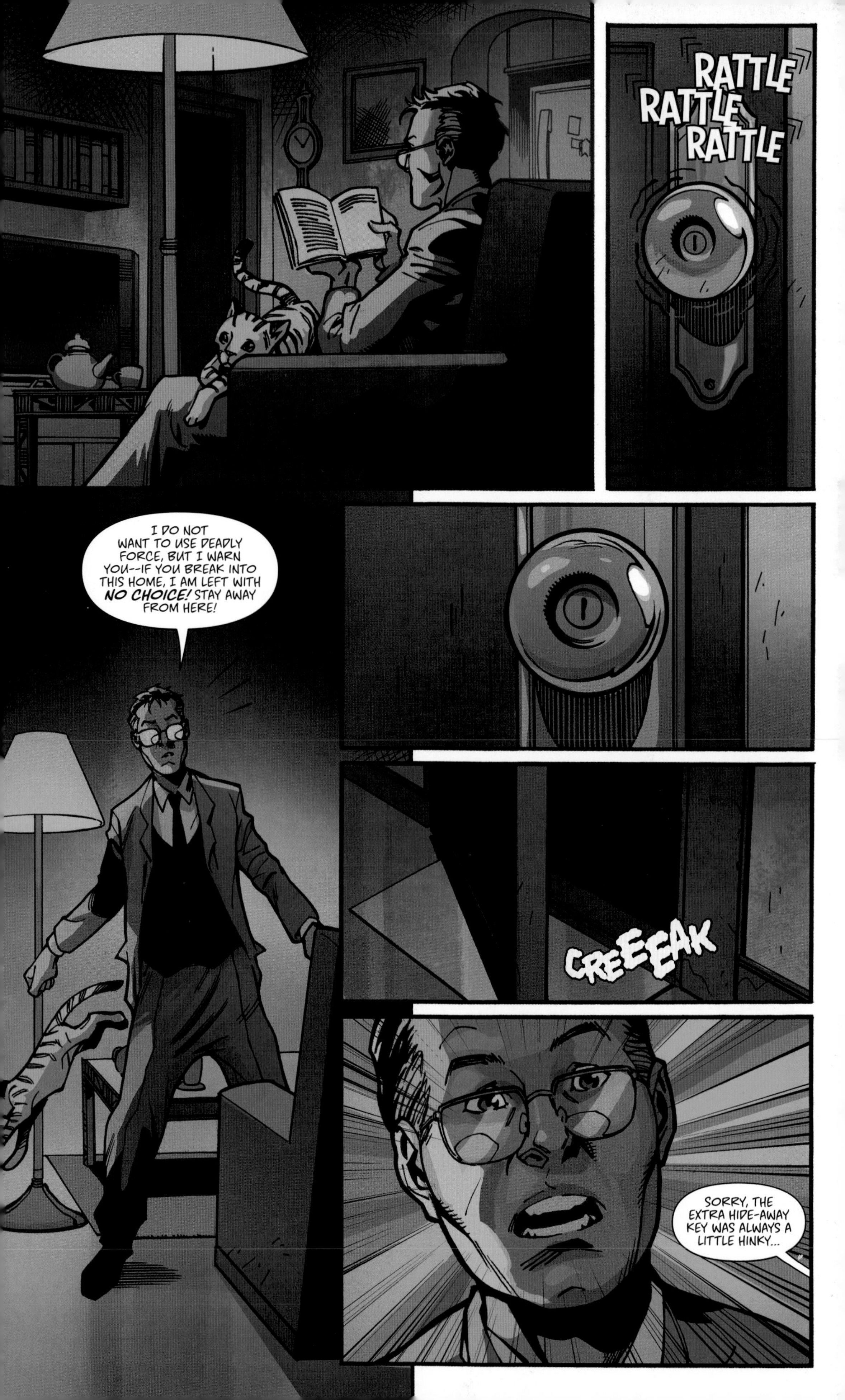
RATTLE
RATTLE
RATTLE
I DO NOT WANT TO USE DEADLY FORCE, BUT I WARN YOU--IF YOU BREAK INTO THIS HOME, I AM LEFT WITH NO CHOICE! STAY AWAY FROM HERE!
CREEEAK
SORRY, THE EXTRA HIDE-AWAY KEY WAS ALWAYS A LITTLE HINKY...

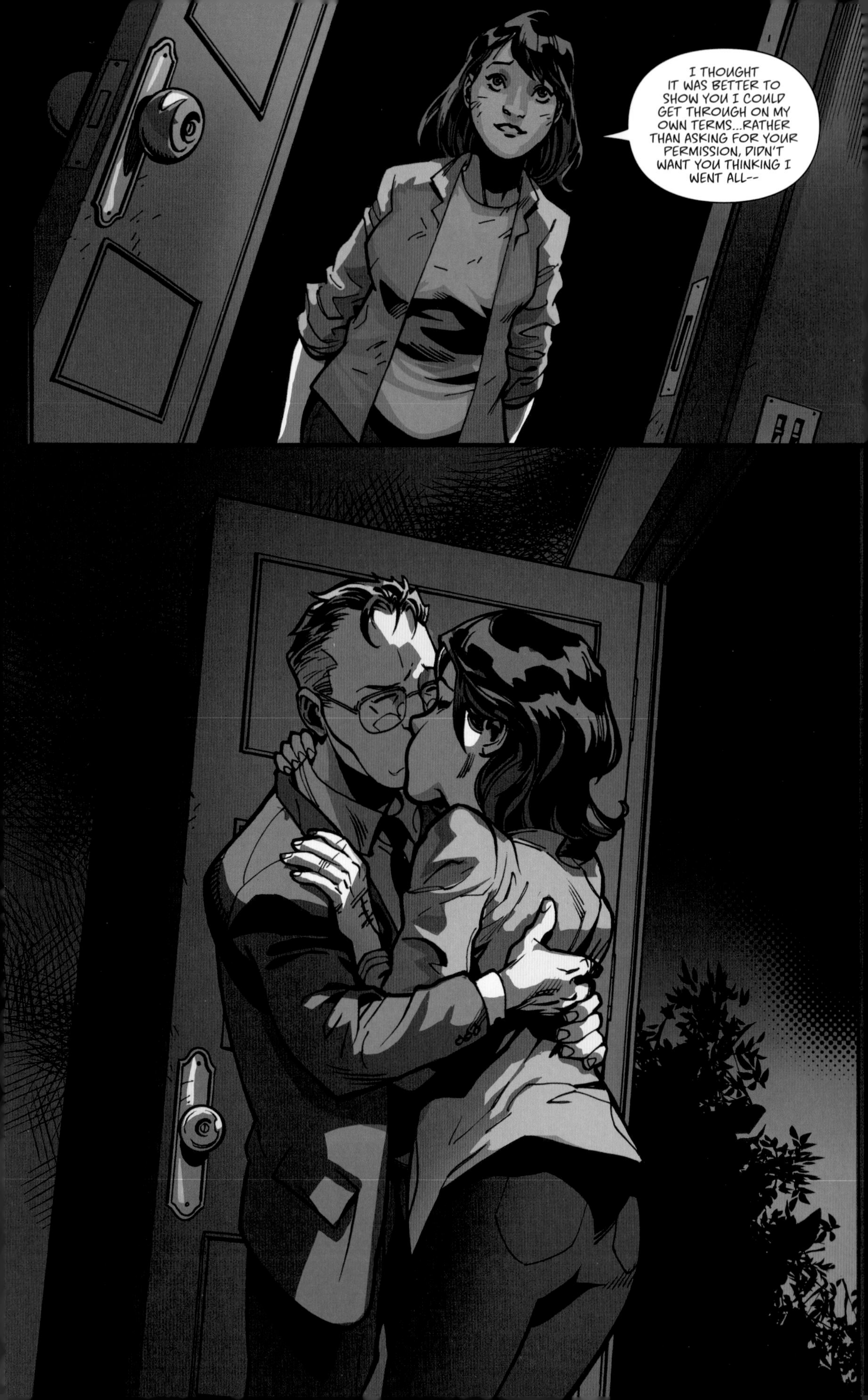
I THOUGHT IT WAS BETTER TO SHOW YOU I COULD GET THROUGH ON MY OWN TERMS...RATHER THAN ASKING FOR YOUR PERMISSION, DIDN'T WANT YOU THINKING I WENT ALL--

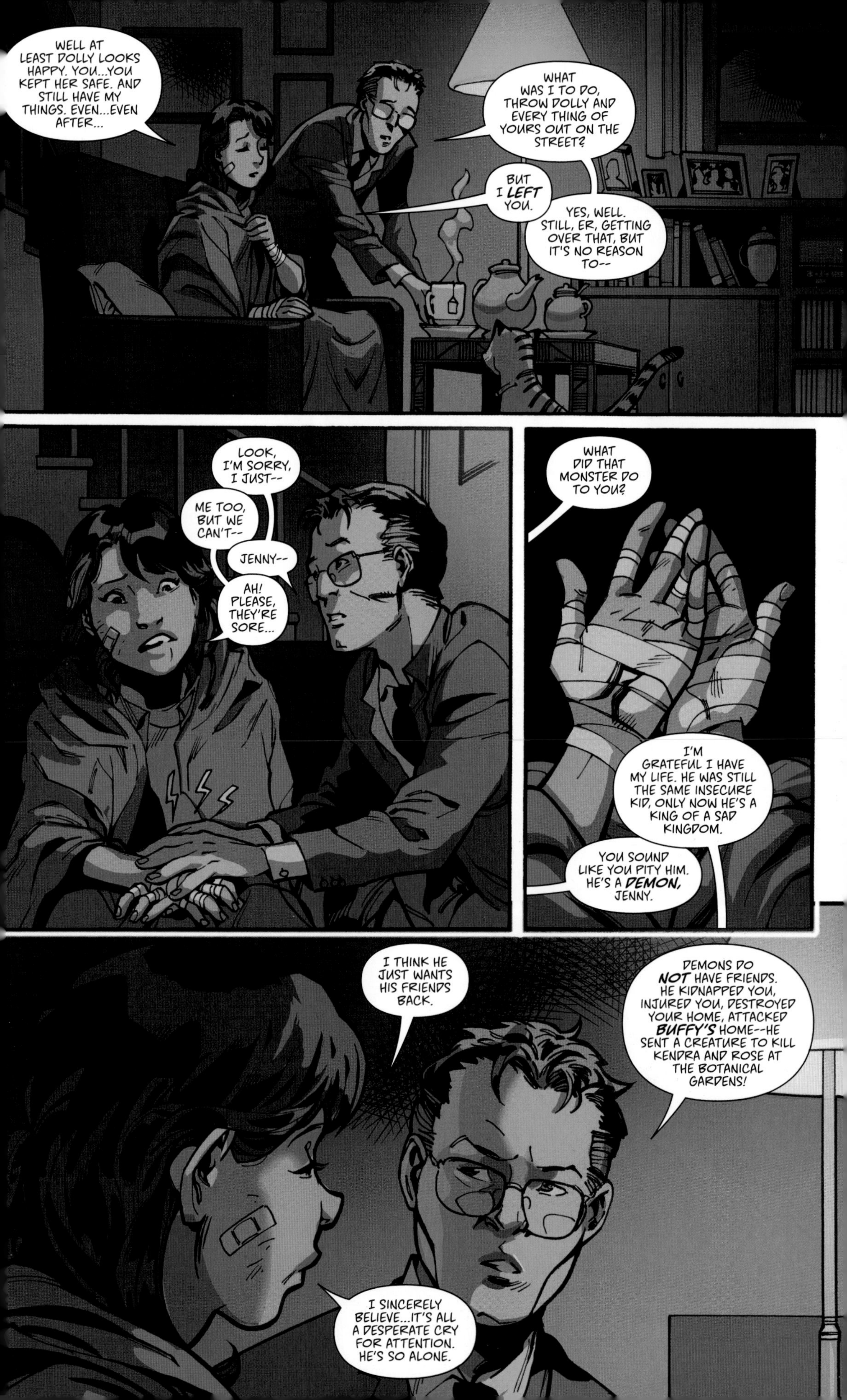
WELL AT LEAST DOLLY LOOKS HAPPY. YOU...YOU KEPT HER SAFE. AND STILL HAVE MY THINGS. EVEN...EVEN AFTER...
WHAT WAS I TO DO, THROW DOLLY AND EVERY THING OF YOURS OUT ON THE STREET?
BUT I *LEFT* YOU.
YES, WELL. STILL, ER, GETTING OVER THAT, BUT IT'S NO REASON TO--
LOOK, I'M SORRY, I JUST--
ME TOO, BUT WE CAN'T--
JENNY--
AH! PLEASE, THEY'RE SORE...
WHAT DID THAT MONSTER DO TO YOU?
I'M GRATEFUL I HAVE MY LIFE. HE WAS STILL THE SAME INSECURE KID, ONLY NOW HE'S A KING OF A SAD KINGDOM.
YOU SOUND LIKE YOU PITY HIM. HE'S A ***DEMON,*** JENNY.
I THINK HE JUST WANTS HIS FRIENDS BACK.
DEMONS DO ***NOT*** HAVE FRIENDS. HE KIDNAPPED YOU, INJURED YOU, DESTROYED YOUR HOME, ATTACKED ***BUFFY'S*** HOME--HE SENT A CREATURE TO KILL KENDRA AND ROSE AT THE BOTANICAL GARDENS!
I SINCERELY BELIEVE...IT'S ALL A DESPERATE CRY FOR ATTENTION. HE'S SO ALONE.

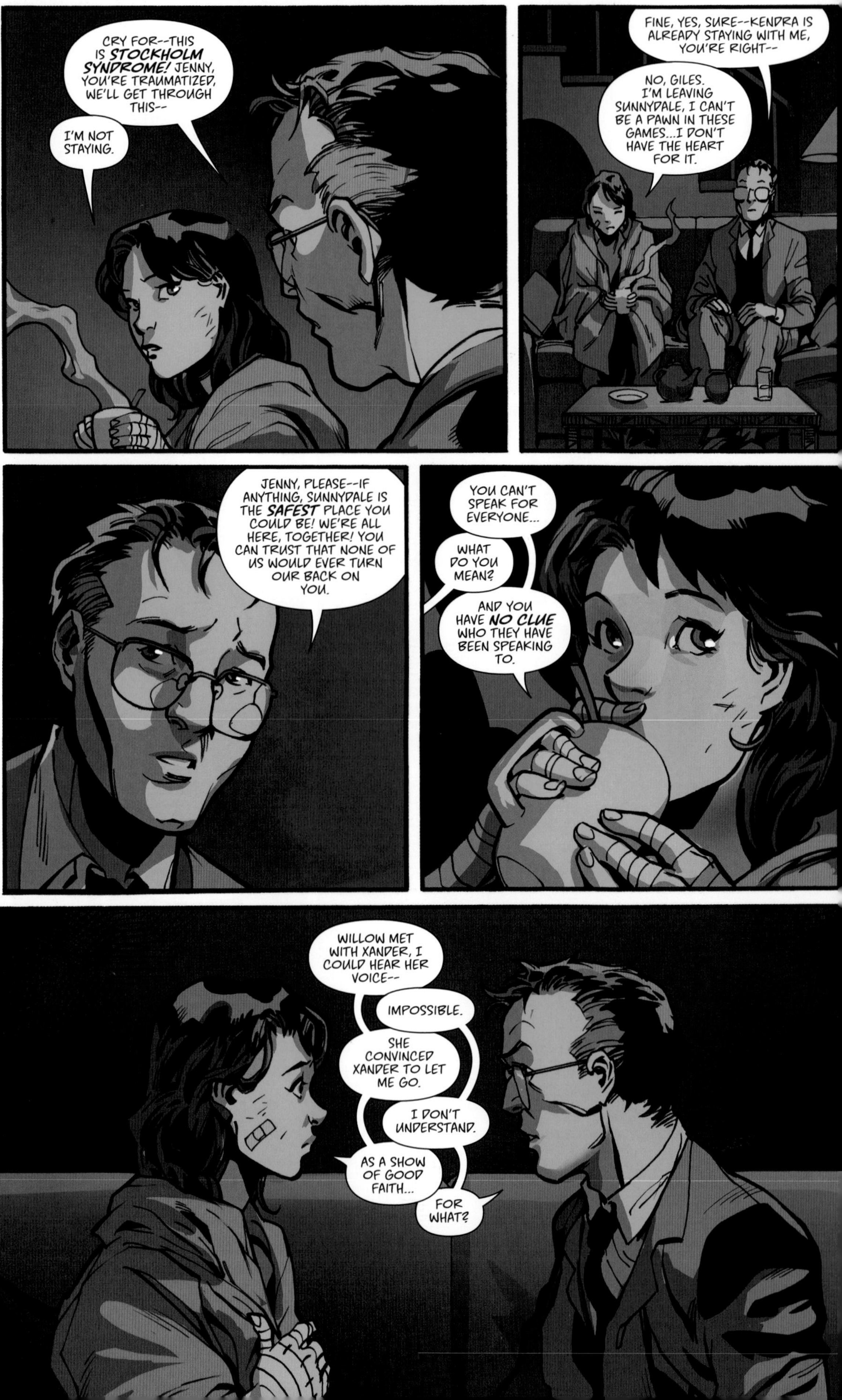
CRY FOR--THIS IS STOCKHOLM SYNDROME! JENNY, YOU'RE TRAUMATIZED, WE'LL GET THROUGH THIS--
I'M NOT STAYING.
FINE, YES, SURE--KENDRA IS ALREADY STAYING WITH ME, YOU'RE RIGHT--
NO, GILES. I'M LEAVING SUNNYDALE, I CAN'T BE A PAWN IN THESE GAMES...I DON'T HAVE THE HEART FOR IT.
JENNY, PLEASE--IF ANYTHING, SUNNYDALE IS THE SAFEST PLACE YOU COULD BE! WE'RE ALL HERE, TOGETHER! YOU CAN TRUST THAT NONE OF US WOULD EVER TURN OUR BACK ON YOU.
YOU CAN'T SPEAK FOR EVERYONE...
WHAT DO YOU MEAN?
AND YOU HAVE NO CLUE WHO THEY HAVE BEEN SPEAKING TO.
WILLOW MET WITH XANDER, I COULD HEAR HER VOICE--
IMPOSSIBLE.
SHE CONVINCED XANDER TO LET ME GO.
I DON'T UNDERSTAND.
AS A SHOW OF GOOD FAITH...
FOR WHAT?

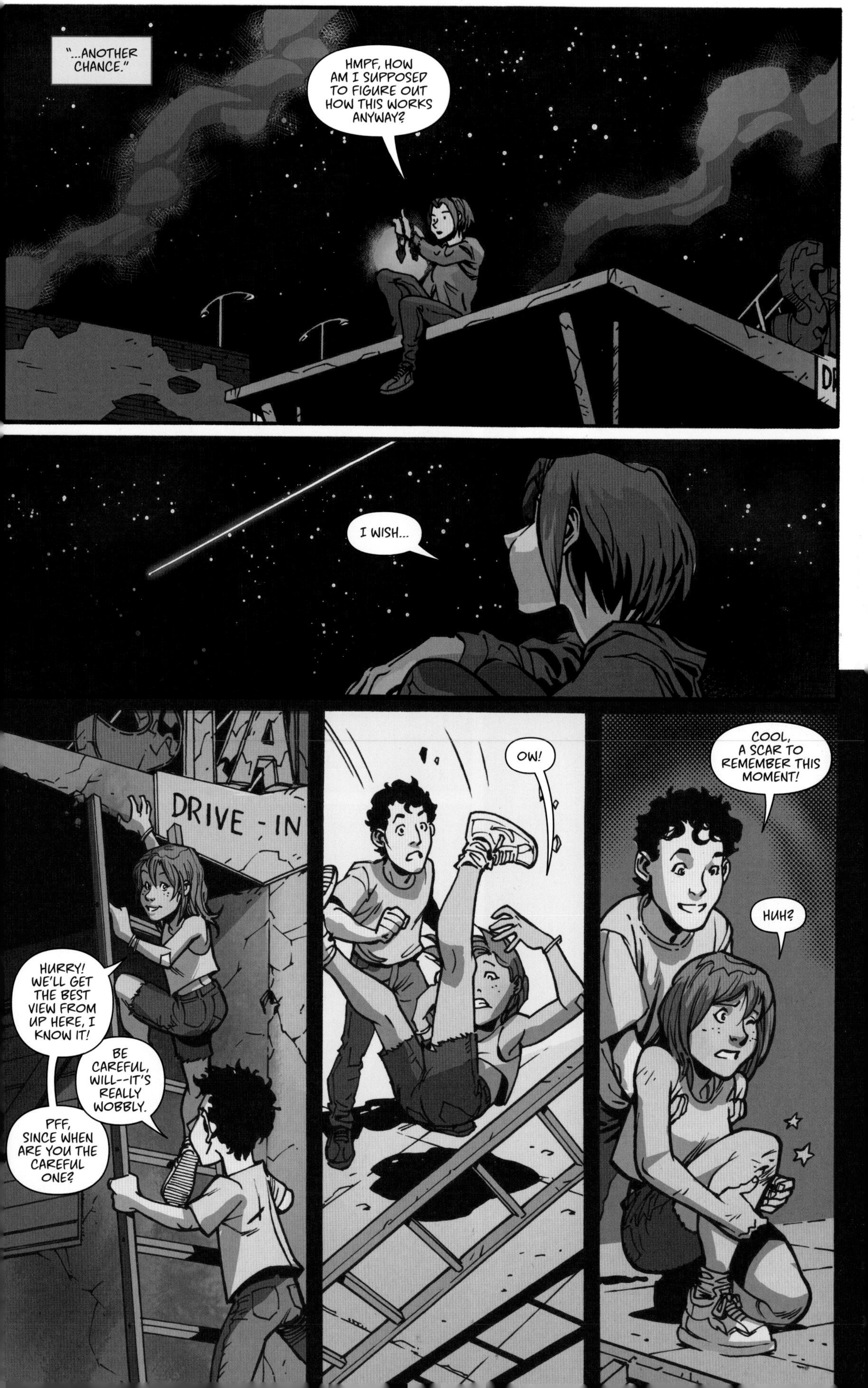
"...ANOTHER CHANCE."
HMPF, HOW AM I SUPPOSED TO FIGURE OUT HOW THIS WORKS ANYWAY?
I WISH...
DRIVE - IN
HURRY! WE'LL GET THE BEST VIEW FROM UP HERE, I KNOW IT!
BE CAREFUL, WILL--IT'S REALLY WOBBLY.
PFF, SINCE WHEN ARE YOU THE CAREFUL ONE?
OW!
COOL, A SCAR TO REMEMBER THIS MOMENT!
HUH?

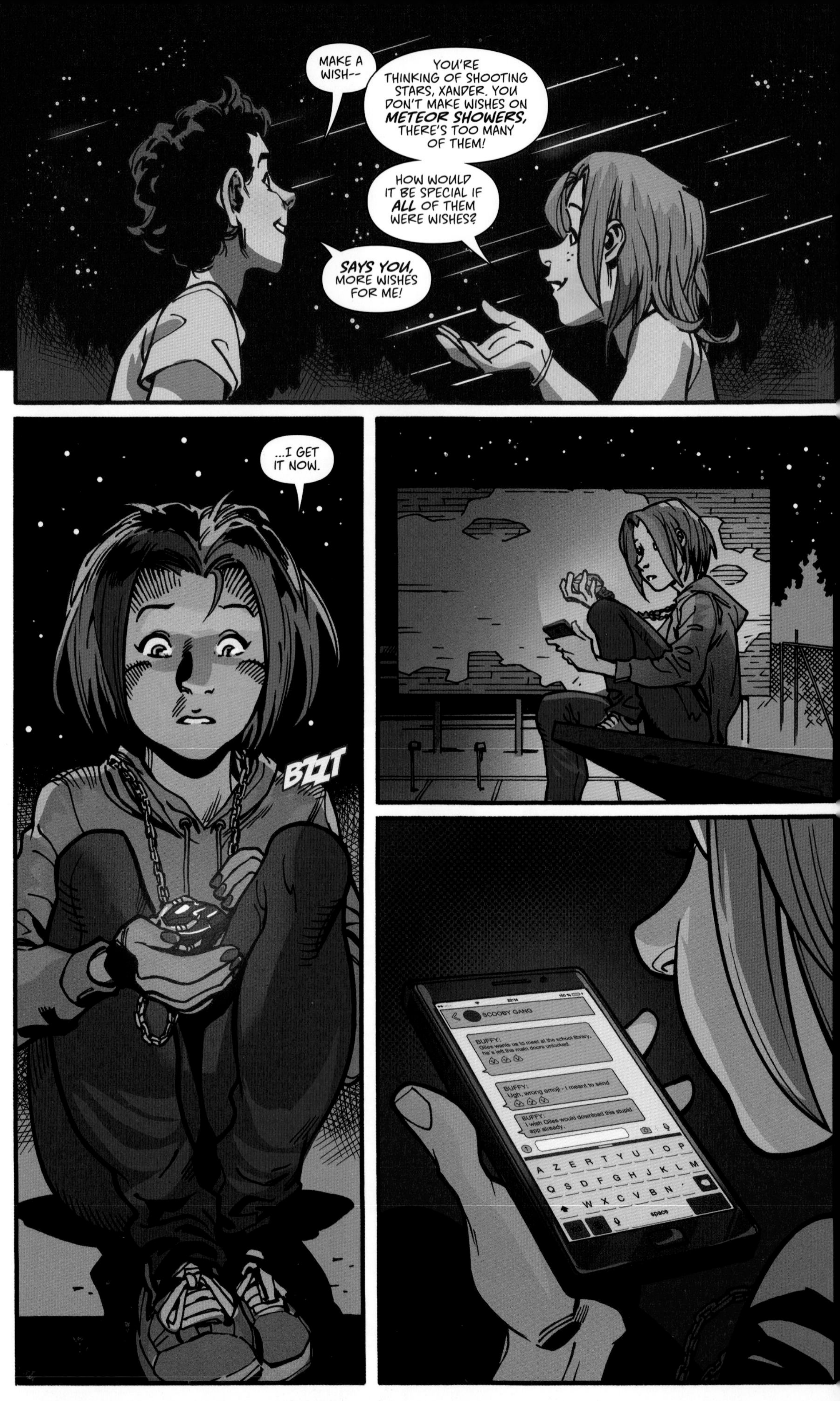
MAKE A WISH--
YOU'RE THINKING OF SHOOTING STARS, XANDER. YOU DON'T MAKE WISHES ON **METEOR SHOWERS,** THERE'S TOO MANY OF THEM!
HOW WOULD IT BE SPECIAL IF ***ALL*** OF THEM WERE WISHES?
SAYS YOU, MORE WISHES FOR ME!
...I GET IT NOW.
BZZT
SCOOBY GANG
BUFFY: Giles wants us to meet at the school library, he's left the main doors unlocked.
BUFFY: Ugh, wrong emoji - I meant to send
BUFFY: I wish Giles would download this stupid app already.

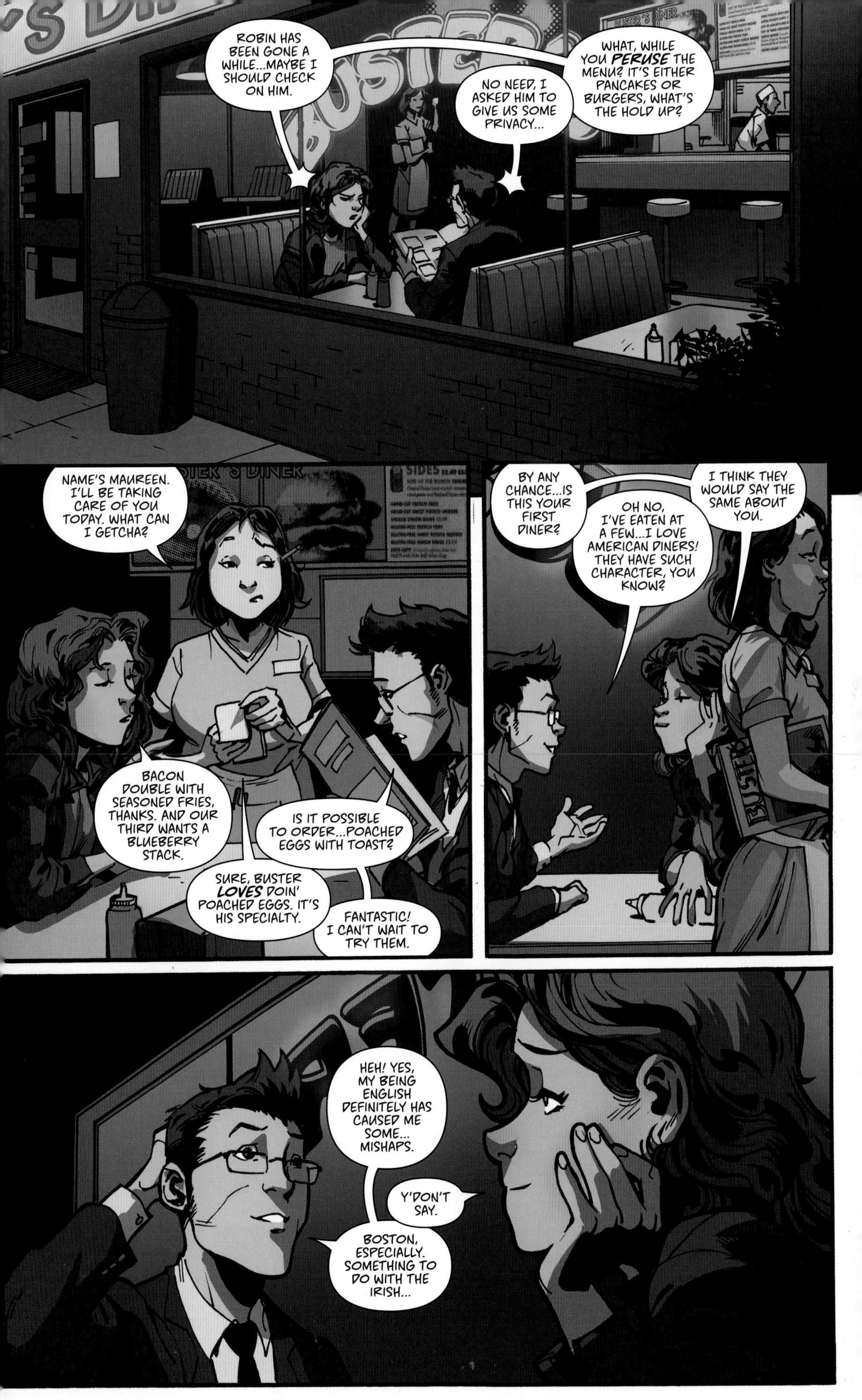
ROBIN HAS BEEN GONE A WHILE...MAYBE I SHOULD CHECK ON HIM.
WHAT, WHILE YOU PERUSE THE MENU? IT'S EITHER PANCAKES OR BURGERS, WHAT'S THE HOLD UP?
NO NEED, I ASKED HIM TO GIVE US SOME PRIVACY...
NAME'S MAUREEN. I'LL BE TAKING CARE OF YOU TODAY. WHAT CAN I GETCHA?
BACON DOUBLE WITH SEASONED FRIES, THANKS. AND OUR THIRD WANTS A BLUEBERRY STACK.
IS IT POSSIBLE TO ORDER...POACHED EGGS WITH TOAST?
SURE, BUSTER LOVES DOIN' POACHED EGGS. IT'S HIS SPECIALTY.
FANTASTIC! I CAN'T WAIT TO TRY THEM.
BY ANY CHANCE...IS THIS YOUR FIRST DINER?
OH NO, I'VE EATEN AT A FEW...I LOVE AMERICAN DINERS! THEY HAVE SUCH CHARACTER, YOU KNOW?
I THINK THEY WOULD SAY THE SAME ABOUT YOU.
HEH! YES, MY BEING ENGLISH DEFINITELY HAS CAUSED ME SOME... MISHAPS.
Y'DON'T SAY.
BOSTON, ESPECIALLY. SOMETHING TO DO WITH THE IRISH...

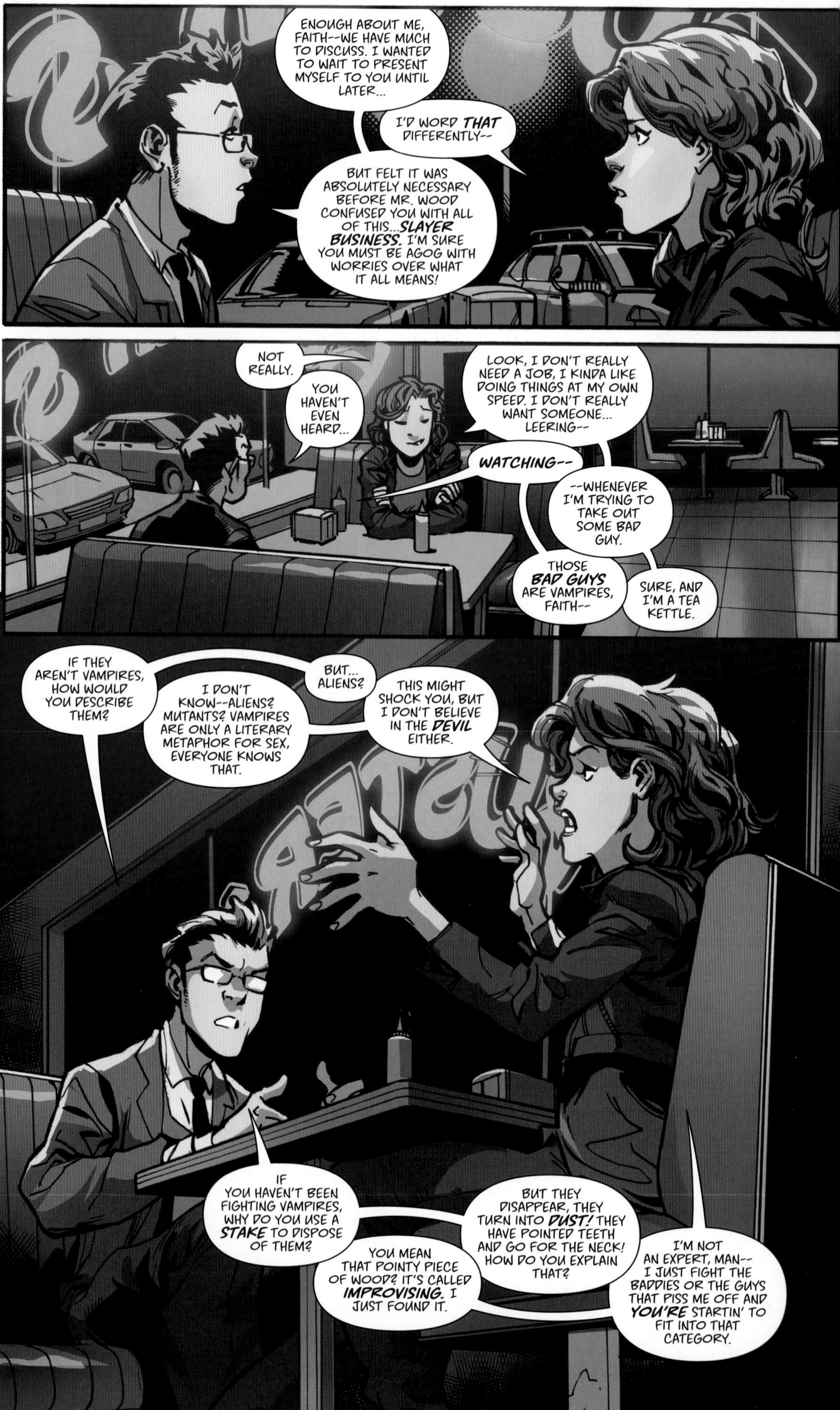

ENOUGH ABOUT ME, FAITH--WE HAVE MUCH TO DISCUSS. I WANTED TO WAIT TO PRESENT MYSELF TO YOU UNTIL LATER...
I'D WORD THAT DIFFERENTLY--
BUT FELT IT WAS ABSOLUTELY NECESSARY BEFORE MR. WOOD CONFUSED YOU WITH ALL OF THIS...SLAYER BUSINESS. I'M SURE YOU MUST BE AGOG WITH WORRIES OVER WHAT IT ALL MEANS!
NOT REALLY.
YOU HAVEN'T EVEN HEARD...
LOOK, I DON'T REALLY NEED A JOB, I KINDA LIKE DOING THINGS AT MY OWN SPEED. I DON'T REALLY WANT SOMEONE... LEERING--
WATCHING--
--WHENEVER I'M TRYING TO TAKE OUT SOME BAD GUY.
THOSE BAD GUYS ARE VAMPIRES, FAITH--
SURE, AND I'M A TEA KETTLE.
IF THEY AREN'T VAMPIRES, HOW WOULD YOU DESCRIBE THEM?
I DON'T KNOW--ALIENS? MUTANTS? VAMPIRES ARE ONLY A LITERARY METAPHOR FOR SEX, EVERYONE KNOWS THAT.
BUT... ALIENS?
THIS MIGHT SHOCK YOU, BUT I DON'T BELIEVE IN THE DEVIL EITHER.
IF YOU HAVEN'T BEEN FIGHTING VAMPIRES, WHY DO YOU USE A STAKE TO DISPOSE OF THEM?
YOU MEAN THAT POINTY PIECE OF WOOD? IT'S CALLED IMPROVISING. I JUST FOUND IT.
BUT THEY DISAPPEAR, THEY TURN INTO DUST! THEY HAVE POINTED TEETH AND GO FOR THE NECK! HOW DO YOU EXPLAIN THAT?
I'M NOT AN EXPERT, MAN-- I JUST FIGHT THE BADDIES OR THE GUYS THAT PISS ME OFF AND YOU'RE STARTIN' TO FIT INTO THAT CATEGORY.

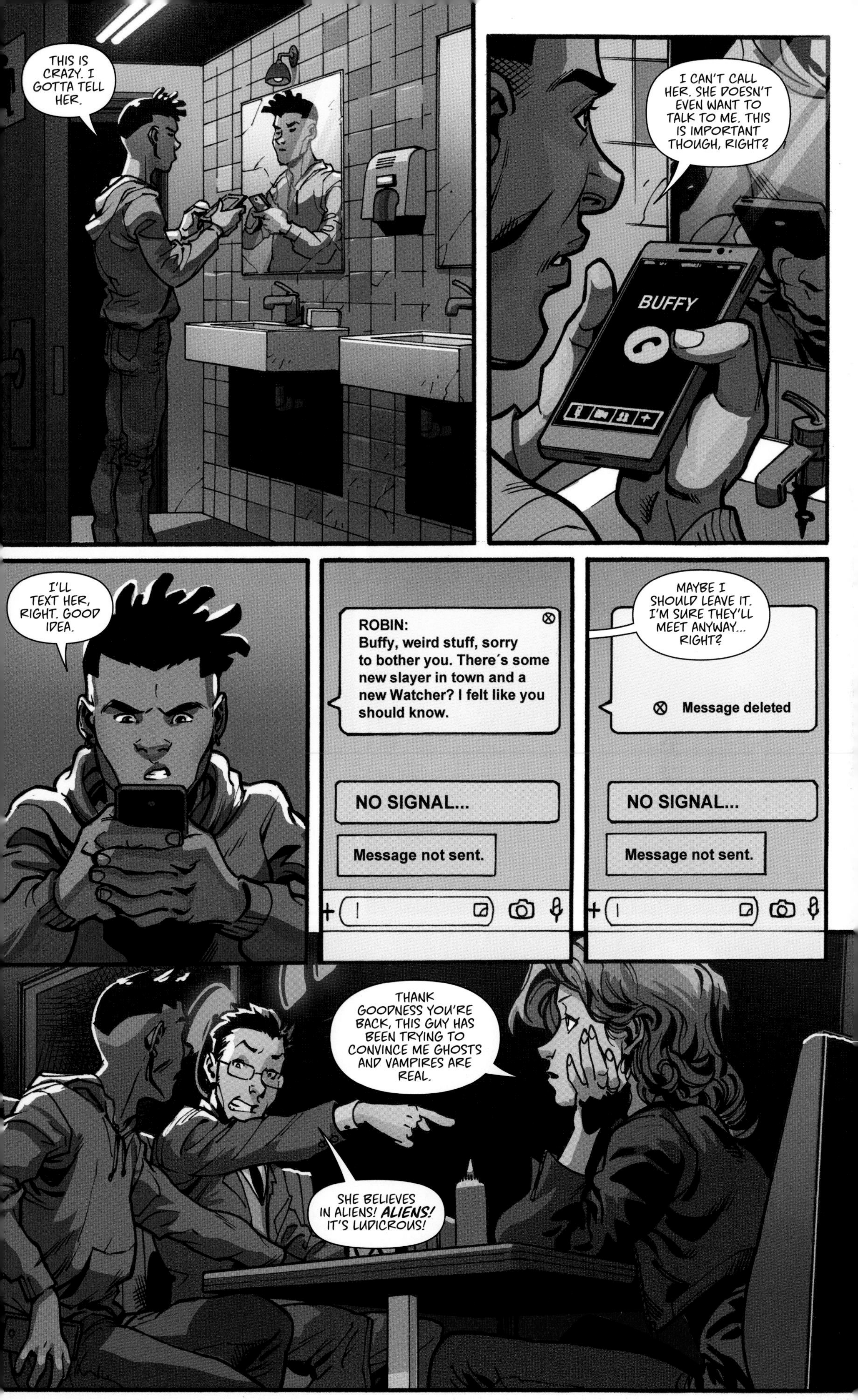
THIS IS CRAZY. I GOTTA TELL HER.
I CAN'T CALL HER. SHE DOESN'T EVEN WANT TO TALK TO ME. THIS IS IMPORTANT THOUGH, RIGHT?
BUFFY
I'LL TEXT HER, RIGHT. GOOD IDEA.
ROBIN:
Buffy, weird stuff, sorry to bother you. There´s some new slayer in town and a new Watcher? I felt like you should know.
NO SIGNAL...
Message not sent.
MAYBE I SHOULD LEAVE IT. I'M SURE THEY'LL MEET ANYWAY... RIGHT?
Message deleted
NO SIGNAL...
Message not sent.
THANK GOODNESS YOU'RE BACK, THIS GUY HAS BEEN TRYING TO CONVINCE ME GHOSTS AND VAMPIRES ARE REAL.
SHE BELIEVES IN ALIENS! ALIENS! IT'S LUDICROUS!

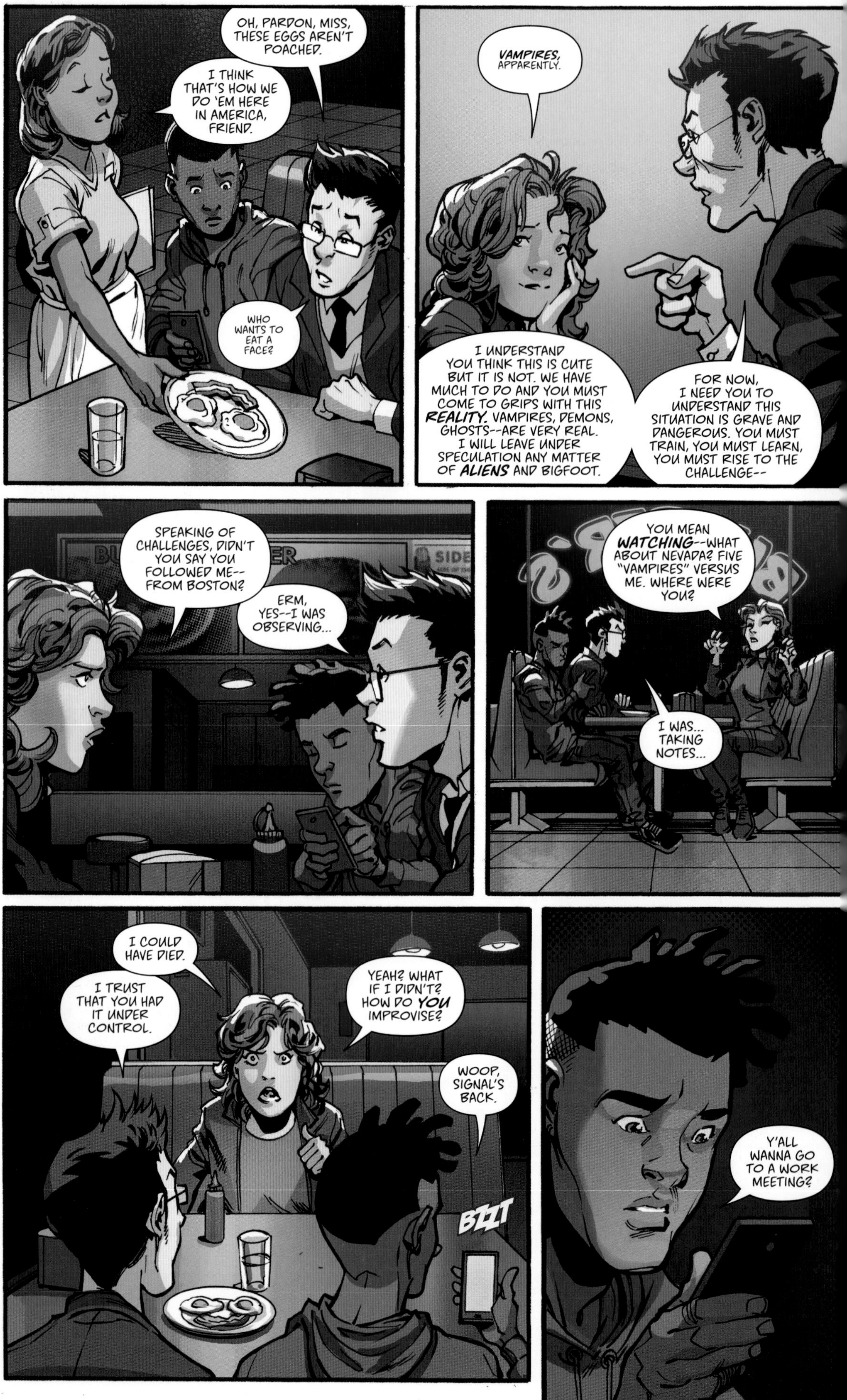
OH, PARDON, MISS, THESE EGGS AREN'T POACHED.
I THINK THAT'S HOW WE DO 'EM HERE IN AMERICA, FRIEND.
WHO WANTS TO EAT A FACE?
VAMPIRES, APPARENTLY.
I UNDERSTAND YOU THINK THIS IS CUTE BUT IT IS NOT. WE HAVE MUCH TO DO AND YOU MUST COME TO GRIPS WITH THIS REALITY. VAMPIRES, DEMONS, GHOSTS--ARE VERY REAL. I WILL LEAVE UNDER SPECULATION ANY MATTER OF ALIENS AND BIGFOOT.
FOR NOW, I NEED YOU TO UNDERSTAND THIS SITUATION IS GRAVE AND DANGEROUS. YOU MUST TRAIN, YOU MUST LEARN, YOU MUST RISE TO THE CHALLENGE--
SPEAKING OF CHALLENGES, DIDN'T YOU SAY YOU FOLLOWED ME-- FROM BOSTON?
ERM, YES--I WAS OBSERVING...
YOU MEAN WATCHING--WHAT ABOUT NEVADA? FIVE "VAMPIRES" VERSUS ME. WHERE WERE YOU?
I WAS... TAKING NOTES...
I COULD HAVE DIED.
I TRUST THAT YOU HAD IT UNDER CONTROL.
YEAH? WHAT IF I DIDN'T? HOW DO YOU IMPROVISE?
WOOP, SIGNAL'S BACK.
BZZT
Y'ALL WANNA GO TO A WORK MEETING?

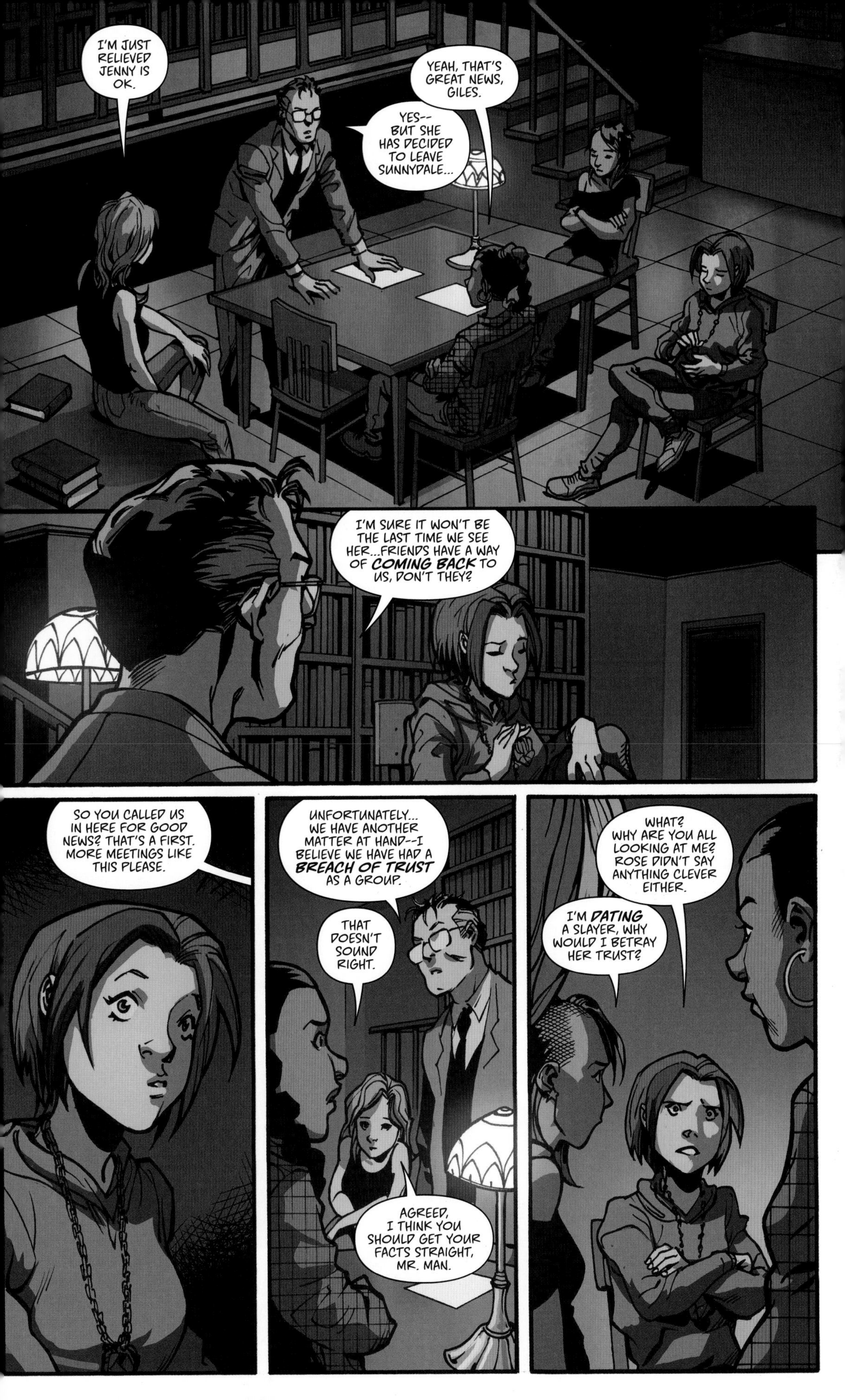

I'M JUST RELIEVED JENNY IS OK.
YEAH, THAT'S GREAT NEWS, GILES.
YES-- BUT SHE HAS DECIDED TO LEAVE SUNNYDALE...
I'M SURE IT WON'T BE THE LAST TIME WE SEE HER...FRIENDS HAVE A WAY OF COMING BACK TO US, DON'T THEY?
SO YOU CALLED US IN HERE FOR GOOD NEWS? THAT'S A FIRST. MORE MEETINGS LIKE THIS PLEASE.
UNFORTUNATELY... WE HAVE ANOTHER MATTER AT HAND--I BELIEVE WE HAVE HAD A BREACH OF TRUST AS A GROUP.
THAT DOESN'T SOUND RIGHT.
AGREED, I THINK YOU SHOULD GET YOUR FACTS STRAIGHT, MR. MAN.
WHAT? WHY ARE YOU ALL LOOKING AT ME? ROSE DIDN'T SAY ANYTHING CLEVER EITHER.
I'M DATING A SLAYER, WHY WOULD I BETRAY HER TRUST?

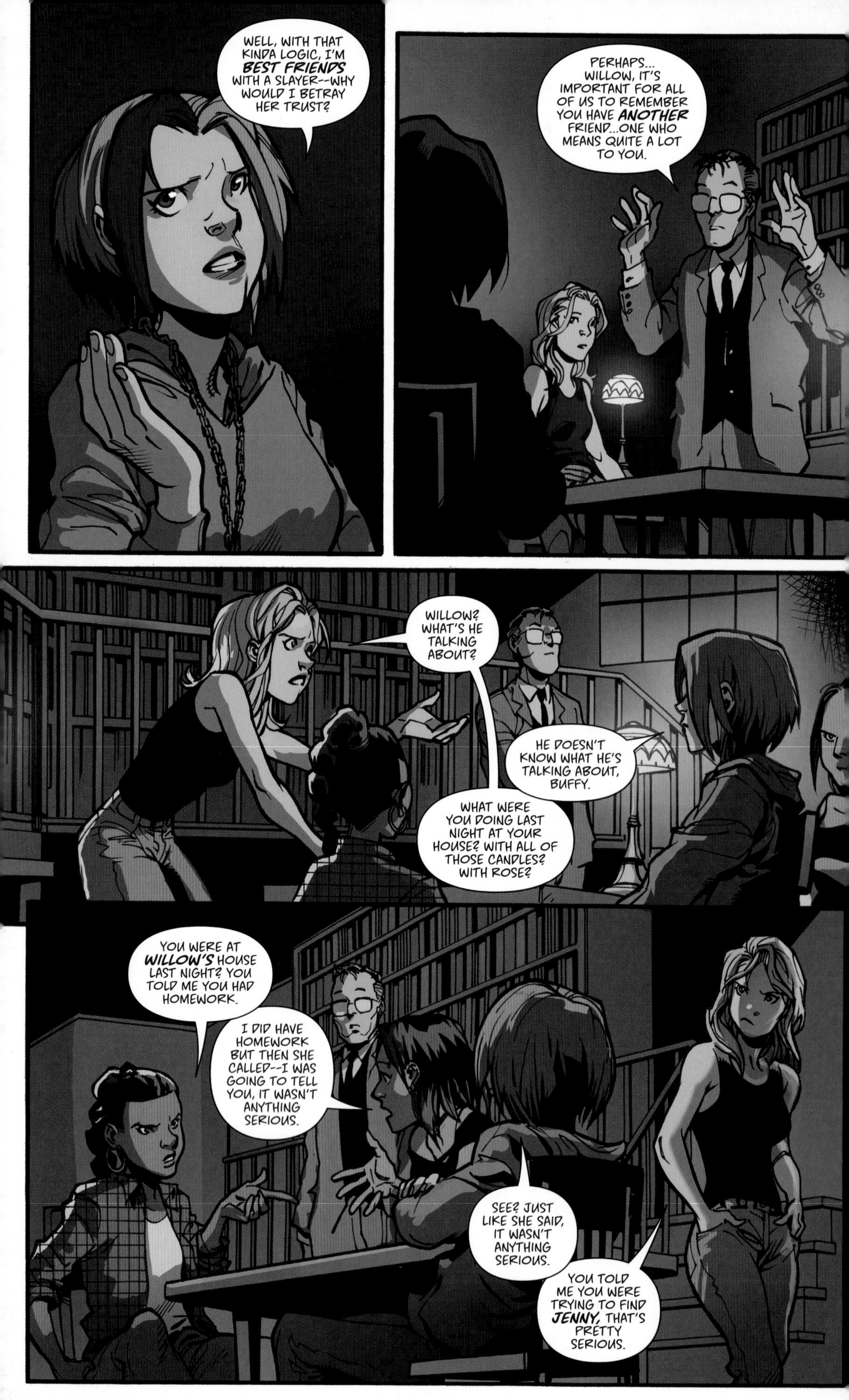

WELL, WITH THAT KINDA LOGIC, I'M **BEST FRIENDS** WITH A SLAYER--WHY WOULD I BETRAY HER TRUST?
PERHAPS... WILLOW, IT'S IMPORTANT FOR ALL OF US TO REMEMBER YOU HAVE **ANOTHER** FRIEND...ONE WHO MEANS QUITE A LOT TO YOU.
WILLOW? WHAT'S HE TALKING ABOUT?
WHAT WERE YOU DOING LAST NIGHT AT YOUR HOUSE? WITH ALL OF THOSE CANDLES? WITH ROSE?
HE DOESN'T KNOW WHAT HE'S TALKING ABOUT, BUFFY.
YOU WERE AT **WILLOW'S** HOUSE LAST NIGHT? YOU TOLD ME YOU HAD HOMEWORK.
I DID HAVE HOMEWORK BUT THEN SHE CALLED--I WAS GOING TO TELL YOU, IT WASN'T ANYTHING SERIOUS.
SEE? JUST LIKE SHE SAID, IT WASN'T ANYTHING SERIOUS.
YOU TOLD ME YOU WERE TRYING TO FIND **JENNY,** THAT'S PRETTY SERIOUS.

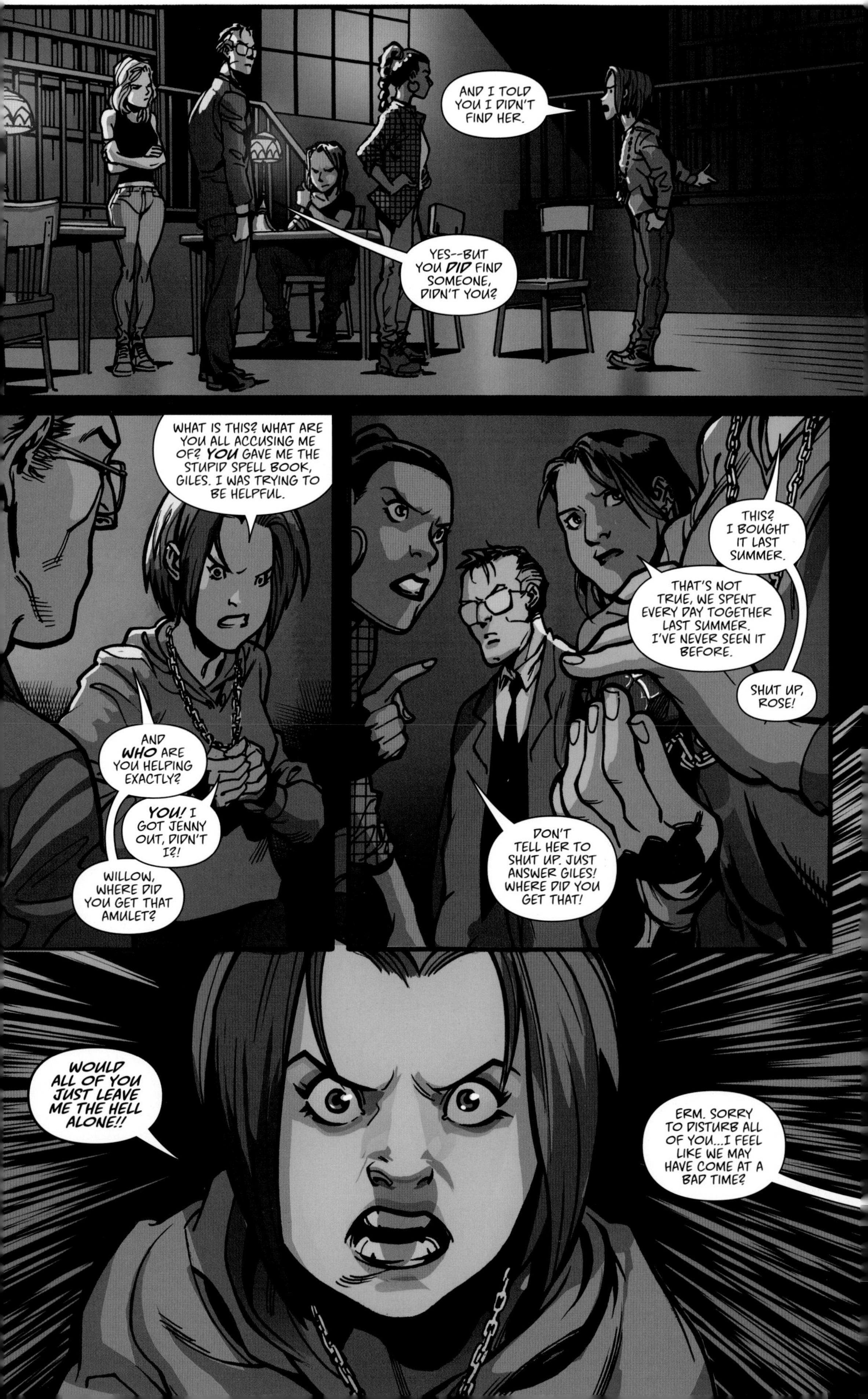
AND I TOLD YOU I DIDN'T FIND HER.
YES--BUT YOU ***DID*** FIND SOMEONE, DIDN'T YOU?
WHAT IS THIS? WHAT ARE YOU ALL ACCUSING ME OF? ***YOU*** GAVE ME THE STUPID SPELL BOOK, GILES. I WAS TRYING TO BE HELPFUL.
AND ***WHO*** ARE YOU HELPING EXACTLY?
YOU! I GOT JENNY OUT, DIDN'T I?!
WILLOW, WHERE DID YOU GET THAT AMULET?
THIS? I BOUGHT IT LAST SUMMER.
THAT'S NOT TRUE, WE SPENT EVERY DAY TOGETHER LAST SUMMER. I'VE NEVER SEEN IT BEFORE.
SHUT UP, ROSE!
DON'T TELL HER TO SHUT UP. JUST ANSWER GILES! WHERE DID YOU GET THAT!
WOULD ALL OF YOU JUST LEAVE ME THE HELL ALONE!!
ERM. SORRY TO DISTURB ALL OF YOU...I FEEL LIKE WE MAY HAVE COME AT A BAD TIME?

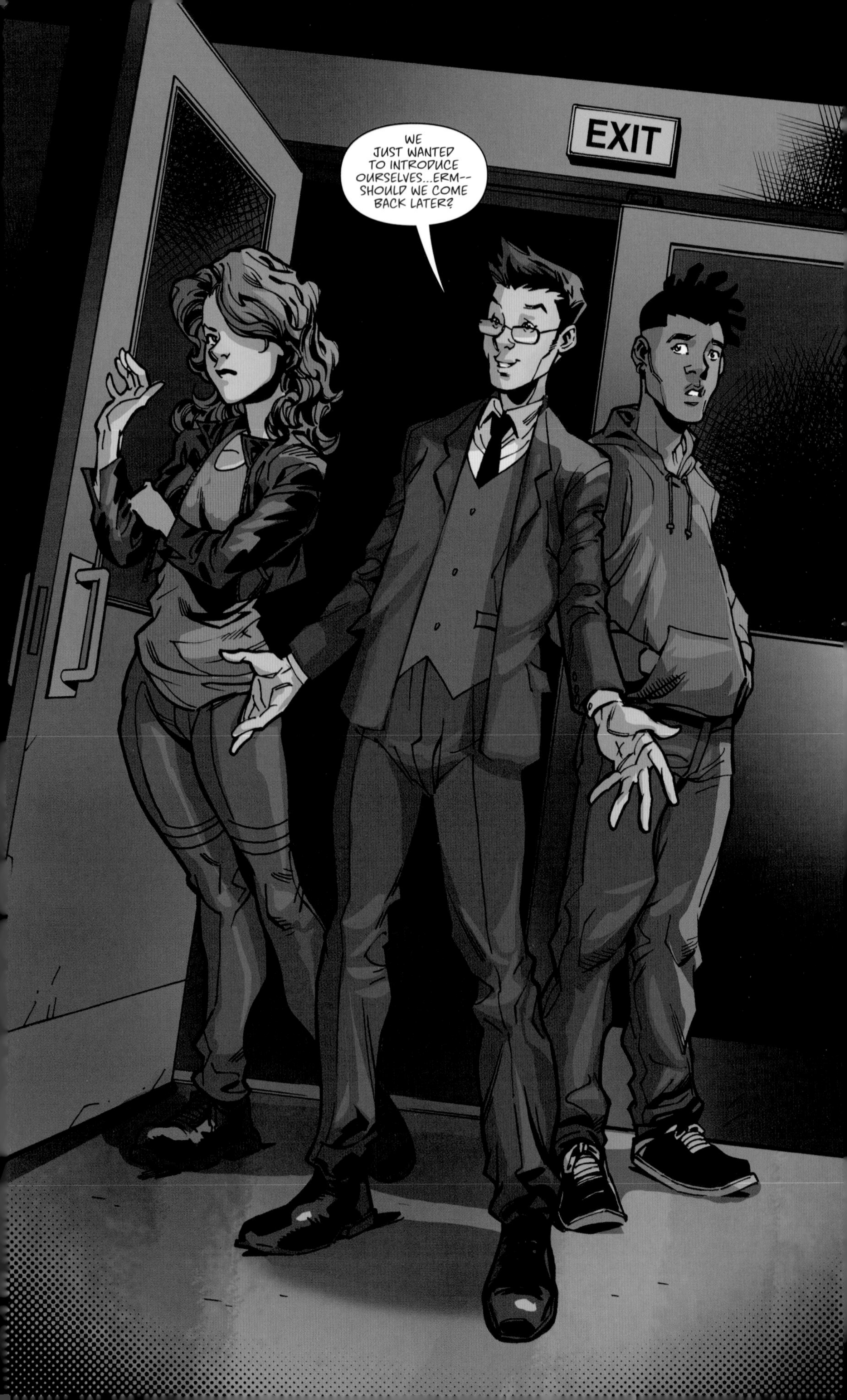
EXIT
WE JUST WANTED TO INTRODUCE OURSELVES...ERM--SHOULD WE COME BACK LATER?

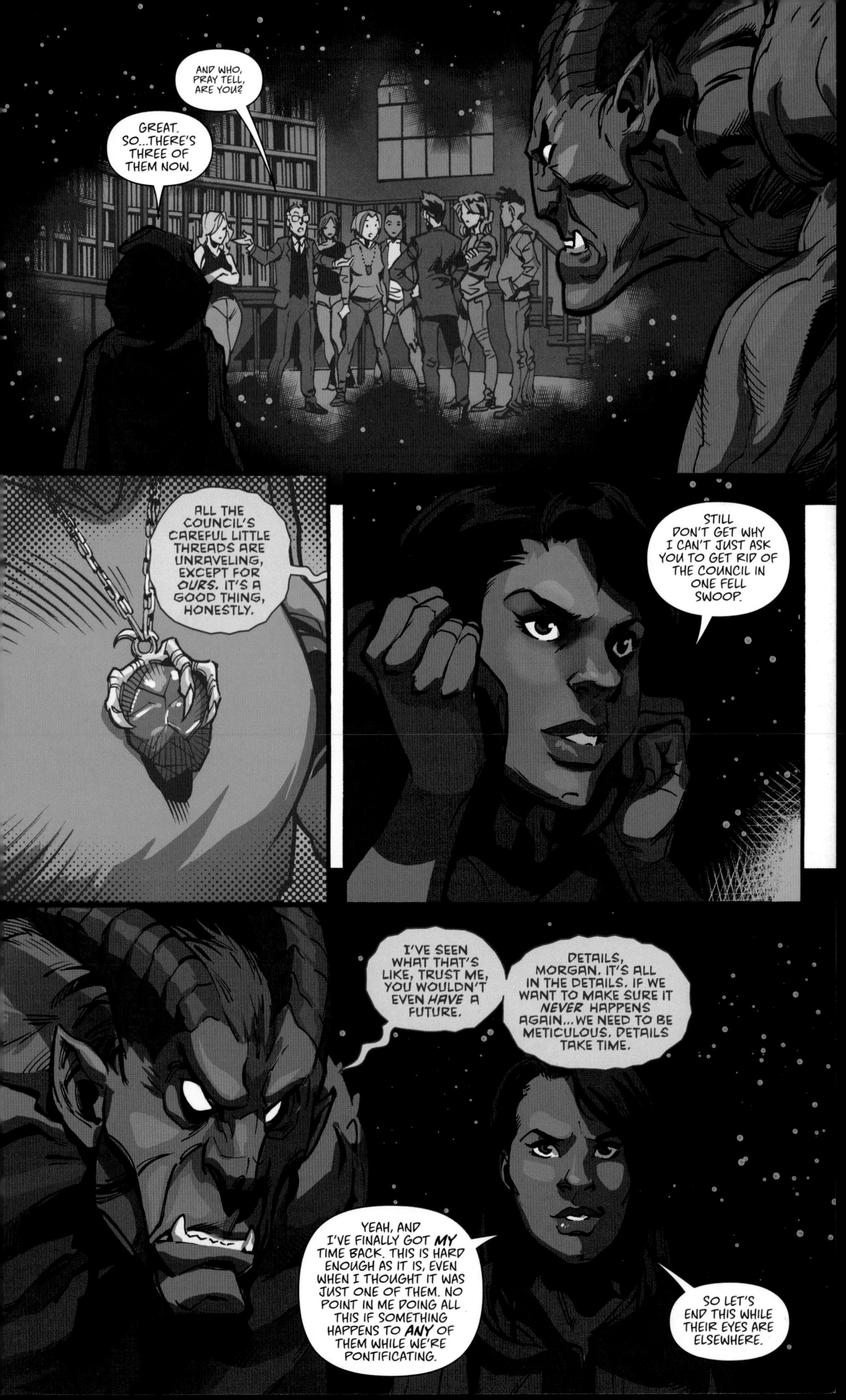

AND WHO, PRAY TELL, ARE YOU?
GREAT. SO...THERE'S THREE OF THEM NOW.
ALL THE COUNCIL'S CAREFUL LITTLE THREADS ARE UNRAVELING, EXCEPT FOR *OURS*. IT'S A GOOD THING, HONESTLY.
STILL DON'T GET WHY I CAN'T JUST ASK YOU TO GET RID OF THE COUNCIL IN ONE FELL SWOOP.
I'VE SEEN WHAT THAT'S LIKE, TRUST ME, YOU WOULDN'T EVEN *HAVE* A FUTURE.
DETAILS, MORGAN. IT'S ALL IN THE DETAILS. IF WE WANT TO MAKE SURE IT *NEVER* HAPPENS AGAIN...WE NEED TO BE METICULOUS. DETAILS TAKE TIME.
YEAH, AND I'VE FINALLY GOT **MY** TIME BACK. THIS IS HARD ENOUGH AS IT IS, EVEN WHEN I THOUGHT IT WAS JUST ONE OF THEM. NO POINT IN ME DOING ALL THIS IF SOMETHING HAPPENS TO ***ANY*** OF THEM WHILE WE'RE PONTIFICATING.
SO LET'S END THIS WHILE THEIR EYES ARE ELSEWHERE.

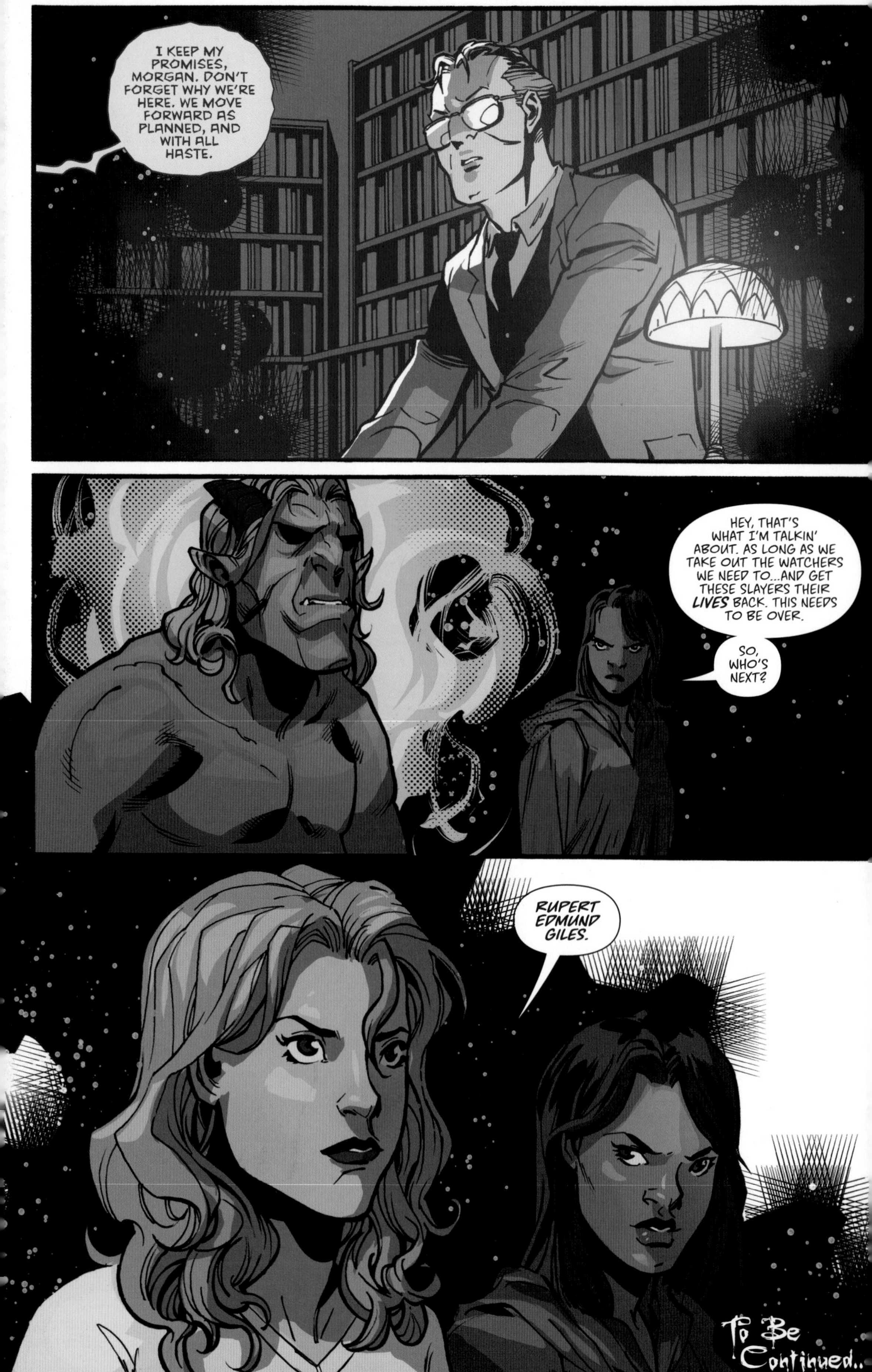
I KEEP MY PROMISES, MORGAN. DON'T FORGET WHY WE'RE HERE. WE MOVE FORWARD AS PLANNED, AND WITH ALL HASTE.
HEY, THAT'S WHAT I'M TALKIN' ABOUT. AS LONG AS WE TAKE OUT THE WATCHERS WE NEED TO...AND GET THESE SLAYERS THEIR LIVES BACK. THIS NEEDS TO BE OVER.
SO, WHO'S NEXT?
RUPERT EDMUND GILES.
To Be Continued..

BUFFY THE VAMPIRE SLAYER #20

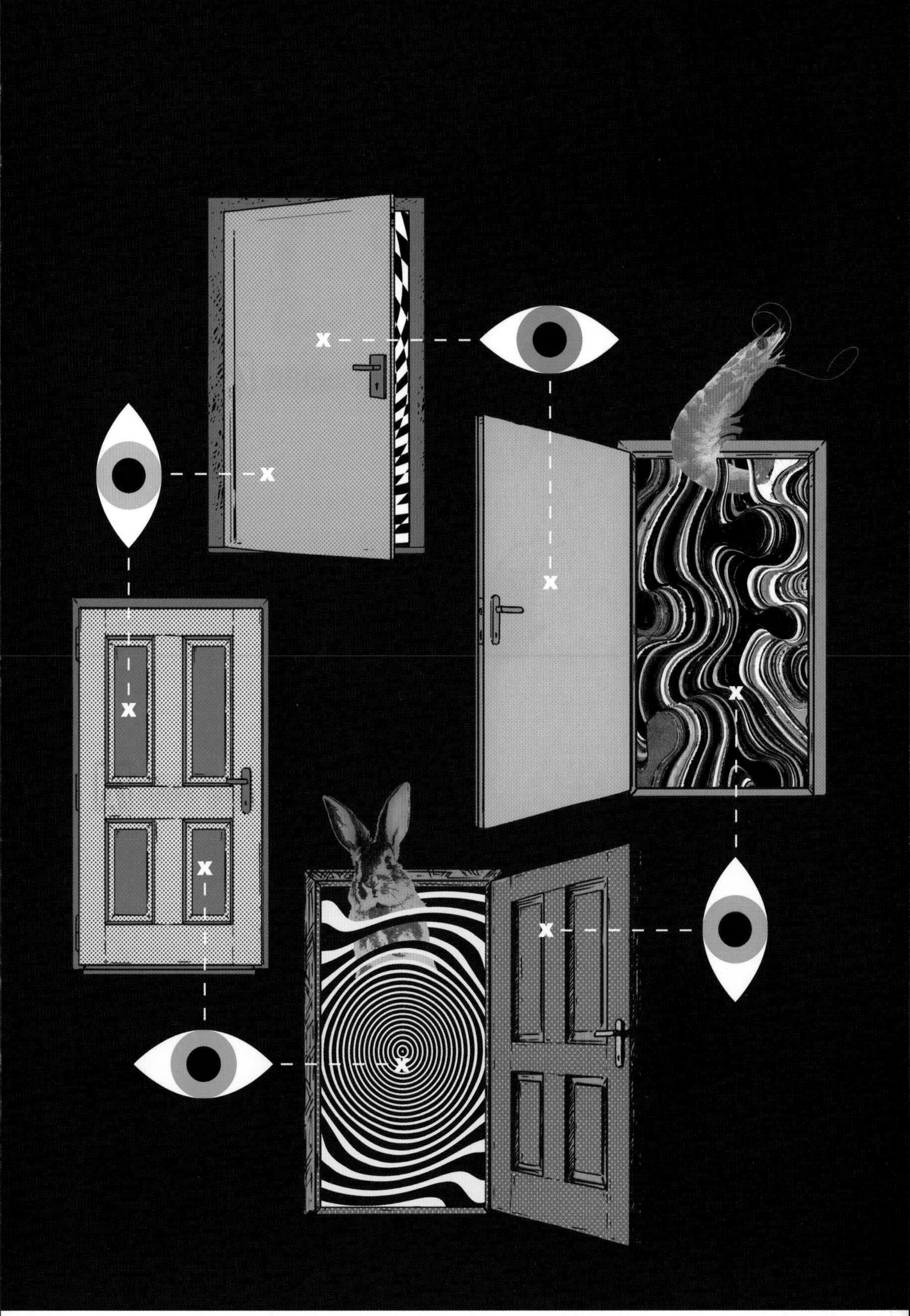

Issue Twenty Ring of Fire Cover by **Becca Carey**

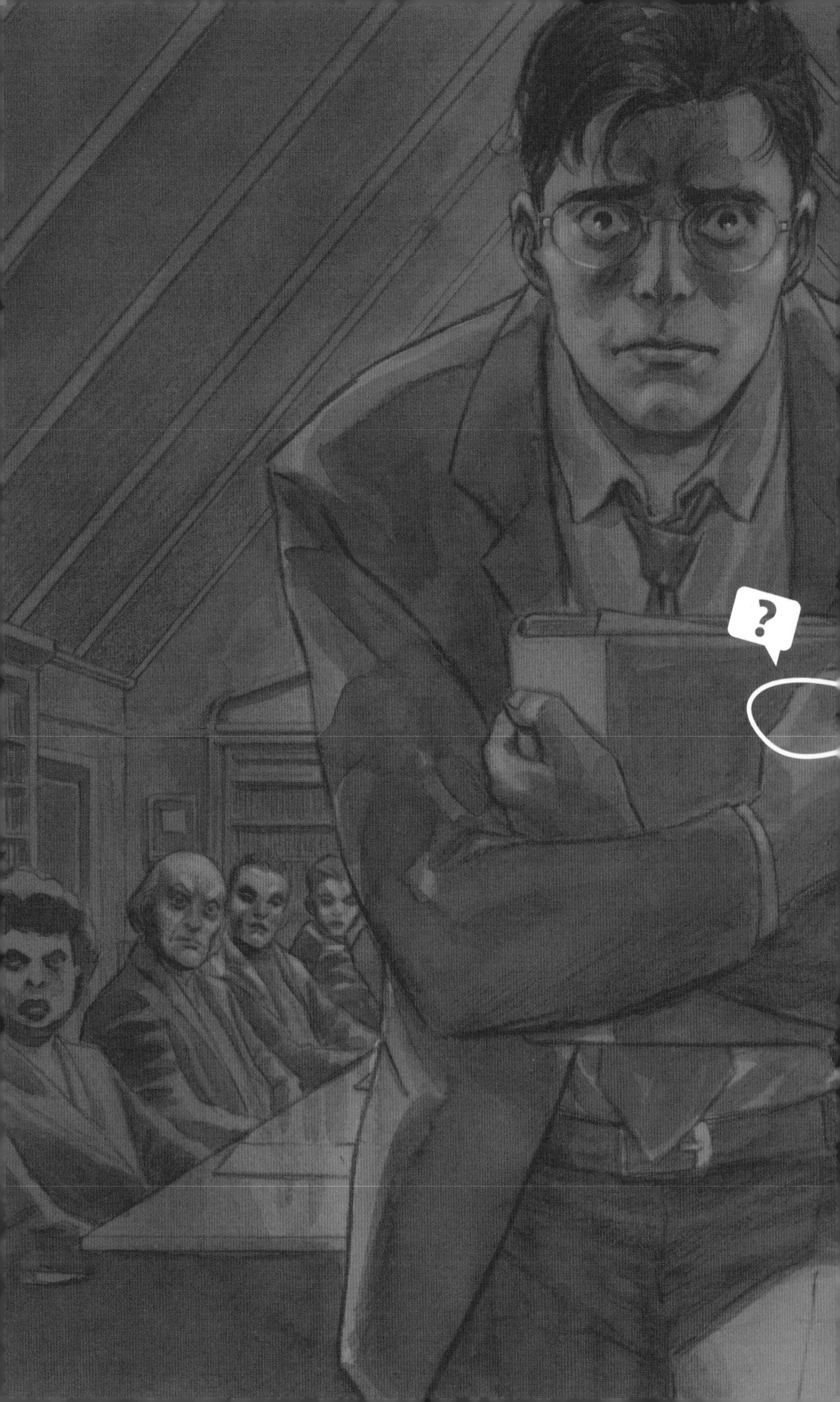
?

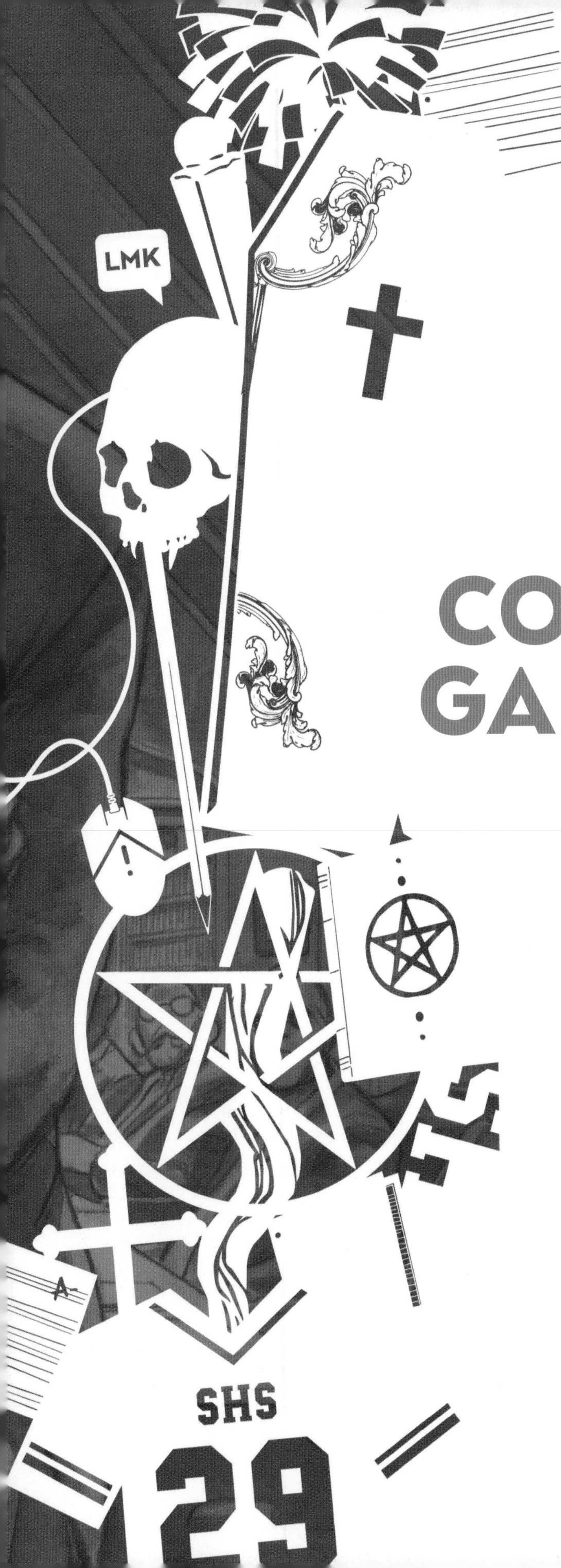
LMK
SHS
29

COVER GALLERY

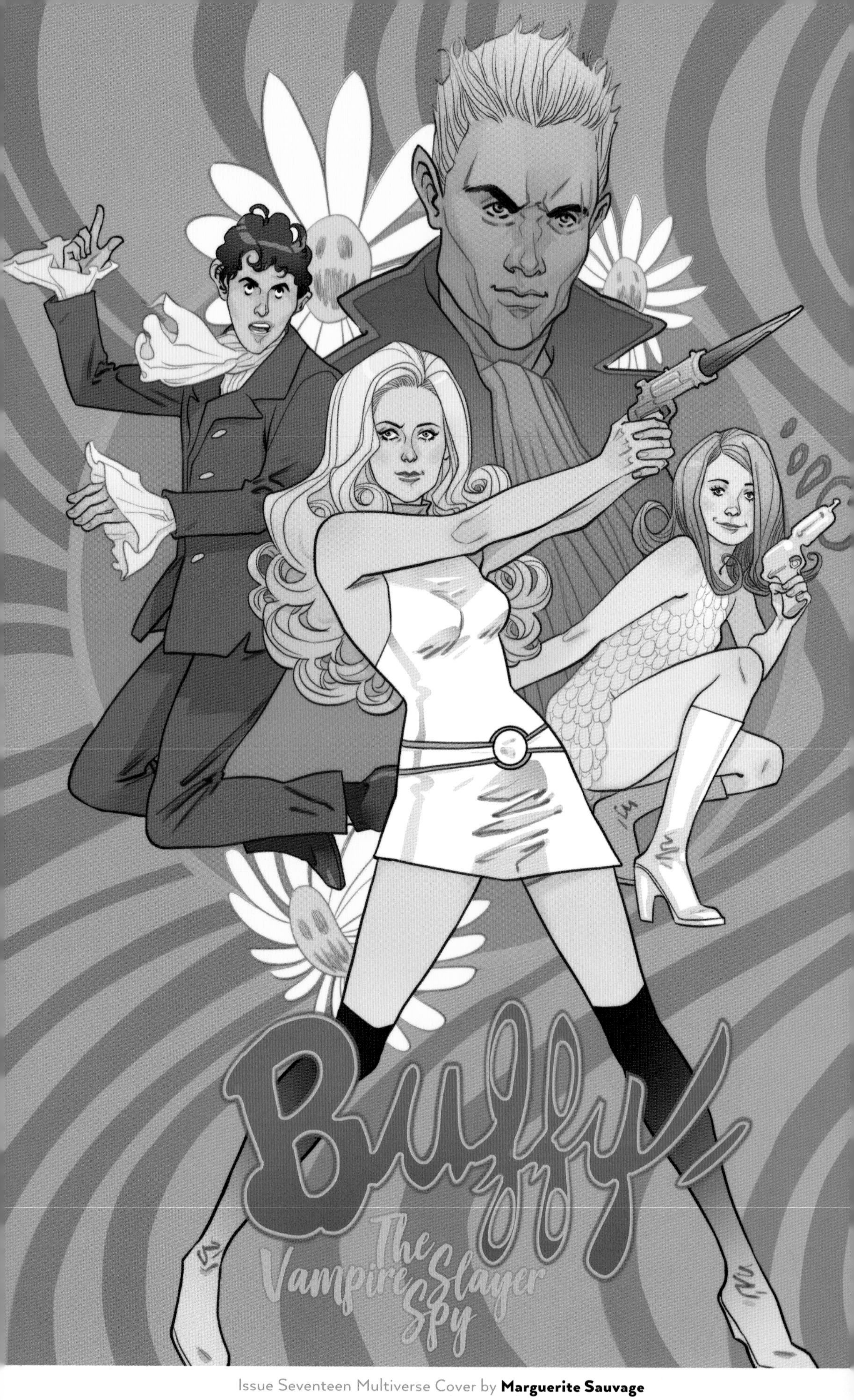
Buffy
The Vampire Slayer Spy
Issue Seventeen Multiverse Cover by **Marguerite Sauvage**

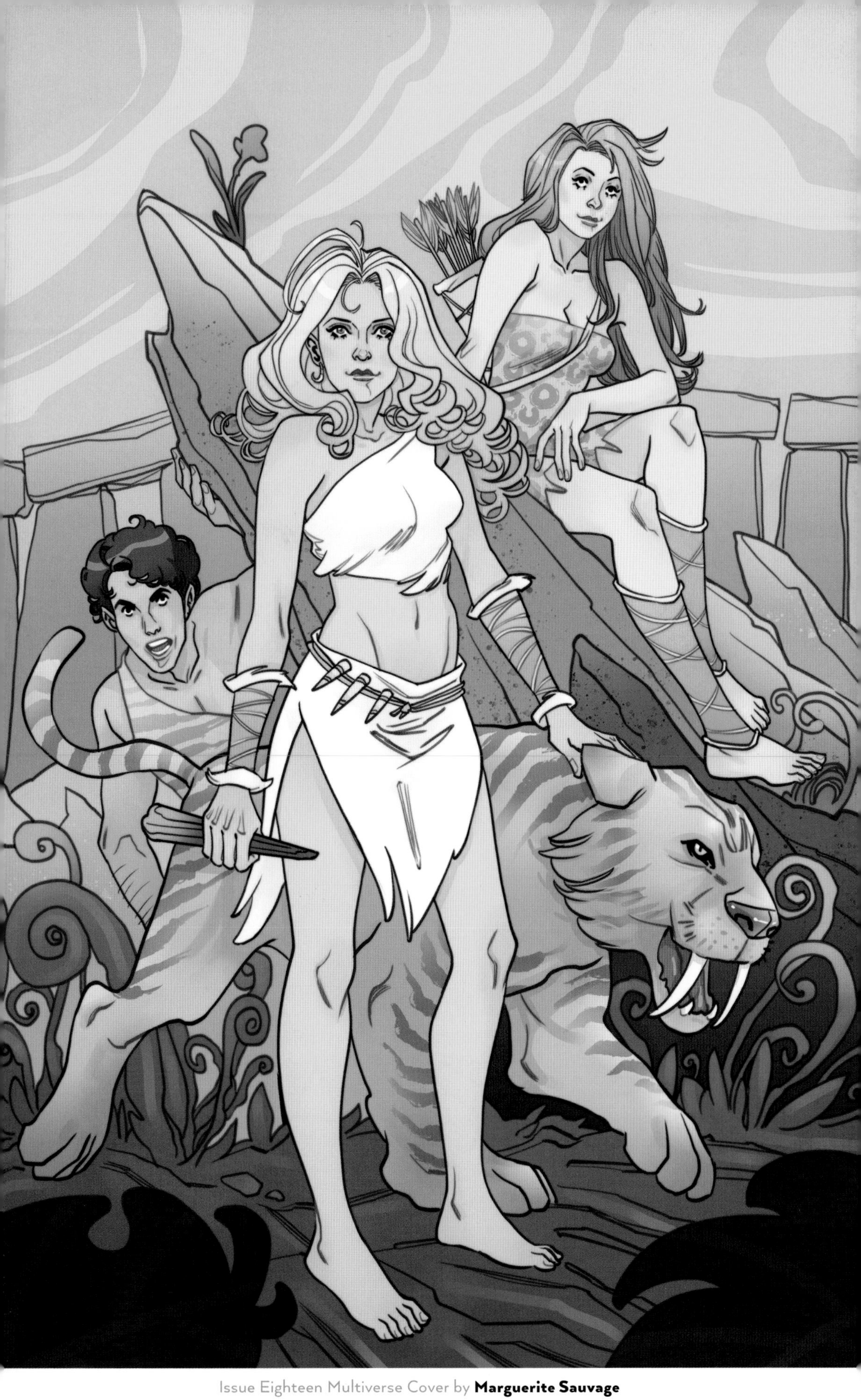

Issue Eighteen Multiverse Cover by **Marguerite Sauvage**

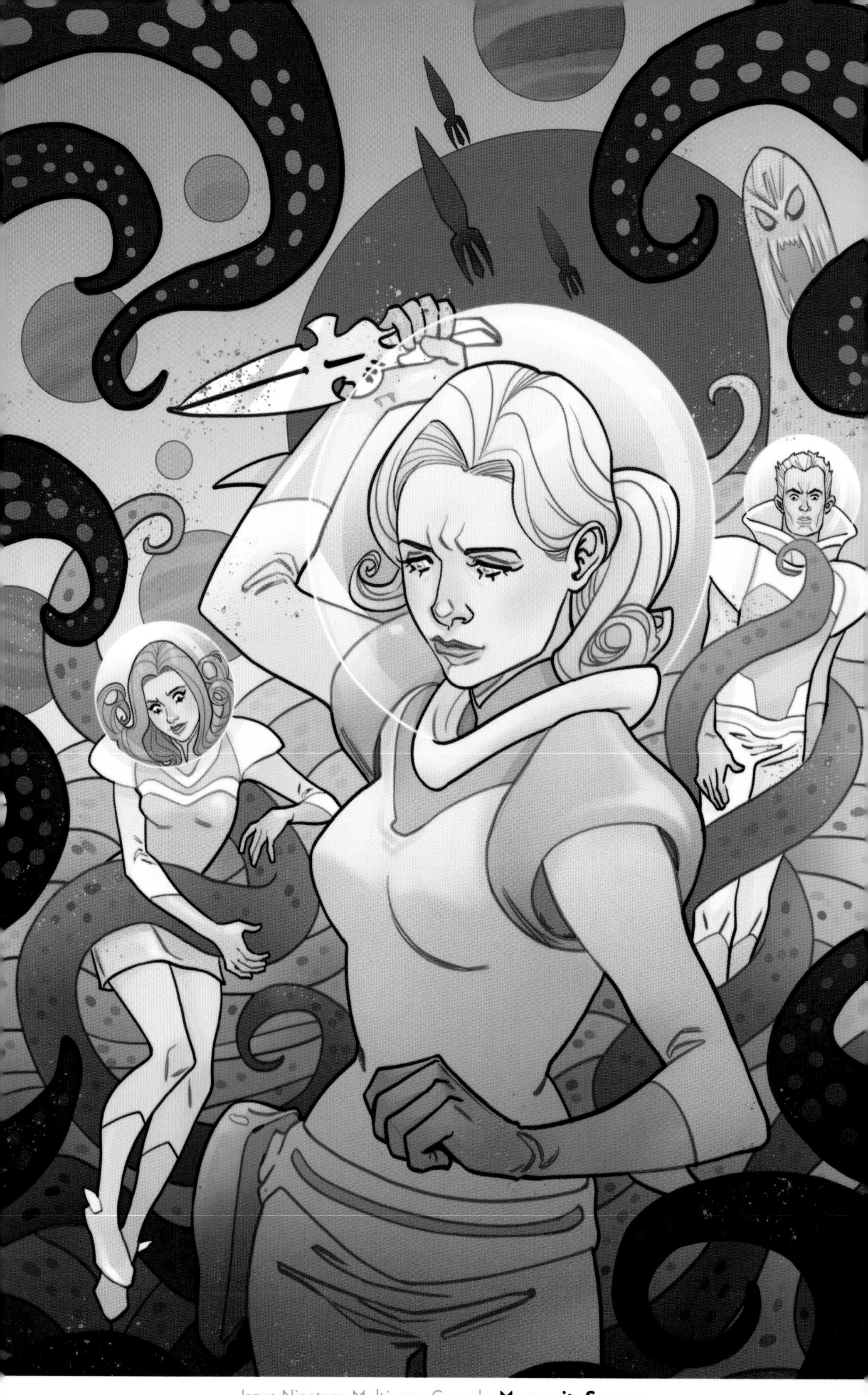

Issue Nineteen Multiverse Cover by **Marguerite Sauvage**

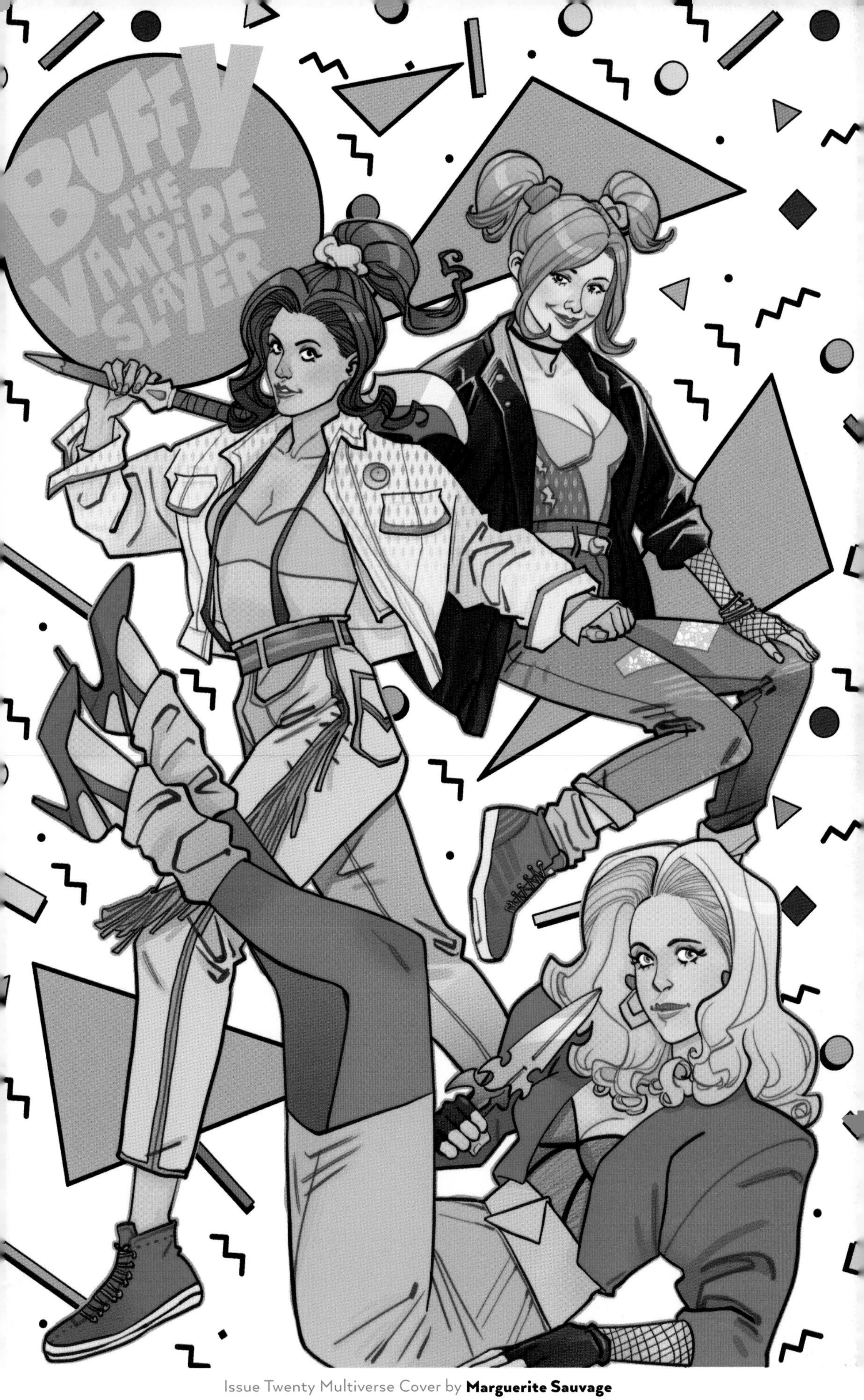
BUFFY
THE
VAMPIRE
SLAYER

Issue Twenty Multiverse Cover by **Marguerite Sauvage**

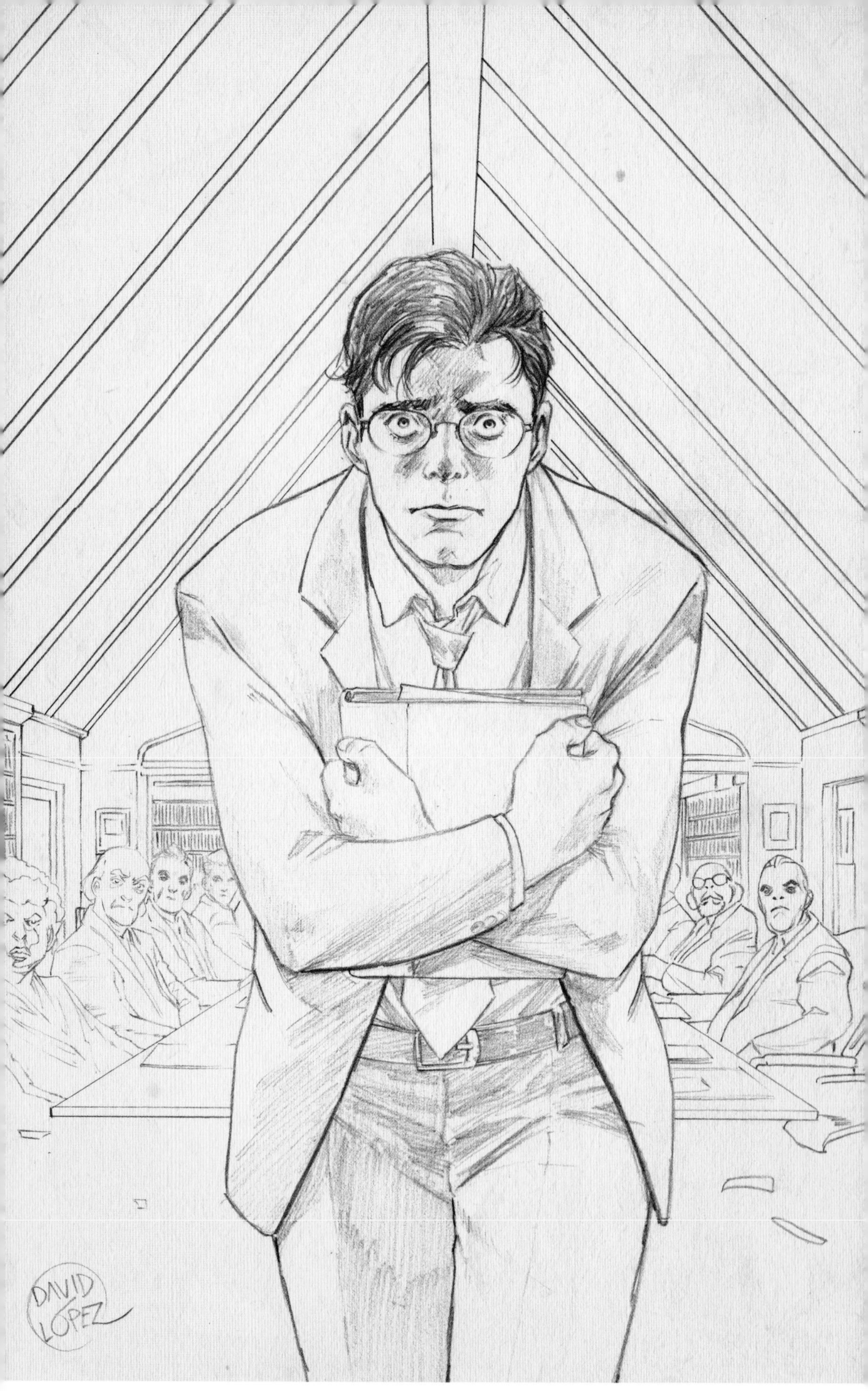
DAVID LÓPEZ

Issue Seventeen Incentive Cover by **David López**

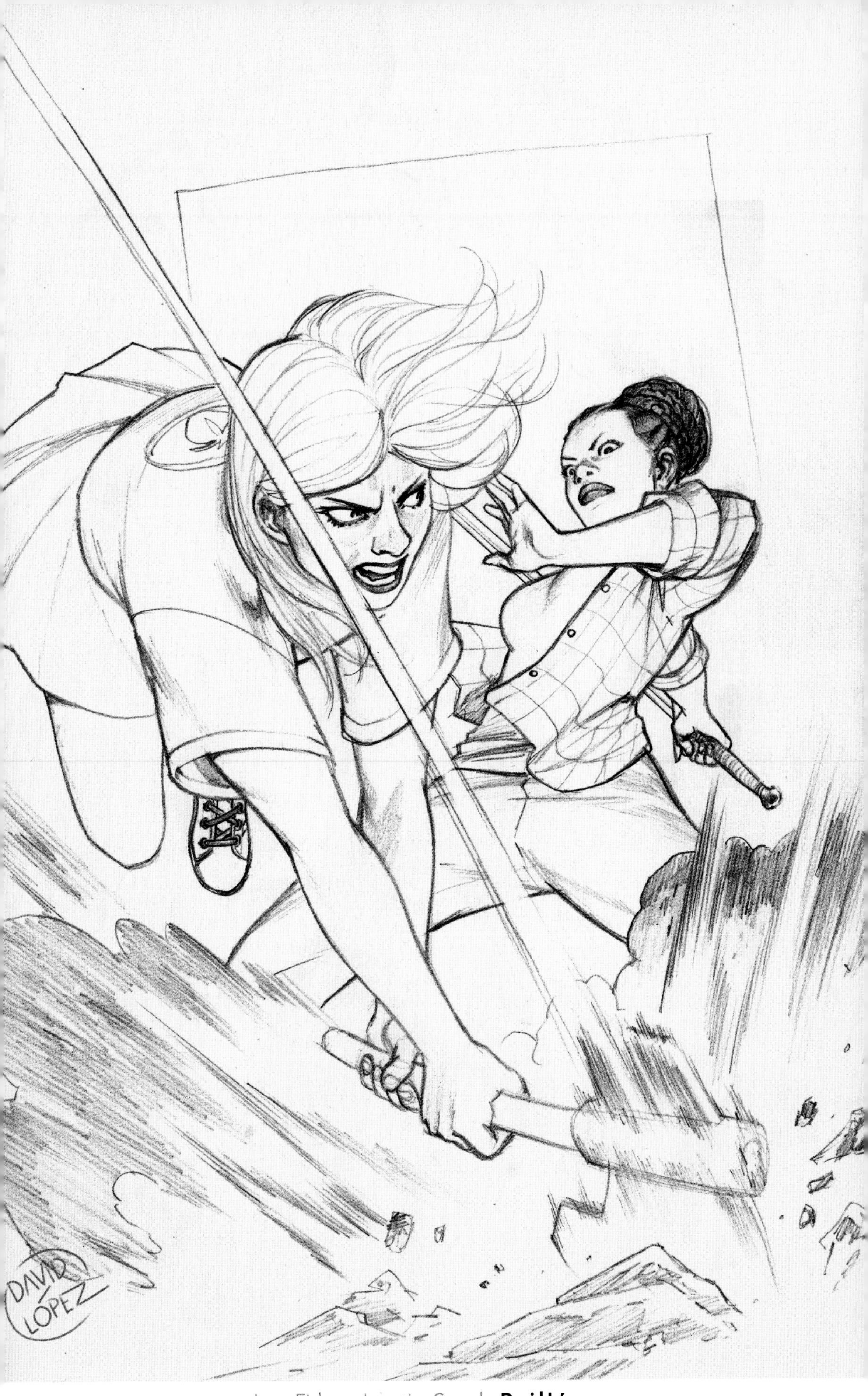
DAVID LÓPEZ

Issue Eighteen Incentive Cover by **David López**

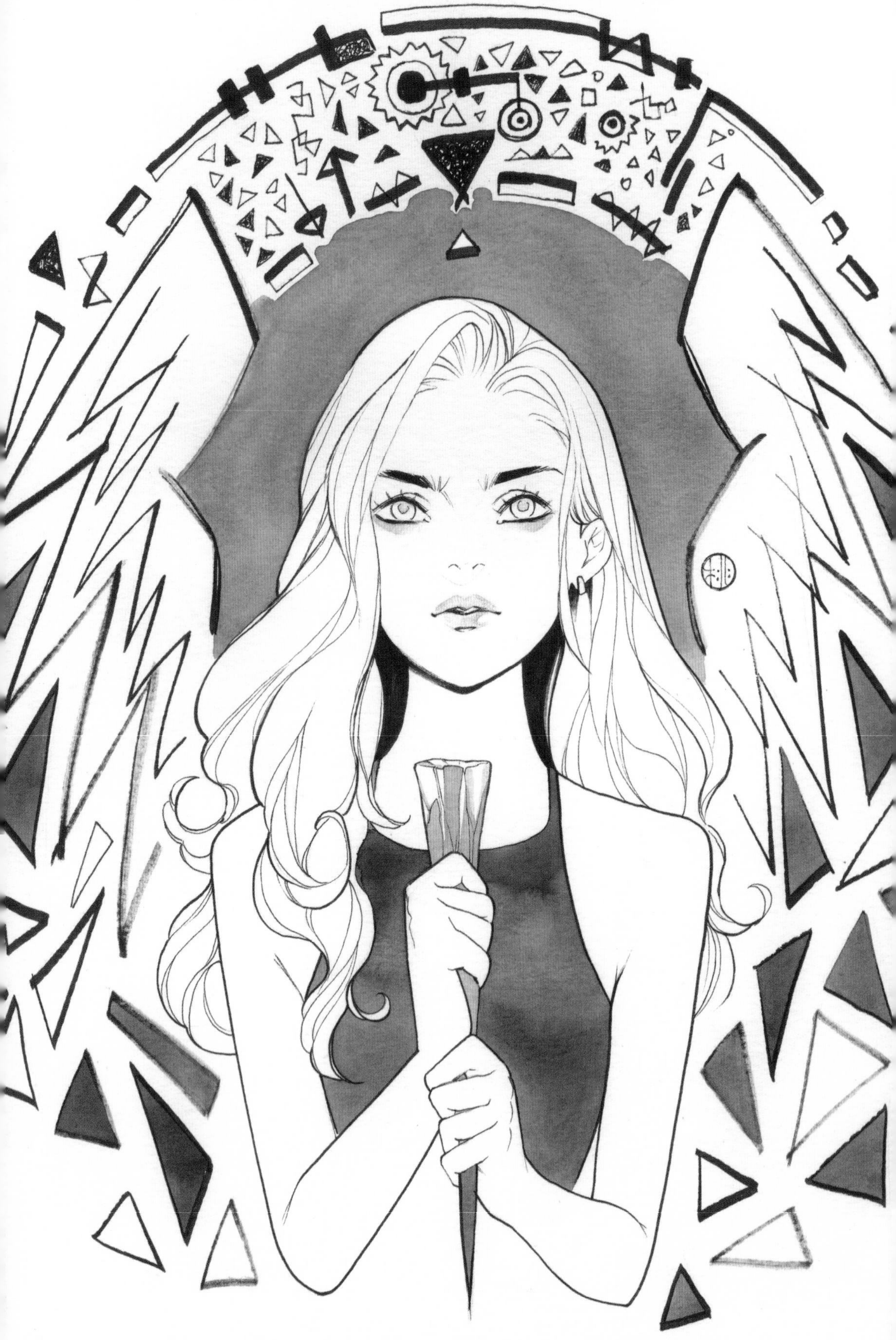

Issue Nineteen Incentive Cover by **Peach Momoko**

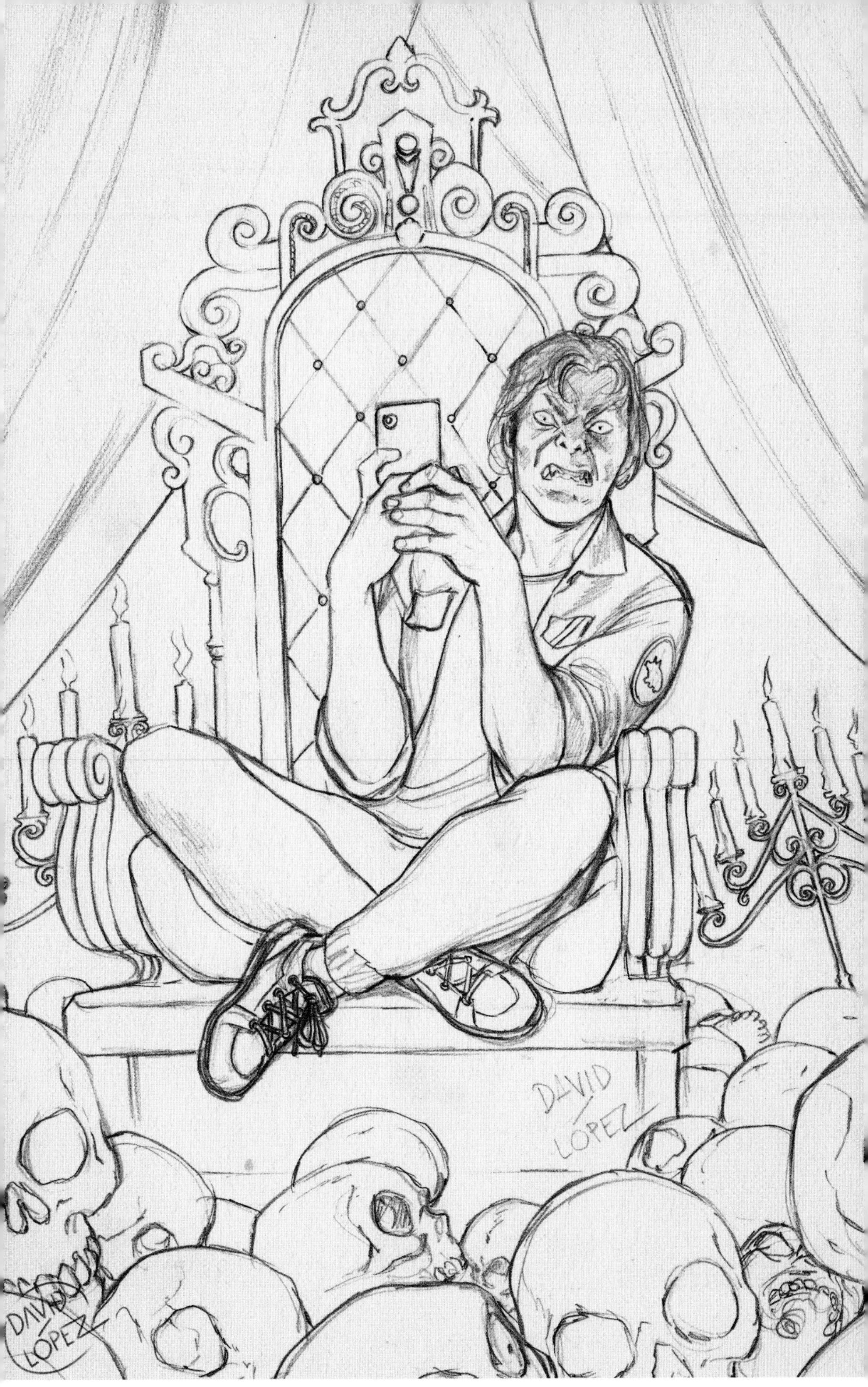
DAVID
LÓPEZ
DAVID
LÓPEZ
Issue Twenty Incentive Cover by **David López**

DISCOVER
VISIONARY CREATORS

KIERON GILLEN DAN MORA
TAMRA BONVILLAIN
ONCE & FUTURE
VOLUME ONE
THE KING IS UNDEAD

JAMES TYNION IV
WERTHER DELL'EDERA
MIQUEL MUERTO
SOMETHING is KILLING the CHILDREN
VOLUME ONE
SCOTT SNYDER

Brian Azzarello · Maria Llovet
FAITHLESS

GRANT MORRISON DAN MORA
Klaus
How Santa Claus Began

SIMON SPURRIER × MATÍAS BERGARA
CODA
VOLUME ONE
"This one is really special!"
—JEFF LEMIRE
(New York Times bestselling writer of Black Hammer)

matt kindt tyler jenkins
GRASS KINGS
volume one

BOOM! STUDIOS

AVAILABLE AT YOUR LOCAL COMICS SHOP AND BOOKSTORE

To find a comics shop in your area, visit www.comicshoplocator.com

WWW.**BOOM-STUDIOS**.COM

Once & Future
Kieron Gillen, Dan Mora
Volume 1
ISBN: 978-1-68415-491-3 | $16.99 US

Something is Killing the Children
James Tynion IV, Werther Dell'Edera
Volume 1
ISBN: 978-1-68415-558-3 | $14.99 US

Faithless
Brian Azzarello, Maria Llovet
ISBN: 978-1-68415-432-6 | $17.99 US

Klaus
Grant Morrison, Dan Mora
Klaus: How Santa Claus Began SC
ISBN: 978-1-68415-393-0 | $15.99 US
Klaus: The New Adventures of Santa Claus HC
ISBN: 978-1-68415-666-5 | $17.99 US

Coda
Simon Spurrier, Matias Bergara
Volume 1
ISBN: 978-1-68415-321-3 | $14.99 US
Volume 2
ISBN: 978-1-68415-369-5 | $14.99 US
Volume 3
ISBN: 978-1-68415-429-6 | $14.99 US

Grass Kings
Matt Kindt, Tyler Jenkins
Volume 1
ISBN: 978-1-64144-362-3 | $17.99 US
Volume 2
ISBN: 978-1-64144-557-3 | $17.99 US
Volume 3
ISBN: 978-1-64144-650-1 | $17.99 US

Bone Parish
Cullen Bunn, Jonas Scharf
Volume 1
ISBN: 978-1-64144-337-1 | $14.99 US
Volume 2
ISBN: 978-1-64144-542-9 | $14.99 US
Volume 3
ISBN: 978-1-64144-543-6 | $14.99 US

Ronin Island
Greg Pak, Giannis Milonogiannis
Volume 1
ISBN: 978-1-64144-576-4 | $14.99 US
Volume 2
ISBN: 978-1-64144-723-2 | $14.99 US
Volume 3
ISBN: 978-1-64668-035-1 | $14.99 US

Victor LaValle's Destroyer
Victor LaValle, Dietrich Smith
ISBN: 978-1-61398-732-2 | $19.99 US

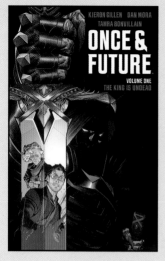

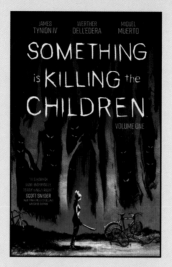

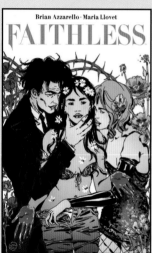

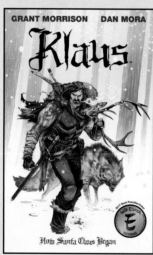

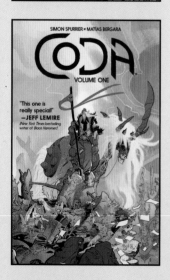

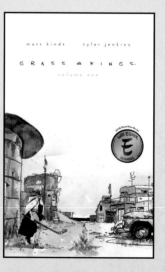

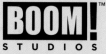